GROWING WISE DAY BY DAY

THOMAS J. SICA

AuthorHouse™ LLC
1663 Liberty Drive
Bloomington, IN 47403
www.authorhouse.com
Phone: 1-800-839-8640

Published by AuthorHouse 09/16/2014

ISBN: 978-1-4969-3394-2 (sc)
ISBN: 978-1-4969-3395-9 (e)

DEDICATION & ACKNOWLEDGEMENTS

This book is dedicated to the most important person in my life, my wife, Connie. Without her help I would not be where I am or who I am. She has stood by me for many years. Someone has said, "Behind every good man is a good woman." I cannot answer to the first part, but I can say that alongside me is a great woman. She certainly walks in wisdom and righteousness.

Proverbs 31:30 says, "Charm is deceptive and beauty is vain, but a woman who fears the Lord is to be praised." It was this verse that I used to guide me as I looked for a girl to date and then in choosing a wife. She is a woman "who fears the Lord", with beauty in addition. Any man who seeks a wife and finds one like the one I have found will be blessed indeed.

I would also like to acknowledge those who helped edit this book, without whose help you could not read my gibberish. Amy Walsh has helped in a major way, and, along with my wife, encouraged me to write this book. James Cooley and Erica Krysko also helped with editing.

FOREWORD

In 1978 I went to Liberty University, then known as Liberty Baptist College. It was there that I first heard Jerry Falwell encourage people to read Proverbs the way I will suggest in this devotional.

Since then, I have made an effort to read Proverbs on a regular basis. I have been encouraging others to do the same. I have topically preached through the book of Proverbs on several occasions. I then put all of the verses in a topical format. As a result, Proverbs has become one of my favorite books in the Bible.

The purpose of the Book of Proverbs is given in Proverbs 1:2-6. We can summarize it this way: Proverbs is for gaining wisdom. It was inspired by God and much of it was written by the wisest man who ever lived, King Solomon. He was told by God that he could have anything he wanted and all he had to do was ask. He asked for wisdom, and God gave it to him in abundance.

Most people will tell you that wisdom is gained by spending years living in this world, so that by the time you are old, you will have it. But, I believe you can get wiser much faster, by spending time reading and applying the words of the wise, as written in Proverbs.

I hope that my words in *Growing Wise Day by Day* will prove helpful in your walk. Yet, the most important words in this book are the words of God found in Proverbs. Put *Growing Wise Day by Day* alongside your Bible. And, as least once a day read Proverbs and this book. I hope the end result will be that you walk in wisdom one day at a time.

INTRODUCTION

There are four sections found on each page of this devotional. The **1st section** is the date and chapter. It is important that you begin each day by reading the chapter of Proverbs for the day. As you will see, each chapter that you read is based on the date. There are 31 chapters in the Book of Proverbs and 31 days in most months. So, for example, on the tenth day of each month, you will read Proverbs 10 and so on. Following this schedule will take you through the entire book of Proverbs each month.

The **2nd section** is the verse or verses for the day. Each verse is taken from the chapter which corresponds to the day of the month. For example, on January 4th, you will find verse 23. Verse 23 is from Proverbs, chapter 4. You will find that no verse in this section is ever repeated in the entire devotional. All verses are taken from the English Standard Version of the Bible.

The **3rd section** is the explanation of the verse or verses for that day. It will not take you long to read these sections, so it would benefit you to take some time each day to meditate on what you have read.

The **4th section** is the application statement. These statements, which are in bold letters, tell you what you should do based on the verse for the day. Growing wise involves reading God's Word and then putting it into practice. This is what Jesus said is true of the wise (Matthew 7:24-27).

Day by Day, you will learn the principles of wisdom. As you continue to learn these, and continue to put them into practice, you will find yourself *Growing Wise Day by Day*. You may also find yourself agreeing with the Psalmist's statement -- that God's Word made him wiser than those who were around him (Psalm 119:97-104).

January 1 – Read Proverbs 1

v. 3 to receive instruction in wise dealing, in righteousness, justice, and equity;

Proverbs 1:1-7 tells us the value of the book of Proverbs. With such great value, why don't people continually read it? Might it be that most have never heard of its value? No matter who you are, you can benefit from regularly reading this great book, the Book of Proverbs.

Here in verse three, we are given one of those areas of value. I like the values mentioned in this verse. What a great life it would be if we always did what was right. What a great life we would live if we always did what was just. What a great testimony we would have if we always did what was fair.

Learning to live this way requires knowledge, effort and choice. We need to know what is right, just and fair. We need to choose what is right, just and fair. We need to put forth the effort to do what is right, just and fair. Where do these qualities fit in your life?

Did your last action at work demonstrate these three qualities? Did your last encounter with your neighbors display these qualities? Did you do what was right, just and fair with your family last night? If not, spending time in Proverbs will help you make these qualities an integral part of your life. This is just one example of what receiving instructions in wise dealings will do for you.

Make a commitment to spend time daily in Proverbs and this devotional, and you will grow in wisdom one day at a time.

January 2 – Read Proverbs 2

v. 5 then you will understand the fear of the LORD and find the knowledge of God.
v. 6 For the LORD gives wisdom; from his mouth come knowledge and understanding;

Reading Proverbs 2 makes it clear that wisdom is not easily found. In order to get wisdom, you must search for it. In fact, a reading of verses 1-4 makes it clear that not everyone will even search for it. This is also seen by the number of times the word "if" is used in this passage. Wisdom does not just fall into our laps. So why would people who say that they want to be wise not do the searching required to get it?

In verse 6, God makes it clear that wisdom comes from Him. This is also seen in James 1. If you want wisdom, it begins with a relationship with God. In fact, once you have it, you will understand the fear of the Lord and find the knowledge of God (verse 5). Many people lack wisdom because they lack a relationship with God. Ask God for wisdom and search Proverbs, the Book of Wisdom, and the rest of the Bible for it. God is willing to give it, but like all good things, it does not come easily. It can be found, but it begins with God. The search for wisdom that does not include a relationship with God will fall short.

Are you in need of wisdom? Go to the God of wisdom.

January 3 - Read Proverbs 3

v. 13 Blessed is the one who finds wisdom, and the one who gets understanding,

What value is there is searching for wisdom? What value is there in reading and meditating on Proverbs, the Book of Wisdom, on a regular basis? Well, let's make a list of wisdom's value from Proverbs 3:

1. The one who finds wisdom is blessed. - verses 13 & 18
2. Wisdom is more valuable than silver, gold and rubies. - verses 4-15
3. Long life, riches and honor can come from wisdom. - verse 16
4. Both pleasantness and peace are rewards from gaining wisdom. - verse 17

Once realizing how precious wisdom is, one must keep in mind that wisdom begins with a right relationship with God, not just sitting down and reading a book (Proverbs 1:7). It is not just a matter of reading Proverbs, but of discovering the God who is presented in the Book of Proverbs and the rest of the Bible. It is not just reading Proverbs, but applying its truth to your life and growing in your relationship with the God of the Bible.

God desires to give you life and life to the fullest (John 10:10). Receive it from Him by placing your faith in the power of the person and work of Christ Jesus (1 Corinthians 15:3-4).

If you have never received Jesus as your Savior and Lord, let today be the day. Put your trust in what He did on the cross to save you from your sin. It is the only way to a relationship with God (Acts 4:12; John 14:6).

Put your trust in Jesus Christ. It will be the WISEST thing you will ever do.

January 4 - Read Proverbs 4

v. 23 Keep your heart with all vigilance, for from it flows the springs of life.

In the Bible, the heart, mind, and soul all refer to the same thing, the inner you. The term "heart" is the one that seems to be most often used for who you are inside. Proverbs 4:23 says, "Keep your heart with all vigilance." Why? Because "from it flows the springs of life." The thought is that we need to make sure that the "inner you" is where it should be. If the "inner you" is right, than the "outer you" will be where it should be.

Some people can hide the "inner you" and have a fake "outer you." The Bible calls that hypocrisy. If you pollute the spring, the rest of you will be polluted. Make sure your heart is right with God!

The heart can certainly get messed up, as you can read in Matthew 15:19. The Bible warns us to keep our heart right, so these kinds of hearts should be avoided: a double heart (Psalm 12:2), an unclean heart (Psalms 51:10) a proud heart (Proverbs 21:4), a hard heart (Proverbs 28:14), and an unbelieving heart (Hebrews 3:12). Our desire should be to keep our heart pure before God (2 Timothy 2:22).

All of your actions proceed from your heart (Luke 6:45).

Make sure your heart is right with God and then keep it right with God through daily use of His Word.

January 5 – Read Proverbs 5

v. 18 Let your fountain be blessed, and rejoice in the wife of your youth,
v. 19 a lovely deer, a graceful doe. Let her breasts fill you at all times with delight; be intoxicated always in her love.

You have heard of the "Love Chapter", 1 Corinthians 13, and the "Faith Chapter", Hebrews 11, but let me add a third one, the "Adultery Chapter", Proverbs 5.

There are seven truths in this chapter that tell us how to avoid committing adultery. One of them is found in verses 15-20 and also in 1 Corinthians 7:1-5. It is to find satisfaction in your spouse. Certainly your spouse is not perfect, but neither are you. Your spouse is the one to whom you made a promise before God. Not only should you keep that promise, but do much more. You should seek to make the relationship with your spouse so strong, that no adulterous person would ever have any possibility of destroying your marriage.

We can all be tempted, but build into your life some hedges of protection against temptation. A strong marriage is a wonderful thing.

Don't believe the lie that adultery is OK. It is not, and it will bring God's judgment (1 Thessalonians 4; Ephesians 5). When you said, "I do" you made a commitment before God. It was a commitment, not only to stay married, but to build a strong, loving marriage. It was a commitment to love your spouse, not because she deserves it, but because of your promise to her and to God.

Build a strong marriage and don't allow adultery to ruin it.

January 6 - Read Proverbs 6

v. 6 Go to the ant, O sluggard; consider her ways, and be wise.

Let's consider the ant (Proverbs 6:6-11).

First, you can learn from the ant. Verse 6 tells us that God created it, and we can learn from what God created (See Psalms 19 & Romans 1).

Second, verse 7 tells us that the ant has a message tailor-made for the sluggard: Don't be lazy. If you watch ants, you will notice that they hardly ever seem to be standing still.

Third, verses 7-8 tell us that the ant has no one directing it, but it knows to gather its provisions in summer and its food at harvest. Just look around your house or your yard and you will see ants busily gathering food.

Fourth, verses 7-8 tell us the ant prepares for times when it can't gather food. It gathers in summer, for the most part, and therefore is ready for winter when there is no food to gather. Are you preparing for retirement? Have you set money aside for days when you may be without a job? We need to think ahead so that we are ready for lean times.

Fifth, verses 9-10 tell us that you don't have to be really, really lazy to mess up -- just a little laziness will do. Though you sometimes run across people who work too much, far more people tend to be on the lazy side.

Work hard, plan, and prepare for hard times. See Genesis 41.

January 7 - Read Proverbs 7

v. 1 My son, keep my words and treasure up my commandments with you;
v. 5 to keep you from the forbidden woman, from the adulteress with her smooth words.

This is a story of a youth who lacked judgment. Now that's a new one! No, youths who lack judgment are nothing new, and they are what Proverbs 7 is all about. According to verses 6-9, a young man was headed down the street to the wrong place at the wrong time of day. Because he was in the wrong place at the wrong time, he got himself into trouble with a prostitute. Unfortunately, these were not his only failures.

He also listened to the prostitute (verses 14-22). He did not understand the cost of going with her (verse 23). Furthermore, he did not realize that great men had been brought down by her (verse 26). Even more so, he should have understood that her house was a highway to the grave (verse 27).

Beware! Do not go to places where you should not be, especially at times that make it even worse. Come to grips with the fact that punishment will come to those who reject God's standard of morality.

Chapter 7 is about a father pleading with his son to latch onto wisdom so that he will not fall prey to immorality and immoral people.

Fathers, teach your children about wisdom and morality, and demonstrate both yourselves.

January 8 - Read Proverbs 8

v. 13 The fear of the Lord is hatred of evil. Pride and arrogance and the way of evil and perverted speech I hate.

What is true of those who love God? Well, today people seem to think that anything can be true of a person and that person still love God.

While the Bible says much about those who love God, we are given a summary description in Proverbs 8:13. Loving God can also be described as "the fear of the Lord." In this verse we are given four things that are true of the Fear of the Lord, or four things that are true of those who love God.

First, those who fear the Lord hate evil. Someone can't love God and love evil at the same time. In fact, it even goes further. **Someone who loves God hates evil.**

Secondly, those who fear the Lord hate pride and arrogance. "Pride" and "arrogance" describe someone who does not think he needs God. This could certainly not describe one who loves God.

Thirdly, God-fearing people hate the way of evil. A lover of God hates the behavior that results from evil. Someone who loves God looks to have righteous behavior, not evil behavior.

Lastly, those who fear God hate perverted speech. Perverted speech includes lying, gossiping, backbiting, immoral speech, immoral joking, and using foul words.

Someone who loves God avoids the things that God hates, as described above. Think about it: A lover of God can be known by what he hates, not just by what he loves. Does what you hate demonstrate that you love God?

Hate what God hates.

January 9 – Read Proverbs 9

v. 7 Whoever corrects a scoffer gets himself abuse, and he who reproves a wicked man incurs injury.

v. 8 Do not reprove a scoffer, or he will hate you; reprove a wise man, and he will love you.

v. 9 Give instruction to a wise man, and he will be still wiser; teach a righteous man, and he will increase in learning.

Have you ever wondered how to tell if someone is wise or foolish? I want to be wise. I'm sure you do, too. Well, one way to tell if a person is wise or not, is to see how he responds to a rebuke. Proverbs 9:7-9 tells us that a wise person is receptive to a rebuke and will love the rebuker. However, a wicked person will hate or grow cold towards the rebuker. So, find out how a person responds when he is rebuked, and you will find out if a person is wise or foolish.

When I am in the position where I have to rebuke or counsel someone, these verses always come to mind. When I rebuke a person, I sit back and wait to see if that person will love me or grow cold towards me. By how he responds to me, I can tell if he is wise or wicked.

How about you? How do you respond when you are rebuked?

Proverbs has much to say on this subject. One great project you can do is to read through Proverbs day by day for a month with the sole idea of looking for verses that talk about being rebuked or rebuking. I have done this very study and it has helped me immensely.

Show your wisdom when being rebuked by loving those who loved you enough to rebuke you.

January 10 - Read Proverbs 10

v. 7 The memory of the righteous is a blessing, but the name of the wicked will rot.

How do you want to be remembered? Think of the people of history and how they are remembered. There are those remembered with disdain such as Hitler, Bin Laden, Judas, Joseph Stalin, and Queen Mary I. There are those remembered with great honor, such as Jesus, Abraham Lincoln, Michelangelo, Albert Einstein, Florence Nightingale, and Ruth. We are all making a name for ourselves by what we do and by who we are.

Each day, we are writing a new page concerning how we will be remembered. In Proverbs 10:7, we are told that the memory of the righteous will be a blessing, but the memory of the wicked will rot. When people remember you after you die, will it be a blessing or will it rot? Today you are making the choices that will decide how you will be remembered.

Will the choices you make today endear you to people? Or, cause them to think of you with rottenness? Some people live selfishly and wickedly and so they are not remembered well. Others live selfless and loving lives, and when they are long gone, their memory continues to be a blessing to others.

Live life in such a way that when you are remembered it is a blessing and not a rottenness.

January 11 - Read Proverbs 11

v. 3 The integrity of the upright guides them, but the crookedness of the treacherous destroys them.

v. 21 Be assured, an evil person will not go unpunished, but the offspring of the righteous will be delivered.

Through all of the ages, believers have been disturbed by a seeming contradiction. When we look around, we see those who reject God prosper, but those who seek God fall behind. The fact that the wicked prosper does not make sense, even when we understand that we are living in a world that is ruled by sin.

Yet, the wicked prospering is not the whole story. It is striking to read through Proverbs 11. It is striking because eight of these verses basically say the same thing about the wicked (verses 3, 5, 6, 17, 19, 21, 23, & 27). Those who are wicked and seek to do wicked things in the end only destroy themselves. They may succeed for a time in hurting the righteous. They may succeed for a time in getting ahead in this life. They may look like they are winning. Yet God's Word is clear; in the end they will reap what they have sown.

You have two choices in life: to be led by integrity and righteousness (11:3) or to be tempted to join in with those who would do what is wicked (11:6). Keep in mind that the wage of the wicked is deceptive (11:18). They will not go unpunished (11:21). However, The Lord delights in those whose ways are blameless (11:20).

Choose the right path because it is right and it pleases God.

January 12 – Read Proverbs 12

v. 17 Whoever speaks the truth gives honest evidence, but a false witness utters deceit.
v. 19 Truthful lips endure forever, but a lying tongue is but for a moment.
v. 22 Lying lips are an abomination to the LORD, but those who act faithfully are his delight.

Honesty! Integrity! These things are so missing in our society today. People are willing to lie for just about any reason. Seldom do we find people who have made the commitment to not lie for any reason. These rare people have made the commitment to integrity.

I have made that commitment for a very important reason: God says much about lying and none of it is good.

Proverbs 12:22 says that the Lord detests lying lips. Verse 17 tells us that a false witness tells lies. Verse 19 says that truthful lips endure, but lying lips are but for a moment. Yes, it is clear that lying lips are an abomination to God.

There are many more verses in the Bible on this subject. Look them up. You will find one near the end of the Bible. It is Revelation 21:8. It says that ALL liars will go to hell. Don't buy into this world's view of lying that says that everyone lies and there is nothing wrong with it. If you lie consistently, you may one day find yourself in that one place where you wished you would never go.

Don't lie. Ever.

January 13 - Read Proverbs 13

v. 1 A wise son hears his father's instruction, but a scoffer does not listen to rebuke.
v. 10 By insolence comes nothing but strife, but with those who take advice is wisdom.

If there is one thing that most people like to avoid, it is a rebuke. Most people do not like to rebuke others, and they certainly do not like to be rebuked. But Proverbs has much to say on this subject. What is very clear is that the "fool" or the "mocker" does not listen to a rebuke (verse 1). In fact, he usually ends up "turning cold" towards the rebuker. What we need to know is that we should be open to being rebuked, especially if the rebuke comes from a heart of love.

Much can be learned from a rebuke, and those who are unwilling to listen will pay for it in the end (verse 13). There is great wisdom in listening to a rebuke (verse 10). The next time you are rebuked, don't be quick to react. Take time to mull over what is said. Ask yourself the following questions:

1. Does this come from a person who loves God?
2. Does this come from a person who knows the Word of God?
3. Does this come from a person who loves me?
4. Is the rebuke right?

A rebuke seldom feels good at the time because it says we are doing something wrong. But, we ought to be welcoming towards being rebuked because a rebuke can help us to be wise.

Have an open and receptive heart even when rebuked.

January 14 – Read Proverbs 14

v. 23 In all toil there is profit, but mere talk tends only to poverty.

Do you know anyone who is lazy? We are living in an entitlement society, where people are perfectly willing to sit back and do nothing and let the government, their families or the church take care of them. There are people who are healthy but unwilling to work hard because they can get more from the government while sitting home.

What does the Bible say? "All hard work brings profit." There is value in good hard work. On the other hand, there are those who are always talking about what they will do, but are still lazy. They have great dreams, but they never get from the head to the hand. Mere talk gets you nowhere and leads to poverty. Sometimes wives don't trust their husbands because they are big on talk and little on action. The Bible makes clear that we will do better if we are big on action and little on talk.

Laziness and mere talk are two sides of the same coin that cause you to lose whatever coins you could have had. Be willing to work hard, for in hard work there is profit. See Proverbs 12:11; 28:19 and 2 Thessalonians 2:6-10. If you are busy working hard and not seeing much return in what you are doing, don't give up. All hard work results in profit.

Work hard. Don't just be a talker.

January 15 – Read Proverbs 15

v. 8 The sacrifice of the wicked is an abomination to the LORD, but the prayer of the upright is acceptable to Him.

What does God think of the wicked and the righteous? Let's start with the wicked. Proverbs 15:8 says that God detests their sacrifices. The offerings and religious service of evil people to God is rejected. Why? God hates hypocrisy! Acts done from a heart that is not in agreement with the act is meaningless, and God actually detests them. That is why it is so important to make sure that our actions always come from a heart that is right with God. Verse 9 tells us that God also hates the way of the wicked. The lifestyle of the wicked is not in agreement with God's way. We often see people perform religious acts, but then spend the rest of the week living as if God does not exist. In this case, even religious acts on Sunday are hated by God.

Now God has a different view of the righteous. He loves it when they talk to Him. This is true because He loves them and loves to hear from them. The righteous are those who love and serve God from a hearts that love and seek after God. This kind of heart is reflected in their actions, which are righteous.

We often say, "There is only one person we have to please." Well, is God pleased with you or detesting you? If you love God from the heart, and that love can be seen in your actions, then God loves you and wants to hear from you.

Love God and talk to him often.

January 16 - Read Proverbs 16

v. 6 By steadfast love and faithfulness iniquity is atoned for, and by the fear of the Lord one turns away from evil.

Sometimes in life we do something really dumb or sinful, and we hurt the people we love. When this happens, we wonder whether we could ever get things right with them. In circumstances like these, sometimes the road to healing is a long and hard road. Once trust has been broken, it is hard to repair. But, it can be repaired!

It may take time, but this is understandable when a trust has been crushed. Proverbs gives us an outline of how to get things right. It is found in 16:6, "By steadfast love and faithfulness, iniquity is atoned for." The key words for getting things right are "steadfast love" and "faithfulness." The combination of these two words is found three other times in Proverbs. (See 13:3; 14:22; 20:28.)

Steadfast love means goodness or kindness. Faithfulness means trustworthiness. So when you have messed up and broken someone's trust, the way to get things right is to continually act in love over a period of time so that your trustworthiness will be seen. When you are loving and faithful over a period of time, people begin to trust you again. However, beware that you don't break their trust again. Each time trust is broken, it becomes harder to repair.

Be faithful to the ones you love, in fact to everyone, but if you mess up, correct it in the honest, Biblical way.

January 17 - Read Proverbs 17

v. 28 Even a fool who keeps silent is considered wise; when he closes his lips, he is deemed intelligent.

One of the very first verses I memorized in the book of Proverbs was Proverbs 17:28. The Bible has much to say about how much we talk. The clear teaching of Scripture is that a wise person uses words with restraint. A wise person does not need to tell everyone everything he knows about whatever is being discussed. A wise person is perfectly willing to sit back and listen to what everyone else has to say and does not necessarily feel the need to speak up or respond. The second phrase of this verse paraphrases the first. The words "closes his lips" means to "keep silent."

A foolish person can learn from this. As verse 28 says, "Even a fool who keeps silent is considered wise." A fool proves himself to be a fool when he starts talking. If he remains quiet, people may think he is wise. Some people just seem to want to do all of the talking in every conversation and don't seem to know when to shut up. Have you ever noticed that in a small group meeting? Some people are like waterfalls: Their mouths just keep gushing and gushing. Next time you are in a small group meeting, sit back and watch how much people talk, and make sure you are not the one doing all of the talking.

Act like the wise person who is controlled in his speech and tends to talk less than others.

January 18 - Read Proverbs 18

v. 2 A fool takes no pleasure in understanding, but only in expressing his opinion.

The Book of Proverbs talks a great deal about the person who is called a "fool." We are given many characteristics of this person. In Proverbs 18:2, we are given two more. The first is that a "fool" finds no pleasure in understanding. To take "pleasure" in something means that you are delighting to do it or that you are eager to do it. I take pleasure in preaching and teaching God's Word. I also take pleasure in fishing. I am delighted and eager to do these things.

The fool finds no pleasure in understanding. "Understanding" carries the idea of insight, wisdom, or the capacity to discern right from wrong. Sadly, a foolish person is not eager to learn these things.

There is something he is eager to do. Though he has no desire for wisdom, he does have a desire to tell everyone what he thinks and to air his own opinion. The fool is the person who seems to know everything about anything, yet has no real desire to learn something. It is interesting that Proverbs says that a "fool" loves to talk and that a "wise" person tends to remain quiet.

So what do we learn from this? First, we should be eager to grow in wisdom and knowledge. Second, we should be in no hurry to air our own opinions.

Have you ever walked away from a group conversation without sharing your opinion on the subject in question? The problem with the fool is that he wants everyone to know what he thinks, but he often has no valuable thoughts on the subject in question.

Use your mind and ears more than your mouth.

January 19 - Read Proverbs 19

v. 3 When a man's folly brings his way to ruin, his heart rages against the LORD.

Sadly, and all too often, people follow their own way and end up ruining their lives. They do not follow God, but instead choose the easier road or the road that heads in the wrong direction. There are two paths in life: man's way and God's way. Some turn from God's way to follow man's way.

I have had to watch people head down the road towards the bridge that has been washed out, so that their path is one that ends in disaster. Then, a most interesting thing happens - they blame God. They have not done what God says in His Word. They have rejected God's warnings. They have refused to listen to advice. But, then they blame God.

It would be like building a car. You gather all of your parts and then you consult the instructions for putting it together. You look at them and you say, "These are too complicated." Or "I don't think I will do it this way." Or "I have a better way to do it." Then you set out to build your car. Everything goes well at first but then you begin to run into problems. Things start to go wrong. You finally sit in frustration at your inability to finish your car. Then, you blame the guys who wrote the manual that you didn't follow.

You can't get mad at God when you mess things up because you did not do what He told you to do. People do this very thing with their marriages, raising their children, their finances, and living life in general. They do not do what God commands, and then when what God warned would happen does happen, somehow they find a way to blame God.

If you make a mess of your life, don't blame God.

January 20 – Read Proverbs 20

v. 6 Many a man proclaims his own steadfast love, but a faithful man who can find?

Friends: There are all kinds. They all claim to be true friends. We all hope that all our friends are true, but we know that is not true. If you are married, your best friend should be your spouse, but even this friend can sometimes prove not to be true. The reality is that true, faithful friends are hard to find (Proverbs 20:6). They are few and far between. They are there, but there are not many of them, so two things should be kept in mind.

First, you should seek to be that kind of friend. You should be a friend who is faithful to your friends. You should be a friend who can be trusted by your friends. You should be a friend who is a friend even when your friend is not present. You should be faithful to your friends at all times and in all places.

Second, when you find a friend who is faithful to you, hold onto that friend and treat him with the love he deserves. Remember the most important thing in a friendship is being a friend. You should let your friend know how much you appreciate her friendship. You should be a friend to him or her in the same way he or she is a friend to you.

Have that trait which is the best trait one can find in a friend: faithfulness.

January 21 – Read Proverbs 21

v. 23 Whoever keeps his mouth and his tongue keeps himself out of trouble.

The righteous are always careful and thoughtful in what they say. They know that words spoken without thought can get them into trouble and hurt others.

We must guard our speech! We must be careful in what we say and how we say it. We must be thoughtful every time we open our mouths.

Words spoken without thought are words that have a much greater chance to cause trouble. In fact, the more we speak, the greater chance there is that we will get ourselves into trouble. Look at your life. Have you stuck your foot in your mouth lately? It is so easy to do, and once done, so hard to fix. Once our words have left our mouths, they are out there for all to hear. This is especially true with things like email, texting and Facebook. In the case of cyberspace, they are not only out there, but they are out there to stay and for everyone to see.

Our words must be chosen carefully. Two great verses in the New Testament give us some guidelines for the words we use. They are Colossians 4:6 and Ephesians 4:29. If we will commit these verses to memory and recall them before we speak, they can save us from a great deal of trouble.

Control your mouth and tongue. Consider what comes out of them so that you will keep yourself out of trouble.

January 22 - Read Proverbs 22

v. 24 Make no friendship with a man given to anger, nor go with a wrathful man,
v. 25 lest you learn his ways and entangle yourself in a snare.

When people are not living the way they should, their lives have a negative impact on those around them. Even the best of people can be hurt by those with whom they choose to make close friends (See 1 Corinthians 15:33). Hence, we find the warning in Proverbs 22:24-25. It warns us not to make friends with hot-tempered people. It repeats it by telling us to not associate with people who are easily angered. The old saying is true, "Run with the wolves and you will learn to howl."

You may ask, "Why?" Your gut may say, "But I want to minister to them." That is a different issue. Your heart may say, "But they are already my friend." That is a difficulty, but it does not nullify the warning. Your head may say, "But I will not be affected by them." That is naive. The warning is that choosing these kinds of people to be close associates may cause you to learn their ways and get you ensnared, either in their trouble, or your own trouble because you became like them. If you have friends who are hot-tempered, spend your time helping them to overcome it. If they are unwilling to change, find new friends.

Be careful in friendship, especially with people who are hot-headed and easily angered.

January 23 - Read Proverbs 23

v. 29 Who has woe? Who has sorrow? Who has strife? Who has complaining? Who has wounds without cause? Who has redness of eyes?
v. 30 Those who tarry long over wine; those who go to try mixed wine.

Christians sometimes debate about whether drinking alcohol is OK. I'm on the side that it is not for a number of reasons. One of these reasons is the potential damage that it could cause in our lives. For example, reduced inhibitions have caused accidents, and abetted murder, rape and other crimes. I have seen this damage in people's lives and will continue to see it. Sadly, I have seen whole families destroyed because of alcohol and I'm sure you have too.

Proverbs 23 tells us of some of the damage that alcohol could cause. Here is a list:

1. Poverty – verses 19-21
2. Misery – verses 29-30
3. Poisons – verses 31-32
4. Hallucinations – verse 33
5. Dizziness – verse 34
6. Numbness – verse 35
7. Enslavement – verse 35

This list is not exhaustive. So many lives are destroyed when a glass of water, or even a Pepsi, would have been a better choice. Ephesians 5:18 says, "And do not get drunk with wine, for that is debauchery, but be filled with the Spirit." (Debauchery means reckless behavior or what one does when the mind is absent.)

Be wise. Be filled with the Spirit, not alcohol. Know this: It is harder to stop then to have never started.

January 24 - Read Proverbs 24

v. 12 If you say, "Behold, we did not know this," does not he who weighs the heart perceive it? Does not he who keeps watch over your soul know it, and will he not repay man according to his work?

v. 15 Lie not in wait as a wicked man against the dwelling of the righteous; do no violence to his home;

v. 19 Fret not yourself because of evildoers, and be not envious of the wicked,

v. 23 for disaster will arise suddenly from them, and who knows the ruin that will come from them both?

There is great value in wisdom. Unfortunately, some people seem to think that there is great value in remaining simple-minded. Proverbs 24:12, 15, 19 & 23 speak of doing all we can to become wise.

The greatest wisdom book ever written is the Bible. By not spending time in it, we are saying that there is great value in remaining simple. According to Hebrews 5:11-14, those who constantly use this book of wisdom learn to distinguish good from evil (See Psalms. 119). The Bible is needed for a believer to grow into what God desires for our lives (1 Peter 2:2).

While wisdom in itself is not the end goal, it helps to get us to the end goal. The end goal is to come to know God and to become like His Son (Romans 8:29). God wants us to love and obey Him. The end goal is a life that mirrors His Word and is lived for His glory. A wise person is one who does what God desires.

Spend much time in the Bible and grow in wisdom,

January 25 - Read Proverbs 25

v. 28 A man without self-control is like a city broken into and left without walls.

Lack of self-control is a very dangerous thing. Walls are built around a city to protect the city from outside dangers coming into the city. Without walls a city is in danger from all kinds of bad things entering into it. Without walls a city is open to all of its enemies.

Not being able to control ourselves can get us into all sorts of sin and trouble. The person spoken of in Proverbs 5:23 committed adultery because he lacked self-control. Also Proverbs 17:27 says, "Whoever restrains his words has knowledge." This same lack of self-control can be seen in the person who allows his or her anger to get out of control. The end result of not being in control of ourselves can lead to becoming a failure, no longer useful for the master (1 Corinthians 9:24-27). Beware of living a life with no control or little control.

All of us need to learn to control ourselves. We can do this in many different ways. For example, get out of bed even if you don't have to. Don't eat that snack, even if you really desire it. Start exercising, even if it is not Monday. Teach your body that you have control over its passions.

Be wise, and with the help of the Holy Spirit (Galatians 5:15), control yourself.

January 26 – Read Proverbs 26

v. 12 Do you see a man who is wise in his own eyes? There is more hope for a fool than for him.

Beware of looking good to yourself in the mirror. It would be like running to the mirror and saying, "Mirror, mirror on the wall who is the wisest in all the land?" And then responding to yourself, "Me."

Proverbs 26:12 tells us that one who is wise in his own eyes has very little hope. In fact, there is more hope for a fool. Now, that is a really strong statement when you consider all that Proverbs says about the fool. In Proverbs a fool is described as having very little hope, so the one who is wise in their own eyes has even less.

Be ever learning, and no matter what the topic is, always be ready to learn more. To say that a person is wise in his own eyes is just another way of describing a person who is full of pride. It is fine if others see you as being wise, but seeing yourself this way is not a good thing. God desires that we look at ourselves with humility. We can be confident, but pride is a dangerous thing. If you contlnually keep God's truth in front of you, seeing yourself as you really are, then you can keep yourself where you should be.

Beware of looking too good to yourself in your own mirror.

January 27 - Read Proverbs 27

v. 6 Faithful are the wounds of a friend; profuse are the kisses of an enemy.
v. 9 Oil and perfume make the heart glad, and the sweetness of a friend comes from his earnest counsel.

Sometimes we get it wrong. We think our friend is the person who never hurts us, and our enemy is the one who hurts us. But a true friend is the one who is always honest with us. This means they will sometimes have to say tough things to us, or they may sometimes disagree with us and not be silent about it. We need to understand that sometimes when a true friend hurts us, the wounds come from his love. These kinds of wounds can be trusted because he is our friend. The reality is that a TRUE friend will tell us what we need to hear. (verse 9)

What we need to be careful of is the enemy who is constantly telling us how good we are or how much he loves us. Often it is our enemy who kisses our faces, but then slaps us on the back of our heads (verse 6). A false friend talks about how good we are to our faces and then gossips and slanders. Our enemy wants to look like our best buddy.

We often find out how good of a friendship we have when problems arise in a friendship. Friends can argue and disagree and still be friends, but supposed friendships fall apart when problems arise. Beware of the person who is always buttering you up. He may not be the friend you thought he was. Gravitate towards the person who is willing to be honest with you even if it may cost your friendship. You will find in the end that this is the kind of friend that is truly a friend.

Know this: true friends sometimes wound us, but enemies love to kiss us.

January 28 - Read Proverbs 28

v. 13 Whoever conceals his transgressions will not prosper, but he who confesses and forsakes them will obtain mercy.

When we do something wrong, the desire of most is to cover it up. We don't want anyone to see our mistake, so we hide it. We don't want anyone to confront our mistake so we hide it. We don't want to deal with the consequences of our sin, so we hide it. But, all of that hiding is the very thing we should not do. Proverbs 28:13 says that one who conceals his sin does not prosper. If we want to find mercy from God, we must do two things concerning our sin: confess it & forsake it.

We confess our sin by saying the same thing that God does concerning our sin. We say, "It is sin." We don't make excuses for it. We don't blame others for it. We don't look at it as some small thing. We see it for what it is. We are open and honest about it.

To forsake our sin, means to walk away from it. It means that we stop doing it. It means that we head in a different direction. This verse is very similar to what we read in 1 John 1:9, which says, "If we confess our sins, he is faithful and just to forgive us our sins and to cleanse us from all unrighteousness." The Bible is very clear that concealing sin is the wrong road to take (See 2 Samuel 11-12).

Don't hide your sin, confess it and forsake it.

January 29 - Read Proverbs 29

v. 20 Do you see a man who is hasty in his words? There is more hope for a fool than for him.

This verse is similar to Proverbs 26:12 and speaks of things you can do that will give you less hope than a fool has. In that verse, being wise in your own eyes made you less than a fool. In this verse speaking in haste places you lower than a fool. Both of these are the actions of an unwise person.

Have you ever thought to yourself that some people talk without thinking? It seems like before you get your words out, the other person is already responding. Some people start talking before you have answered fully their first statement or question. The reality is that some people "speak in haste." (Proverbs 29:20) And, sometimes we are included in that group of hasty speakers.

How difficult of a problem is this? Well, consider what Proverbs says about the "fool." According to Proverbs, the "fool" sits pretty low on the totem pole. Yet, Proverbs says that there is more hope for a fool than someone who speaks in haste. (Proverbs 29:20)

Don't be in a hurry to talk or respond to people. Take time to listen to what others are saying. Take time to think over what you have heard. Take time to consider what you will say and how you will say it. It is much wiser to talk slow than to talk to fast.

Don't talk in haste. Read Ecclesiastes 5.

January 30 - Read Proverbs 30

v. 8 Remove far from me falsehood and lying; give me neither poverty nor riches; feed me with the food that is needful for me,

v. 9 lest I be full and deny you and say, "Who is the LORD?" or lest I be poor and steal and profane the name of my God.

If you could only ask God for one or two things for yourself, what would you ask? Of course we know that Solomon asked for wisdom. Maybe you would ask for something different. Here is the request of Agur. "Agur?" You ask. Yes, Agur. He, also, had a request of God in which he asked God for two things before he died. His requests are found in Proverbs 30:8-9.

The first request was that God would keep lies and falsehood far from him. His desire was to be a man of integrity. He wanted to be honest always. The Bible tells us that God hates lying and that those who make it their way of life will not join him in Heaven (Revelation 21:8).

His second request was that God would give him neither poverty nor riches. His fear was that if he was poor he might steal and so dishonor God's name. On the other hand, his fear was that he would get rich and forget God. Jesus said that this is a real problem for the rich. It is an interesting thought in a world that seems so desirous of being rich that people are willing to do anything to get there.

Be truthful and don't forget God or dishonor His Name by stealing from others.

January 31 - Read Proverbs 31

v. 10 An excellent wife who can find? She is far more precious than jewels.

Proverbs 31 is considered the "Wife Chapter" in the Bible. The section on wives begins in verse 10 and it begins with an explosion. The wife that is described here is definitely hard to find. Since this is true, she is very valuable when found. She is worth far more than rubies when discovered.

How sad that most wives claim to be this kind of wife, when according to verse 10, most wives are not. That makes them either seeking to deceive or being deceived. What is even sadder is that when this kind of wife is found, she is not treated like the rare jewel that she is. Proverbs 31; Ephesians 5 and 1 Peter 3 tells us how to treat this kind of wife.

If you are a wife, or hope to be one some day, realize that this kind of wife does not happen by accident. Many wives, who are not this kind of wife, are busy trying to make their husbands better. Yet, this Proverbs 31 kind of woman knows that she must begin with herself and her own character before she points fingers at her spouse. Wives, and wives-to-be, read Proverbs 31, Ephesians 5 and 1 Peter 3. Read and make note of the kind of wife God wants you to be.

Husbands, are you treating your wife like a rare jewel? You may say that your wife is not like the wife described here. Instead of complaining, pray for her to become that kind of women. Remember, a rare jewel is not perfect, just very valuable and rare.

Men, look for or pray for this kind of wife. Ladies, be this kind of woman or wife.

February 1 - Read Proverbs 1

v. 10 My son, if sinners entice you, do not consent.

We are constantly being invited by people to join them in their sin. They might not ask us to join in on murder or robbery, but they certainly try to share their gossip or worry. Maybe you had someone inviting you to skip worship this Sunday. Perhaps you were given an invitation to some immoral act. The invitation could be so many things since we live in a world that has been so captivated by sin. Proverbs 1 tells us how to deal with these invitations to sin. For example, verse 10 tells us to refuse sinners' enticements. Here the enticement is to steal. Verse 15 tells us not to go along with the evildoers. Verse 18 warns us that the end result of joining them hurts all who join their path.

It is surprising how many times in a day we can be enticed to join in with others to sin. They make it sound really good. It often sounds like it is the best thing in the whole world and that, without it, we may fall short of eternal joy. But, the opposite is true; those who join in only hurt themselves. Such is the end of those who make the decision to disobey God. Sooner or later, those who do evil will hurt themselves. I can hear a father telling his child, "Stay away from that crowd, for they are up to no good." This is what is happening here; a father is talking to his son.

Be sure to refuse all enticements to sin today, no matter how good they may sound.

February 2 - Read Proverbs 2

v. 3 yes, if you call out for insight and raise your voice for understanding,
v. 4 if you seek it like silver and search for it as for hidden treasures,

Proverbs 2 tells us to get wisdom. It says that you should call out for it (v. 3), raise your voice for it (v. 3), seek it like silver and search for it as hidden treasure (v. 4). Why? Well, in Proverbs 2 we are given six reasons for getting wisdom. Here they are:

1. You will understand the fear of the Lord. - v. 5
2. You will find the knowledge of God. - v. 5
3. You will understand righteousness, justice and equity, every good path. - v. 9
4. It will deliver you from the way of evil and men of perverted speech. – v. 12
5. You will be delivered from the forbidden woman (adulteress). – v. 16
6. You will walk in the way of good and keep to the paths of righteousness – v. 20

Wow! The results of getting biblical wisdom are awesome! Certainly the results should energize us to pursue this path. With these results, why doesn't everyone pursue this path? The reason is that it takes some effort. Notice you have to look for it as if looking for silver or hidden treasure. But, it is worth the effort. Anything of value is worth the effort. We need to be willing to do what it takes to get it.

Seek biblical wisdom for it has great value.

February 3 - Read Proverbs 3

v. 9 Honor the LORD with your wealth and with the first fruits of all your produce;
v. 10 then your barns will be filled with plenty, and your vats will be bursting with wine.

How we handle money tells something about where we are spiritually (Luke 16:10-13; Matthew 6). Both the Old and New Testaments are consistent on this subject. First, as Proverbs 3:9 says, God wants us to give to Him from the top. That is, God wants us to give Him the "first fruits" of all we have. God must be first in our lives. Whether we give to Him from the first, or from the leftovers, says a great deal about His place in our lives.

Second, when we give from the top, God blesses (Proverbs 3:10). Scripture is full of God's promise to bless those who give in this manner. Check out Malachi 3:6-12 and 2 Corinthians 8-9 for some examples of these blessings.

Now certainly we should not give solely for the blessing. We also should not give solely because we are commanded. We should give out of a heart that is thankful to God for His great blessings. Also, we should give because we want to support His work in the world. When we give Him our first fruits with a right heart attitude, God will indeed bless in so many ways. He always does!

Put God first in your life and show it by giving Him your "first fruits."

February 4 - Read Proverbs 4

v. 14 Do not enter the path of the wicked, and do not walk in the way of the evil.

Proverbs 4:14-19 tells us that there is a difference between the path of the wicked and the path of the righteous. People today want us to think that life is gray and there is no black and white. However, there is a difference between how the wicked live and how the righteous live. They are on two separate paths. These paths are not the same at all. The path of the righteous is bright, and the path of the wicked is deep darkness. Those on the path of the wicked will stumble.

The choice of how we will live our lives is in our hands. Choose the right path! The problem with paths is where they lead. Some paths lead to good places and some to bad places. People think that all paths lead to good places, but this is not true. A couple of years ago my son and I chose a path to walk on because it looked like the right one. It was only when we got to the end that we realized we chose the wrong path and ended up in the wrong place. Because of this we ended up walking a few miles in the wrong direction.

You don't have to wait until the end of the path to know if your path is the right one or the wrong one. God tells us in His Word. All we have to do is look. Check out Matthew 7:13-14 and note the warning about the paths we can choose.

Heed the warnings of the Bible and choose the right path.

February 5 - Read Proverbs 5

v. 3 For the lips of a forbidden woman drip honey, and her speech is smoother than oil,

v. 4 but in the end she is as bitter as wormwood, sharp as a two-edged sword.

We are living in a world where sex outside of marriage is no longer thought to be wrong. But, Proverbs 5 talks about the WISDOM of avoiding adultery and being faithful to your spouse. In fact, in verse 22, adultery is referred to as "iniquities" and a "sin."

God's moral standard has not changed on the issue of sex. It was created to be enjoyed inside of marriage (1 Corinthians 7; Hebrews 13). Outside of marriage, it is to be avoided because it will bring the judgment of God (Ephesians 5; 1 Thessalonians 4) on those who are immoral. Don't let this world's thinking fool you into believing there is nothing wrong with sex outside of marriage.

People today tell us that no one will get hurt. Take a look at those devastated by the sin of adultery, even a small look, and you will know that has been a lie from the first time it was said. Sin always hurts people, and this sin is no different. There are physical (verses 9-10), financial (v. 10) and emotional (v. 11) consequences to sexual sin.

The fact that our present world is driven by sex and lust is nothing new. The fact that so few still call it "sin" is new. Everything has become a "disease" for which we are helpless to overcome, or so is it said. When we look at life the way God does, then we will see life with wisdom.

Reject sexual immorality. See it the way God sees it.

February 6 - Read Proverbs 6

v. 12 A worthless person, a wicked man, goes about with crooked speech,

A worthless and wicked man is described in Proverbs 6:12-15. We are told that this kind of person has crooked speech, which means morally corrupt language (v. 12). He is also sneaky (v. 13). All of this comes from a heart that is perverted and seeks evil (v. 14). This kind of person also continually sows discord or dissension (v. 14). This person is seeking to cause division, which is something God hates (v. 19). This is not a description you should ever want to be true of you. This person is surely a sinful person.

The problem with wickedness is that, for a season, it may seem to be the way to go. For a season, it may seem to gain victory in this life. For a season, it may look like this way of living gets you ahead. But the reality is that, in a moment, it will all fall apart. In a moment, what looked so well in this world will suddenly come crashing down. The crash may happen in this world, or it may not until the next. But, be sure of this, it will happen.

People sometimes wonder why the crash takes so long to come. Because it takes so long to come, people become tempted to join in with the wicked (Psalm 73). Don't join them. Listen to the warning found in verse 15.

Avoid wickedness, no matter how tempting it may sometimes be.

February 7 - Read Proverbs 7

v. 15 so now I have come out to meet you, to seek you eagerly, and I have found you.

In Proverbs 7:15, we find a prostitute telling a young man that she came looking for him. This is a warning to us not to be naïve. We sometimes think that everyone is nice and kind, but that is being naïve. We find it hard to imagine that someone would come looking for us to invite us into sin or to hurt us. Yet, we see this truth throughout the Bible.

In this case, the prostitute is inviting the young man to join him in sin. The particular sin here is adultery. This is a sin that just keeps popping up in society. Notice that she is not only inviting him to sin with her, but she is doing so eagerly. We need to take the warning of Jesus to "watch and pray" seriously.

We are told in Genesis 3 that Eve ate of the tree, and then invited Adam to do the same thing. This would be the first example in the Bible of this "invitation" happening. But it surely was not the last.

I was told just the other day that people are basically "good." Yet, this is not what God says in Romans 3:10-16. People not only sin, but they eagerly invite us to sin, sometimes in the most wicked ways. I wish we would base our thinking on what God states in His Word. We would be far wiser if we understood things His way.

Stay alert and don't fall for invitations to sin.

February 8 - Read Proverbs 8

v. 1 Does not wisdom call? Does not understanding raise her voice?
v. 4 "To you, O men, I call, and my cry is to the children of man.

Do you want to be wise? Do you want to live life with understanding? It is not as hard as you might think. In fact, wisdom is calling out to you. We see this in Proverbs 8:1,4. The problem with not being wise is not that wisdom can't be found. The problem is that people either look in the wrong places, do not look at all, or are not willing to take some effort to find it. Wisdom is available to all mankind according to verse 4.

True wisdom, wisdom for life, is found in the Word of God (See Psalms 119:97-104). If you want wisdom and are willing to dig for it as for gold, it is there for the taking. God wants you to become wise; He even tells us to ask Him for it and He will give it to us (James 1). Yet, people chase after the wrong things (silver, gold & rubies). However, wisdom is more valuable than riches (Proverbs 8:10-11). Don't spend your whole life chasing after the wrong things. Seek the wisdom that comes from God.

At the end of your life, you will see the folly of chasing after those things that don't provide value, real value. It is much wiser to learn that lesson before you regret your decisions.

Seek wisdom from God. As you open the Bible ask Him to fill you with His wisdom.

February 9 - Read Proverbs 9

v. 10 The fear of the Lord *is the beginning of wisdom, and the knowledge of the Holy One is insight.*

The world has turned away from the Creator, and in doing so, it has thought itself wise. We see this truth in Romans 1, where God describes how men have turned away from Him. It says in verses 22 and 23, "Claiming to be wise, they became fools, and exchanged the glory of the immortal god for images resembling mortal man and birds and animals." In Psalm 14:1 it says, "the fool says in his heart, 'There is no God.'" This world has turned away from God and has seen itself as wise in its actions. But this world has totally missed what is really wise.

It is in a relationship with God where wisdom actually starts. It is in knowing God that insight begins. Rejecting God or avoiding God does not get a person to the place of wisdom. It only pushes you further away from that place. God is wisdom and wisdom comes from Him, so without Him, how can there be any wisdom at all? Wisdom starts with Him! If you want it, you must go to Him. You can't turn away from Him and expect to find it. This world trots out all of these brilliant men before us and claims they have all sorts of wisdom. These are men who reject God. These are men who are not as wise as this world thinks.

Do you want to be truly wise? Then begin with a relationship with God.

February 10 - Read Proverbs 10

v. 17 Whoever heeds instruction is on the path to life, but he who rejects reproof leads others astray.

How are you affecting others by the way you live? Are you helping or hurting others? One area that often is missed when considering our impact on others is how we respond to correction. For example, when a couple comes for marriage counseling, often the attitude of one or both is:

1. "Counselor, agree with me that my spouse is the problem and needs to change."
2. "I want my marriage to be fixed, but I don't want to change. I hope my spouse will."

These kinds of attitudes affect others. Proverbs 10:17 helps us to understand this.

It says that the person who listens to instruction is on the right path. This we know. It also says that the person who does not rightly respond to reproof or correction leads others down the wrong path. In other words, the way we respond to truth has an effect on others. When you do what is right, it helps others around you. When you do not do what is right, it hurts others around you.

Parents want their kids to listen to them all of the time and every time. Yet, parents sometimes come home from work in an uproar because their bosses at work reproved them. What are you teaching your children about life? By your response, are you leading them towards the path of life? Or, are you leading them astray?

Consider how your lifestyle affects those around you.

February 11 - Read Proverbs 11

v. 4 Riches do not profit in the day of wrath, but righteousness delivers from death.

It seems in life that people seek wealth far more often then they seek righteousness. People think that wealth is far more important than righteousness. People think that wealth has far more value than righteousness. People play the lottery with the hope that it will make them wealthy and give them everything they want. When is that last time you heard someone say, "The thing I want most in my life is righteousness"?

We would think that in the day of trouble, the greater thing to have would be wealth. Yet Proverbs 11:4 says that in that day "riches do not profit" but "righteousness delivers from death." Maybe people are searching and hoping for the wrong thing. Just maybe the thing that is thought to be of the greatest value really isn't.

True righteousness can only come from God. We get it by placing our trust in what Jesus did for us on the cross. It is then lived out daily in life. Righteousness is simply right living. God determines what right living is, and He tells us what it is in His Word. Live daily doing what God says in His Word, and you can be sure that you are living righteously. If you are living righteously, you have gained something far more valuable than wealth.

Spend more time seeking righteousness than you do wealth, for it is of greater value.

February 12 - Read Proverbs 12

v. 1 Whoever loves discipline loves knowledge, but he who hates reproof is stupid.

I think the vast majority of people would say that they hate to be corrected. But did you know that the Bible says in Proverbs 12:1, "...He who hates reproof is stupid"? If I said that, I would have most people mad or disagreeing with me, for most people do not like to call anything stupid. But, that is what God says, and if God says it, it is true.

To be reproved here means to be rebuked. It means that someone has come to you and pointed out your sin or pointed out that you are wrong. Who wants that? I will answer that - the one who wants to be right with God. While no one needs anyone walking behind him, attacking him for every wrong thing, we all need someone who loves us enough to rebuke us in love. Second Timothy 3:16 and 2 Timothy 4:2 tell us that the Bible and biblical preaching are to be used for this very purpose.

We don't like to be corrected because our sinful, proud hearts desire no part of that. But, our sin and pride are the things that can keep us from spiritual maturity. When you are rebuked in love and respond well, you are on the path towards maturity. If you attack the one rebuking you, you are called a "fool" in Proverbs. In fact, in our present verse you are called "stupid." The word stupid means senseless or lacking understanding.

Don't be stupid! Humbly respond to rebuke.

February 13 - Read Proverbs 13

v. 20 Whoever walks with the wise becomes wise, but the companion of fools will suffer harm.

Take a look at all the people who you consider to be close friends. Consider their character, actions and words. Consider their goals, priorities and desires. Consider their effect on you. Are these friends helping you to grow wise? Is it possible for this group of friends to help you grow wise?

Proverbs 13:20 tells us that we should choose wise friends and avoid fools for friends. Choosing fools for friends will cause harm. 1 Corinthians 15:33 states that bad friends can ruin good morals. Also, consider the kind of friend you are. Do you make a good choice for a friend based on your character, actions and words?

Reading the book of Proverbs with one thought in mind can be valuable. Try reading it looking for the kinds of friends you should not choose. The result of this kind of study can have great value in light of Proverbs 13:20. There is an old saying that goes like this, "Run with the dogs and you will get fleas." Another says, "Run with the wolves and you will learn to howl." Well, you get the idea. Choose wise friends, friends with good moral character, who are headed in the right direction.

Be wise in your choice of friends.

February 14 - Read Proverbs 14

v. 1 The wisest of women builds her house, but folly with her own hands tears it down.

They are seen over and over. Women who build and women who tear down their homes. We see these women in the Bible. We see these women in history. We see these women today. It is heartwarming to see a wise woman build her house, and it is heart wrenching to see a foolish woman tearing hers down.

A wise woman is a woman who follows God's Word in every part of her life. She is the woman who is seen in Proverbs 31, Ephesians 5 & 1 Peter 3. She is a woman like Ruth or Esther. She is a woman who seeks and listens to advice. She is a woman who sees her children with a balanced view. She is a woman who submits to, loves and respects her husband.

The foolish woman is the opposite of the above. I have also seen the following characteristics in the foolish woman:

1. Cares more about how clean her house is than much else
2. Is more concerned with self than others
3. Has a heart that is caught up with money, clothes and the things of this world
4. Usually has few friends because she doesn't know how to make friends
5. Often blames others for where she or her kids are in life

Sadly, the foolish woman often does not realize how foolish she is until the damage has been done, until the house has been torn down.

Women, don't tear down your house! Build it up!

February 15 - Read Proverbs 15

v. 12 A scoffer does not like to be reproved; he will not go to the wise.

A "scoffer" is a person who resents correction and will not consult the wise (v. 12). He does not like to be corrected. "Reproved" in verse 12 may be defined as "rebuke." So, a scoffer is a person who does not like being rebuked and also is not the kind of person who looks for wise counsel. He may seek counsel, but it is just to get people to agree with him, not a search for truth. He is the kind of person that shows by his actions that he is not wise (v. 31-32).

It is so sad to see that those who need counsel, help, or a rebuke most often seek it the least. In fact, you can even learn from an enemy's rebuke. The scoffer generally finds ways to excuse his behavior and even reject the rebuke.

The scoffer will not go to the wise, so the wise often end up going to him to help him. But, the scoffer sees their help as an attack. The scoffer tends not to listen to the wise and so is not at home among the wise. This makes the whole situation extremely hard for the wise. They want to help the scoffer, but at the same time know that the scoffer will not listen.

No one would ever admit to being a scoffer, but you can tell if you are by your response to a rebuke. So, always keep your heart open to a Biblical rebuke.

Seek wise counsel, and when rebuked, respond with love and so be at home among the wise.

February 16 - Read Proverbs 16

v. 18 Pride goes before destruction, and a haughty spirit before a fall.

Pride! We all know it is wrong, but we all have a hard time seeing it in our own lives. Of course, it is easy to see in others, but pride is in us and is seen whenever we get puffed up with ourselves. We must learn to detect it in ourselves. God sees it as an ugly sin. The Bible tells us that God stands opposed to the proud in heart.

There are many problems with pride. It tends to cause us to treat people differently than we would if we did not have it. Another problem with pride is what it does to our hearts. Pride fills one up with self, and the end result of that is not good. The end result is destruction and a fall. There are plenty of examples of this in the Bible and in life. In Acts 12, we see the example of Herod, whom God killed because of it. Even Solomon, the writer of most of Proverbs, finally succumbed to it.

I find that keeping our focus on God is a way of keeping pride from filling our hearts. If your eyes are full of God and His holiness and greatness, your eyes tend to see your own sin. See Isaiah 6 for an example of this.

Detect pride in yourself so that it will not bring about your fall.

February 17 - Read Proverbs 17

v. 9 Whoever covers an offense seeks love, but he who repeats a matter separates close friends.

How do you respond when people offend you? The fool shows his annoyance immediately. Not so the wise! In fact, they respond much differently than the fool to an offense. The response of the wise and the fool is different because they focus on different people in offending situations. The fool focuses on himself and his hurt. The wise person focuses on the offender and his love for him. The wise person seeks love, while the foolish person is selfish. The wise seek love and so cover over an offense (See also 10:12). The wise seek love because they know that is what God wants. The wise seek to love not only those who love them but even those who have offended them.

Secondly, the wise do not repeat matters to others, for they know that doing so will separate people, even close friends. The wise do not want division; they want harmony. They only speak of offenses when given no choice. They only speak of offenses when keeping quiet would cause more harm than talking about it. Sadly, the foolish even cover their desire to gossip in the form of prayer requests. When offended, what do you seek? Do you want to bring people together or help pull them apart?

Seek harmony by covering offenses against you and refusing to repeat them to others.

February 18 - Read Proverbs 18

v. 9 Whoever is slack in his work is a brother to him who destroys.

We are living in a welfare state. We are living in a day when "everyone wants something for nothing." We are living in a day when people would rather get a "handout" than go to work. We are living in a day when people should commit to memory Proverbs 18:9. These words are strong and startling. They should stir believers to proper actions. They should cause us to consider how bad being lazy really is. It is pretty bad as stated in this verse.

The word "slack" means "idle." Throughout the Bible, God makes clear that He expects people to work and to work hard. We see this truth in the New Testament in 2 Thessalonians 3:6-15 and elsewhere. This is one of the reasons we should avoid gambling, which seeks to escape work with a get-rich-quick scheme.

How bad is it to be lazy or idle? We are told that one who is lazy or idle is the brother to one who destroys. Here the word "destroy" means "to corrupt." So if you are a slacker, your brother is a corrupter, meaning that the slacker corrupts. These are strong words concerning our work ethic. While everyone needs to get rest, being slack or idle or lazy is a whole different issue.

It would be better to be accused of working too hard than to be accused of working too little. Either extreme is not good. Yet, the Bible is full of verses that warn of working too little and none of working too much.

Don't be a slacker and therefore a brother to one who destroys.

February 19 - Read Proverbs 19

v. 2 Desire without knowledge is not good, and whoever makes haste with his feet misses his way.

So often we are in a hurry. If our computer is not flying, we get mad. If the girl at Burger King doesn't get our order quickly enough, we fret. If the TV remote isn't flipping channels at soaring speeds, we scream. This is often how we run through life. We do everything at breakneck speed. The problem with that way of living is that we can "be hasty and miss the way." When we get in a hurry, we can miss the right thing or do the right thing in a wrong way.

This is also true of zeal. Just because you are excited about doing something does not mean it is the right thing to do or that you will do it in the right way. Zeal is great, but zeal without knowledge is not. There are many people who are zealous about religion but have missed the right way (See Romans 10:1-2). Zeal must go hand-in-hand with knowledge. When our knowledge is correct, we should be zealous about what we do. The wise person combines zeal with knowledge and then connects it with careful steps, not haste.

Merge zeal with knowledge, and don't be hasty or you may miss the way.

February 20 - Read Proverbs 20

v. 22 Do not say, "I will repay evil"; wait for the LORD, and he will deliver you.

It is no surprise for me to say, "Sometimes people hurt us." We all know that, and we all know that it will always be a part of life. People can hurt us either intentionally or by accident. Even our best of friends can hurt us unintentionally. Sadly, even at times, they may do so intentionally. This is a reality of life. So, the issue we need to consider is not whether we will or will not be hurt by people. The issue we need to deal with is how we choose to respond when we are hurt by people. God tells us to never seek revenge (verse 22). When we are hurt, the wise thing to do is not to return evil for evil. We should never seek revenge.

When you find yourself hurt by others, especially if it is intentional, trust God to deal with the person who is hurting you. Don't ever seek to retaliate against someone who is personally attacking you. You may have to correct the situation, but you don't need to retaliate against the person who has hurt you. God will do that (See Numbers 12.). Romans 12:14-21 and Matthew 5:43-48 give us further revelation on this important subject.

Also, notice that this truth is found both in the Old and New Testament. This principle has always been true. Let God deal with people who hurt you! Follow Jesus' example when He even prayed for those who physically put Him on the cross.

Love your enemies, don't retaliate against them.

February 21 - Read Proverbs 21

v. 3 To do righteousness and justice is more acceptable to the LORD than sacrifice.

People in our society often live life by going to church on Sunday or Saturday and then living "like the devil" during the week. They think that "devil living" is OK because they go to church on Sunday. But, God says that worship that is not seen in our lifestyle is hypocritical and worthless. People think that their religious activity on Sunday makes up for all of their unrighteous living during the week. Sunday church services become just a play that people go to see, not reality in their lives.

Some people think that immorality, greed, idolatry, slander, drunkenness, theft, and other such things are OK as long as you show up for church or do some religious things. But that is not what God says in verse 3. For a clear-cut illustration of this truth, see 1 Samuel 15. The value of worship on Sunday is determined by what we do during the week. It is not the other way around. One hour of worship that is not seen in how we live all of the other hours of the week is worthless worship, no matter how emotional it may be. This was one of the problems with the religious leaders of Jesus' day (See Matthew 23).

Religion is not true religion unless it influences every day of the week and every hour of the day. Worship must be a daily activity that is seen in the way one walks, talks and thinks. That kind of true worship is seen in righteous and just living.

Make worship mean something by doing what is right and just every day of the week.

February 22 - Read Proverbs 22

v. 1 A good name is to be chosen rather than great riches, and favor is better than silver or gold.

Many people spend their lives trying to get rich. People work many hours just to have more money or more things money can buy. Look at all of the people playing the lottery or gambling. This, along with others things, tells us that for many people, money, along with the things it buys, must be the most valuable thing in the whole world. It is not! There are many things more valuable than money, so it is a shame that people will often sell their souls for money. Verse 1 tells us of one of those things that are more valuable than money or wealth.

It is having a good name! There are many who have missed this, for there are many who chase after riches at the expense of their names and the respect of others.

Don't miss out on having a good name! Live in such a way so that you earn the respect of others so that your name is one that is honored. Do the things today that will cause people to respect you tomorrow. Avoid the things that will cause people to smirk when they hear your name mentioned.

One more thing... When people try to smear your name, entrust yourself to God and continue to do what is right.

Be more concerned about how people view your name than how much is in your wallet.

February 23 – Read Proverbs 23

v. 4 Do not toil to acquire wealth; be discerning enough to desist.
v. 5 When your eyes light on it, it is gone, for suddenly it sprouts wings, flying like an eagle toward heaven.

Beware of working too much. Yes, working too much! The end of the road in life is not riches. Wealth does not hold the happiness that so many people think it does. We should be careful that we don't work to the point of ruining our lives just to get rich. Riches can be gone in a moment. There may be times when you have to work long hours, but be careful.

There are numerous rich people who have had great wealth then lost it, often while still counting it. Verse 5 tells us that it can fly away like an eagle. In life, wisdom is often seen in restraint: the restraint of holding one's anger, the restraint of not eating too much, the restraint of not wearing yourself out to get rich. You must have the wisdom to show restraint. Don't wear yourself out to get rich. Have the wisdom to show restraint.

There are all kinds of dangers from working too much. You can spend too much time away from your family. You can spend too much time away from your church. You can destroy your health. You can get rich and forget God. While it is hard to figure out how much is too much, if you see any of the just mentioned dangers, you may be working too much.

Be wise, don't work too much and for the wrong reasons.

February 24 – Read Proverbs 24:10

v. 10 If you faint in the day of adversity, your strength is small.

Life is tough! This world is not for the faint of heart. Life is tough because our world has been saturated with sin. Many, because of how tough this world is, try to hide from it. They run to drugs, alcohol, pills, work, or some other thing which helps them hide. Some people even create their own little worlds in their minds and you can see in their eyes that no one is home.

Yet, verse ten says that if we falter in times of trouble, our strength is small. Life's troubles can make us want to quit. People quit all the time. They quit on their marriages, churches, jobs and even life itself. I have been ready to quit being a Pastor on several occasions. Statistics tell us that 1,500 pastors are leaving the ministry every MONTH. But if there has been one verse that keeps me from quitting more than any other, it is Proverbs 24:16, which says, "for though a righteous man falls sevens times, he rises again, but the wicked are brought down by calamity."

I want to be numbered among the righteous. The righteous don't quit; they keep on keeping on. One of the marks of a mature believer is perseverance (James 1:2-4). A mature believer knows where to go when life is tough (Philippians 4:10-13). Life may be hitting you full force today, but be numbered among the righteous. Be numbered among the mature. Whatever you do today - DON'T QUIT! Meet life in the strength of Christ.

When adversity comes - don't quit! Run to Jesus for strength.

February 25 – Read Proverbs 25

v. 28 A man without self-control is like a city broken into and left without walls.

The power of self-control... Do you have that power? So many sins, so many mistakes in life are directly related to the inability to control oneself. It is seen when temptation comes our way and we are unable to say no. Something happens out of the blue, and we are not ready for it. We debate whether we should buy that thing that we can't afford or wait until we can and end up spending foolishly. We know we should refrain, but the pull is too strong. Have you been there?

A city with broken-down walls is a city that is indefensible. A city with broken-down walls is a city that can't keep anything out. A city with broken-down walls is a city that is open to trouble. Do you lack self-control? If you do, then you are open to all kinds of temptation and probably have too weak of a defense to say, "No!" You are like a city with broken-down walls.

Paul disciplined his body so that he would become self-controlled and not give into temptation. For the Christian, self-control finds its foundation in the strength of Christ (Philippians 4:13) and the filling of the Holy Spirit (Ephesians 5:18; Galatians 5:17). Don't let your inability to control yourself cause you to lose your testimony (Matthew 5:13-16). Self-control is a great form of protection against all sorts of sin and evil.

Control yourself so that you will not be like a city without walls.

February 26 - Read Proverbs 26

v. 4 Answer not a fool according to his folly, lest you be like him yourself.
v. 5 Answer a fool according to his folly, lest he be wise in his own eyes.

Could it be? Might there be a contradiction in the Bible? Verse four tells us not to answer a fool and verse five tells us to answer a fool. Is this a contradiction? People look for contradictions in the Bible all of the time to try to prove it wrong.

There is no contradiction. The book of wisdom is telling us that sometimes we need to refrain from answering the fool and sometimes we need to answer the fool. Sometimes if we respond to a person who is acting like a fool, we will be just like them. Yet, there are times if we just let the foolish person go, he will think that his actions are right and wise. So, he must be refuted and proven unwise.

How do we know when to do which? That is where wisdom comes in. There are times when we need to respond to people, and there are times when we just need to keep our mouths shut. Today you may find yourself in both situations. Knock, seek and pray, asking God to help you to know when to do which. Knowing how to respond to people shows the difference between a mature person and one who is not. There are times when you need to respond to people to keep them from thinking their foolishness is wise, and there are times to remain silent.

Be wise and know when to answer people and when to keep quiet.

February 27 - Read Proverbs 27

v. 2 Let another praise you, and not your own mouth; a stranger, and not your own lips.

There are all sorts of reasons why someone might want to praise himself to others. It happens all of the time. Some do so to get ahead in life. Some do so to brag about what they have accomplished. Some do it to get "one-upmanship" on another person. Some do it because they have very low self-esteem. Some do so to show their value to others. As I said, there are many reasons why someone might praise himself to others.

This verse tells us not to do it. If you are going to be praised, let someone else do it, even a stranger. You might say, "If I waited for someone to praise me, it would never happen." That may be true, but self-praise never sounds wise or good. Commending yourself to others is not well-received. Generally speaking, it is improper to applaud yourself. Matthew Henry wrote, "There may be a just occasion for us to vindicate ourselves, but it does not become us to applaud ourselves.[2]"

On the other hand, some people have been praised so little that, when it comes, they don't know how to respond to it. That may be an area that will also take some work.

Second Corinthians 10:18 says, "For it is not the one who commends himself who is approved, but the one whom the Lord commends." The reality is that self-praise means very little. It is only when God, or even others, speaks well of us that it counts.

Avoid self-praise!

February 28 - Read Proverbs 28

v. 9 If one turns away his ear from hearing the law, even his prayer is an abomination.

The Bible tells us in many places that God loves to hear us pray. For example, Matthew 7:7-12 tells us about that. Yet, there are times when God hates to hear some people pray. This verse tells us that the one who rejects God's Word (the Bible) is the one whose prayers are detestable to God. The word "abomination" means an offense or something that is disgusting. So when some people pray to God, God sees their prayers as disgusting. Why? Because they have rejected His Word by not obeying it. These are the people who turn a deaf ear to the law (the Bible).

If you do not listen to God, God does not want to listen to you. Are you listening to what God says in the Bible? Is His Word the final authority for all that you think, say and do? Do you live life in obedience to His Word?

Think about it. If you are the disobedient person, than you are the one whose prayers are disgusting to God. I remember a question that was asked years ago during a race for president. It was this one: "Does God hear the prayers of everyone?" The answer is yes! But, some of the prayers that God hears are offensive to Him. Are they yours?

Live in a manner pleasing to God so that your prayers will not be an abomination.

February 29 - Read Proverbs 29

v. 25 The fear of man lays a snare, but whoever trusts in the Lord *is safe.*

O for a heart that only "fears God." We mess up far more than we think because of the fear of man. Even the apostle Paul asked for prayer concerning this issue. In Ephesians 5:19-20, he asked for prayer so that he would fearlessly preach. Peter, out of his fear of man, denied the Lord right before he heard the rooster, and he did it again later on in his life (Matthew 26:69-75; Galatians 2:11-14). The sad thing is that we often fear man more than we fear God. Because this is true, we often don't do what God wants us to do. We see this happen all throughout the Bible. This proverb is so true!

We need to stop fearing man and start trusting God (Proverbs 29:25). So we learn here that the way to overcome our fear of man is to trust God. As I so often say, the opposite of fear is faith and vise versa. We often fear what we see (man) and fail to trust what we do not see (God). Faith brings us to the opposite of this: trusting what we do not see (God) and not fearing what we do see (man). This is not an easy task, and that is why Paul asked for prayer concerning this very issue.

We all need help in this area of our lives, and we all need to keep in mind what God said concerning faith: "And without faith it is impossible to please him…" (Hebrews 11:6).

Trust God more than you fear man.

March 1 - Read Proverbs 1

v. 7 The fear of the LORD is the beginning of knowledge; fools despise wisdom and instruction.

If a young person were to ask, "Where do I need to begin life to make sure I get where I need to be at the end of my life?" I think the answer for many people would be all over the place. I think the advice of people concerning this issue would be all over the place.

Proverbs is not all over the place. It has a very clear answer to this question. It states in 1:7, "The fear of the Lord is the beginning of knowledge." Without getting into great detail, let me say that "the fear of the Lord" refers to a right relationship with God. Notice that this is the place where knowledge begins. So this is the answer to the question I first gave. There is no more important thing in life than a right relationship with God. Do you want to be wise? Get right with God! Do you want your life to be where it should be at the end of your life? Get right with God!

Unfortunately, though this is the correct starting place in life, many people reject the answer. Note that the fool despises wisdom and discipline. Christians are often looked on as fools, but that is not how God sees it. It is the one who rejects God who really is the fool (See Psalm 14:1). Some have told me that they want to live their life whatever way they want and then before they die, they will get right with God. That thinking is backwards and will not work.

Above all else, seek to have a right relationship with God through the person and work of His Son (Jesus).

March 2 - Read Proverbs 2

v. 4 if you seek it like silver and search for it as for hidden treasures,

Have you ever considered how you approach God's Word? Do you go to it as if searching for treasure? There are those whose approach to God's Word can be summed up in Proverbs 2:4.

Our approach to God's Word should be the same as one who is carefully searching for treasure. We are to go to God's Word looking for precious and rare jewels. Those kinds of things are not easily found. It takes careful digging and searching. Most will never find valuable jewels because they just don't put forth the effort that it takes to find them.

Can you imagine what it must be like to search and search and then one day you finally find something that is very rare and valuable? I think you would walk away with great excitement. When is the last time you walked away from God's Word having found a rare treasure of truth? When is the last time you walked away from God's Word with excitement over what you found? While we all go through dry-spells because silver is so hard to find, there ought to be times when we walk away from our time in God's Word with great excitement because of what we have found. This kind of excitement takes silver-seeking and treasure-hunting.

Search God's Word today for truth, as if searching for treasure. You may find something very valuable.

March 3 - Read Proverbs 3

v. 25 Do not be afraid of sudden terror or of the ruin of the wicked, when it comes,
v.26 for the LORD will be your confidence and will keep your foot from being caught.

Some fear is proper and right because it keeps us from doing wrong or dangerous things. Proper fear can even motivate us to do the right thing. Yet, far too many people are driven and controlled by the wrong kind of fear. Fear often keeps them from doing the right thing. It often causes them to do the wrong thing.

One example of sinful fear is the fear of "sudden terror or of the ruin of the wicked." "Sudden terror" refers to bad things that come our way quickly or unexpectedly. This is the kind of fear that can keep people up all night. This is the fear that keeps people afraid of what may happen tomorrow. This is the fear of what lurks around every corner.

The one who walks in wisdom knows that God is watching over him (Psalms 121). He trusts in the promises of God, promises such as the one Jesus gave in Matthew 7:24-27. He knows that God has his back; therefore, he can walk or lie down and not be afraid. He knows that nothing can harm us unless God allows it, and if God allows it, there is nothing that he can do to stop it. He knows that God is at work in his life, so everything that happens in his life is under the control of a sovereign God who is working everything together for his good (Romans 8:28).

Don't allow fear to be the thing that controls you. Place your confidence in God.

March 4 - Read Proverbs 4

v. 1 Hear, O sons, a father's instruction
v. 3-4 When I was a son with my father...he taught me....

There is a principle in the Bible that is laid out in both the Old Testament and New Testament. It is a principle that is vitally important. Sadly, churches, families, and individuals miss it all too often. It is the principle of **discipleship.** It may also be called the principle of **legacy**. Stated simply, it means that all of us should be investing our lives in the next generation, who in turn invest their lives in the next generation. This can refer to physical generations or to spiritual generations.

We find this principle in Proverbs 4. In verse 1, we see Solomon speaking to his sons. In verses 3-4, we see that the thing he is teaching his son is what he learned at the feet of his own father. So the trail goes from father to son to grandson. This may be seen in a church where one person invests his life in another person, who then invests his life in another person and so on.

In the New Testament, we see this principle in 2 Timothy 2:2. We also see it in Titus 2:3-4, where the pastor is teaching the older women and then the older women are teaching the younger women. Can this principle also be seen in your life? Are you investing your life in others and then seeing them invest their lives in still others? Are you inviting people to follow you as you follow Christ?

Invest your life in someone and then encourage them to do the same.

March 5 - Read Proverbs 5

v. 21 For a man's ways are before the eyes of the Lord, and he ponders all his paths.

Proverbs 5 is about avoiding immorality. One of the reasons people still get involved in such relationships is that they think they can do so and no one will know. In fact, this is why people continue to do so many wrong things in our world. But sooner or later everyone gets caught. For example, I saw a crime show on TV where the cop said, "Thank God for dumb criminals." The criminal thought he would not get caught, but he did.

Here is the thing we need to think about: We get caught far sooner and far more often than we think. Our ways are before the eyes of God, which means that God sees everything we do. This truth is spelled out in Psalm 139. God sees everything you do, no matter where and no matter when. This truth is stated, in this chapter, as a deterrent so that you will avoid sexual sin. You may hide from others, but you cannot hide from God. Think of it this way: Would you do wrong, would you sin sexually, if God were sitting right next to you? Or, how would you act differently if you knew someone was watching you? With this truth in mind, we should also keep in mind what God thinks about sexual sin (Ephesians 5:3-7; 1 Thessalonians 4:1-8).

Flee sexual immorality, for God is always watching you and he sees everything you do.

March 6 - Read Proverbs 6

v. 16 There are six things that the LORD hates, seven that are an abomination to him:

There are six things God hates, yes, that God hates. There are seven that are an abomination to him. The 6/7 formula stresses that the final sin is the culmination of the first six. They are listed in Proverbs 6:16-19. Notice that the first five are associated with body parts and move from top to bottom.

1. Haughty eyes = pride
2. Lying tongue = to tell lies, be deceptive
3. Hands that shed innocent blood = intentional harming of the innocent
4. Heart that devises wicked plans = evil that begins in the heart, Mark 7:14-23
5. Feet that make haste to run to evil = running/hurrying to do evil
6. False witness who breathes out lies = falsehood in a courtroom setting, purgery
   -Note that lying is mentioned twice
7. One who sows discord among brothers = a person who causes division

This is not an exhaustive list of the things God hates. It gives us a list of the things that divide people. God has strong words for those who would divide people or churches (Romans 16:17-18; Titus 3:10-11). Sometimes doing the right thing will cause division. But what is spoken of here is that of causing division by doing evil things from the head right down to the feet.

Beware of doing what God hates, in fact, what to God is an abomination.

March 7 - Read Proverbs 7

v. 7 and I have seen among the simple, I have perceived among the youths, a young man lacking sense,

The son mentioned in Proverbs 7 was a young man who lacked sense. Because he lacked sense, he ended up with a prostitute. All of us lack sense (wisdom), and we often do not get it until it is too late to be of value. But, it does not have to be that way. We can gain wisdom long before we would naturally gain it through the school of hard knocks. Here are some of the ways mentioned in the Bible to gain wisdom so that we do not make mistakes in life.

1. Listen to your parents – Proverbs 7:1-5.
   -This very chapter is a father trying to teach his son wisdom.
2. Read the Bible – Psalms 119:97-104; Proverbs 1
   -Go to a church where the Bible is faithfully taught.
3. Learn from history – 1 Corinthians 10.
   -As has been said, "Those who don't learn from history are doomed to repeat it."
4. Learn from the trials God brings you through – James 1:1-4
5. Pray for wisdom – James 1:5-8
6. Have counselors, advisors and friends with whom you can get advice – 11:14; 12:15

Wisdom is not the same as knowledge. Wisdom is the correct use of knowledge. It includes making good choices over bad ones. We all need wisdom, and we all need more of it. The list above provides ways where you can gain wisdom.

Choose to be wise and then go the place where you can learn to be wise.

March 8 - Read Proverbs 8

v. 7 from my mouth will utter truth, wickedness is an abomination to my lips
v. 8 All the words of my mouth are righteous; there is nothing twisted or crooked in them.
v. 13 The fear of the Lord is hatred of evil...

We are living in a day when the world thinks that immorality is wise. The world thinks that those who are moral are not wise. The world thinks that we are unwise to say that alternate lifestyles are immoral, but, wisdom and morality go hand in hand. Proverbs 8 speaks of the qualities of wisdom, and from it we can see that wisdom and morality go together. One cannot be immoral and wise at the same time. The two do not go together. They are like water and oil and do not mix. Wise living is moral living and immoral living is just not wise, no matter how you look at it.

We are only wise when we live the way God calls us to live. Moral living is living according to the Word of God. Any lifestyle that is lived any other way is not moral and therefore not wise. It really is that simple. Moral living is living that avoids wickedness or evil In any form. You may ask, "Who sets the standard of what is moral and what is not?" The answer is easy! God does. And He has told us what is moral and what is not in the Bible.

Be wise. Be moral!

March 9 - Read Proverbs 9

v. 1 Wisdom has built her house; she has hewn her seven pillars.
v. 4 "Whoever is simple, let him turn in here!" ...

All of us are in need wisdom. None of us has enough. This world is confusing and sin makes it even more complicated. I have sat at many kitchen tables and talked with parents and families who wished that they had more wisdom. We search for it and read dozens of books and watch loads of TV shows hoping to get it (Ecclesiastes 12:12b). The only people who I meet who think they don't need more wisdom are those who are full of pride.

The reality is that wisdom is not something that is lost and can't be found. Wisdom is ever before us, wanting to fill us. Verses 1-6 tells us that Wisdom has prepared her house and is inviting everyone over for a meal. The meal is on the table. She has gone out to the highest points in the city. She calls out to everyone in need of wisdom and bids them to come in. Wisdom is there for anyone and everyone who desires it.

The problem is that people have been looking in the wrong places and listening to the wrong people during their quest for wisdom. The right place is the Word of God. God invites us to come in and eat of its treasure.

Seek wisdom where it is found, in the Word of God (1:1-7).

March 10 - Read Proverbs 10

v. 4 A slack hand causes poverty, but the hand of the diligent makes rich.
v. 5 He who gathers in summer is a prudent son, but he who sleeps in harvest is a son who brings shame.

There are times when jobs are plentiful and times when they are not. What is interesting is that when they are not, it seems like people are not in a hurry to get one. When they are not, people should be rushing to the door to be able to provide for themselves and their families, but often they are not. Why would this be? I think the answer is twofold: laziness and foolishness.

"A slack hand" is a reference to laziness. A person who sleeps during harvest is not only lazy but stupid (not wise). America was built on the backs of people willing to work hard and be wise. America will die from many things including laziness and foolishness. The work ethic in America, along with many other countries, is dying. People want to sit back and take life easily and they do so most of the time. It reminds me of what God said it was like right before the flood (See Matthew 24:38).

Don't be the one who "brings shame." This is often seen when a man or woman builds a great business. Then, the children take over and destroy their business. This is due to not having the work ethic or the wisdom of the parent who built it.

Be wise! Work hard and work smart.

March 11 - Read Proverbs 11

v. 7 When the wicked dies, his hope will perish, and the expectation of wealth perishes too.

Death, what a thought! For most, death is a scary thing. For many, death ends hopes and dreams. This verse is full of sadness. The wicked have hope only in this life. How sad. People often look at the wicked (ungodly) and envy them because of their wealth. But our hearts ought to bleed for them because what they have is only for this lifetime and it does not last long. Those who reject God fill up on this world's goods, but no matter how much they have when they die, "they can't take it with them." This ought to change your view towards those who are ungodly and who have more of what this world offers than you do. (See Psalm 73.)

If you are living for God, and maybe don't have as much as those who are not serving God, don't go in the corner and cry for yourself. You still have all eternity to spend with God. You still have all eternity to walk on streets of gold. You still have all eternity to enjoy a life free of disease and sickness and pain. You still have all eternity enjoying all of God's blessings. Some say that is "pie in the sky thinking." It may be, but God makes a really good pie!

Don't get caught envying the wicked because of their wealth, you still have all eternity ahead of you.

March 12 - Read Proverbs 12

v. 15 The way of a fool is right in his own eyes, but a wise man listens to advice.

Sometimes you come across people who think they know all of the answers. This is especially true when it comes to knowing their path in life. They know they are doing the right thing, while everyone around them can see they are doing the wrong thing. Some people truly believe they are right when everything and everyone says they are wrong. This is the way of a "fool" as seen in Proverbs 12:15. The fool doesn't want anyone to tell them anything and if they do, they don't listen. They think they have everything under control. How sad!

The thing about a wise person is that he is always open to advice. He doesn't see advice as an attack on him. He sees advice as an opportunity to become wiser still. In fact, the wise person usually is the one who seeks and asks for advice. The wise person sees love in advice, but the fool only sees criticism. There is wisdom in a multitude of counselors, but there is only foolishness when your only counselor is you.

So which camp do you fit in with: the camp of the fool or the camp of the wise? Which characteristic describes you? I hope it is the camp of the wise.

Be open and willing to listen to advice, especially that which is biblical and given with love.

March 13 - Read Proverbs 13

v. 3 Whoever guards his mouth preserves his life; he who opens wide his lips comes to ruin.

"Open mouth. Insert foot." Have you ever done that? I'm sure you have. We all have, but, we should not just laugh it off. We should take warning from doing so. We should guard our lips, and in doing so, we will guard our life. So many people just say whatever is on their minds, often talking without thinking. This kind of speech is neither wise nor loving.

There is a warning in Proverbs 13:3 of doing that. It says that the one "who opens wide his lips (hastily & thoughtlessly) will come to ruin." This person just blurts out everything. Nothing is held in. Some people just let it all out and some think that there is nothing wrong with doing just that. But the person who does this will come to ruin. This is so true, but who would ever think it? Who would ever think that mere words could ruin a life? Who would ever think that rash words would ruin a life? The reality is that rash words cannot only ruin the life of the speaker, but they can ruin the lives of those spoken to or about. We need to carefully consider what we are going to say before we say it. It is better to speak slowly than to speak swiftly if what comes out of our mouths hurts others.

Speak with caution, and give thought to what comes from your mouth before it comes from your mouth.

March 14 - Read Proverbs 14

v. 2 Whoever walks in uprightness fears the LORD, but he who is devious in his ways despises him.

People often equate religion and love for God with religious activity. While this can be true, it is not always so. God states it differently in His Word, for He equates true religion and love of God with righteous living.

In the Old Testament, Israel was often rebuked when they fasted and presented offerings while, at the same time, not living righteously. The two must go hand in hand. When a person is living the way that God wants him to live, it establishes that he loves God (v. 2a). Daniel would be a classic example of someone whose love for God could be seen in his righteous walk (Daniel 6:4-5).

At the same time, one who is not living righteously proves he does not love God (v. 2b). The Old and New Testaments are full of people who claimed to love God, while at the same time rejecting God's call for righteous living. The very act of rejecting righteous living demonstrates one's lack of love for God. This is stated in 1 John 5:3, "For this is the love of God, that we keep his commandments. And his commandments are not burdensome." So, the way you live is a demonstration of whether you truly love God or whether you despise Him. An abundance of professions of love cannot silence how you live. Love of God is more verified by how we live than by what we declare.

Show your love for God by living righteously.

March 15 - Read Proverbs 15

v. 28 The heart of the righteous ponders how to answer, but the mouth of the wicked pours out evil things.

Righteous people think about what they are going to say before they say it. They don't just say everything that is in their heads. They are careful how they say things, too. A righteous person "ponders" before he speaks. To "ponder" means to meditate. In other words, the righteous person's answers are thought out, not just blurted out. The righteous are careful about their words because they know the power of words.

The wicked could care less: Out it comes! There is no thought given because they often only care about themselves. So, the wicked person says evil things. We see this truth in this verse. "Pours" means to gush out or bubble out, like a geyser bubbling up. As soon as a thought hits, out it comes.

So are you going to talk like a righteous person or a wicked person? Are you going to do your best to give thought to what you say before speaking? Are you going to pour out truths that build up or are evil? Will people be better off for having heard what you say, or will they be worse off? I once heard someone say that he is brutally honest but in love. The reality is that he is just brutal. Sometimes giving thought to what we say before we say it means that we may not say it at all.

Speak like a righteous person, not a wicked one. Give thought to your words.

March 16 – Read Proverbs 16

v. 1 The plans of the heart belong to man, but the answer of the tongue is from the LORD.

We talk about our plans for work, vacation and the weekend, among other things. We try to get people to set goals and work towards the future. We try to get people to think about tomorrow, but, we often forget that "WE" are not the ones who are in control. God is! Even in this chapter this is stated two more times.

v. 9 The heart of man plans his way, but the LORD establishes his steps.
v. 33 The lot is cast into the lap, but its every decision is from the LORD.

The thought is again stated in Proverbs 19:21. When we talk about the future as if we are in control, it is pure arrogance (James 4:13-17). It is good, even wise, to plan and set goals, but we must always remember that "WE" are not sovereign. God is! In our planning, we must remember that the final answer comes from God, not us. We should be careful in talking, thinking or planning tomorrow, for the truth is that "you do not know what a day may bring" (Proverbs 27:1). All of our plans must be based on the knowledge that God is in control of the final product. What will happen tomorrow is in the hands of God.

Plan for tomorrow, but know that God is in control.

March 17 – Read Proverbs 17

v. 22 A joyful heart is good medicine, but a crushed spirit dries up the bones.

It has always been true, but I don't know if it has always been acknowledged. These days, I think we are becoming more understanding of it. The truth of it is that how you think affects how you feel.

If your thinking is messed up, your body will be messed up also. I have heard it acknowledged numerous times that most people go to the doctor because of stress. Our thinking is hurting our health. Doctors are giving people placebos, not because there really is a problem, but because people's thinking is messed up (crushed spirit means despondency, doom and gloom thinking). Even just getting bad news can have a detrimental effect on your body if you allow it to.

All of this being true, it stands to reason that a joyful heart is good medicine. I think if we could just get people to laugh more or be happy more, they would feel better. That is why people in sunny states tend to be healthier or at least feel healthier. Having sunshine and not darkness tends to get rid of gloom and makes people feel better and even be better. God's Word is true. "Joy" helps our health and a "crushed spirit" hurts our health. I have even been in hospitals where staff members have stated that our thinking can have an effect on our healing ability, and if you go into surgery with negative thoughts, you tend to take longer to get healthy.

Be happy and be healthy!

March 18 - Read Proverbs 18

v. 17 The one who states his case first seems right, until the other comes and examines him.

People often make the mistake of believing the first one to tell their story. If a wife tells about her marriage troubles and how bad her husband is, she is believed and the husband is looked down on. If someone reports an incident, he is believed without checking his story. But both policemen and pastors and the wise have learned that all who are parts of an encounter must be heard before anyone can make a correct judgment. Why? All sides need to be heard. It is important to get it right so that people are not hurt by wrong conclusions.

Proverbs 18:17 tells us that the first to state his case seems right until another comes along and examines him. Beware of listening to just one side of an argument or story, no matter how believable, until you have heard everyone involved. The reality is that the first to run with a story may not be right. He may just be trying to beat everyone else out of the gate so that he will be believed. The first could be the one lying or, at least, not getting the facts correct. The warning here is against making too hasty a judgment. One-sided statements may not be reliable.

Investigate a matter by listening to all involved. Don't be hasty.

March 19 - Read Proverbs 19

v. 20 Listen to advice and accept instruction, that you may gain wisdom in the future.

I am not fully sure why all people are not so willing to accept advice and instruction. Maybe for some it is pride. Maybe for others it is an unwillingness to admit failure. For still others it may be just plain old sinfulness (John 3:19-20). For some others there may be other reasons. This I do know: The more we listen to advice and accept instruction, the wiser we will be in the future (v. 20). The more you read Proverbs, the more you will see the advantage of listening to advice and instruction.

This thought is seen throughout Proverbs. In fact, from this we learn that those who want to live their lives without others or separate themselves from others are living life at a disadvantage. While there may be times when we have social problems in interacting with others, there are far more benefits to be gained by interacting than from trying to live life devoid of others. If we are willing to listen, there is much we can learn from each other, especially from those who know and apply God's Word (Hebrews 5:11-14). If we are willing to listen and learn, we can avoid the pitfalls of life.

Keep your heart open so that your ears will work. When you heart is receptive your feet move in the right direction.

Listen to advice and accept instruction, for there is great value in it.

March 20 - Read Proverbs 20

v. 25 It is a snare to say rashly, "It is holy," and to reflect only after making vows.

Oh how quick we are to make promises! We are far too quick to give our word. We are far too quick to make commitments. In fact, we are far too quick to do a lot of things in life. Though some things must be done quickly, our mouths far too often work too quickly. A quick mouth is a quick way to get into trouble.

We are told in this verse that it is a trap or a snare to say something in a hurry and then, only afterwards, think about what we have done. It is like stepping into an animal trap. For an example of this very issue, look at Judges 11-12. Oh how we must learn to listen more and talk much less and much slower! I would rather have someone do something without telling me than to promise an action and fail to fulfill. That is how God would rather it, too. I think one of the reasons is that we are to be faithful to our word. When we say something and then decide not to do it because we have now thought it through, we end up not being faithful to our word. This is not good! Look at Psalm 15:4 where it basically says that a righteous person keeps his or her word no matter what.

We should be slower in giving our word and faster in thinking about our words. This is the safer and wiser route.

Think through your promise before you make it.

March 21 - Read Proverbs 21

v. 13 Whoever closes his ear to the cry of the poor will himself call out and not be answered.

We expect people to listen to us, and when they don't, we get angry. We expect God to listen to us, and when He doesn't, we get angry. But are we listening? I don't mean listening to people in general, though we should do that. There is another group of people we need to listen to, and, in fact, if we don't, God will not listen to us. That is what is said in this verse.

It is those who are poor that need to be heard by us. We need to hear their cries for help. Yet, at times we are deaf to their needs.

When God speaks of poor people, he does not mean lazy people. He means people who are doing their best, but are poor. God makes clear that we are to reach out to the poor in Jesus' name. No matter how much or little you have, there are usually people who have needs that you can help in some way. Are you listening to their cries for help? If you have needs that no one is helping you with, one possibility may be that you have not listened to the cries of others, so now your cries are not being heard. The cries of the poor must be heard, especially by Christians (Galatians 2:10). Check out: 1 John 3:17; 1 Timothy 6:17-19.

Listen to the cries of those in need (the poor), or your needs may not be heard.

March 22 - Read Proverbs 22

v. 1 A good name is to be chosen rather than great riches, and favor is better than silver or gold.

All too often, what people chase after is money. While some may admit that, most would not. Yet, when people chase after nicer, but not necessarily needed, cars, houses, and things it shows in their actions. What people often don't realize is that there are some things far more important than lots of toys or more riches.

While I could list several things here such as salvation and wisdom, Proverbs 22:1 speaks of having a good name or reputation. What people think of you is far more important than money or even human success. I watched a competition show with my wife called "Top Shot." One of the contestants did not care what anyone thought of him and did everything he could to win no matter what the expense. In the end, he lost both the contest and his reputation.

While money is needed to live in this life, riches are never worth getting if we lose our reputation to attain them. While we cannot control what people think of us, we certainly don't want to throw away our reputation for riches. Sadly, many people are willing to do that very thing. People are often willing to do whatever it takes for riches, but it is not worth the price.

Never forsake your reputation for riches.

March 23 - Read Proverbs 23

v. 9 Do not speak in the hearing of a fool, for he will despise the good sense of your words.

There is a point at which people do not like to think of the sovereignty of God for fear that it might mean we are just puppets with no choice. Yet, at the same time, people want God to be very clear as to what they should do so that they do not have to think. They want God to give them a list of do's and don'ts so that decisions will be easy. But we can't have it both ways.

So, when it comes to life, it is all about growing is wisdom. This is so true when it comes to dealing with people. There are times when we may deal with someone one way and then a different way at a different time. For example, Proverbs tells us to rebuke people when they mess up, but this is not always the case. In this verse, we are cautioned about speaking to a fool or rebuking a fool. The reason is that they will scorn the wisdom of our words.

Here is the idea: When we prepare to speak to people, one of the considerations we must make is the receptiveness of the hearer. If you think you are speaking to a person who will simply scorn the wisdom of your words, your best option is to stay quiet. Jesus said a similar thing in Matthew 7:6.

Calculate the receptivity of your hearer before speaking. It may save you some grief.

March 24 - Read Proverbs 24

v. 17 Do not rejoice when you enemy falls, and let not your heart be glad when he stumbles.
v. 18 lest the Lord see it and be displeased and turn his anger from him.

There is a tendency to want to get revenge when someone has been rotten to us. Yes, we don't want to take literal revenge, but we sure would be happy if God did it for us. We sure would gloat if something happened to that person. We sure might rejoice if "they got theirs."

You must understand that thinking like that is the wrong kind of thinking. In fact, when you think like that, God turns His anger away from the person who did you wrong. He then looks towards you with disapproval. With this in mind, if your enemy falls or even stumbles, don't rejoice.

How do you keep from thinking or feeling that way? Keep in mind what Jesus said about this issue in Matthew 5:43-48. Psalm 73 also gives great advice on this subject. Instead of getting angry or wishing ill on your enemy, pray for them. Jesus said that when your heart gets to the point where you pray for your enemies, you are well on your way to maturity. When Jesus was on the cross, he prayed for his persecutors. When Stephen was being stoned, he did the same.

Pray for your enemies rather than rejoicing at their fall.

March 25 - Read Proverbs 25

v. 26 Like a muddied spring or a polluted fountain is a righteous man who gives way before the wicked.

When is the last time you drank from a muddied spring? My family regularly drinks spring water, but we would not drink from a muddied spring. I like my water to be clear and clean. I would not drink from a polluted fountain or well. Besides having clean water, I also want germ-free water. So drinking from either of these places is not something I would do and probably not something you would do.

Yet, there is something the righteous do all of the time and should not, just like the things just mentioned. It is for the righteous to give way to the wicked. There is an old saying that goes likes this, "All it takes for evil to rein is for the righteous to remain silent." For various reasons, the righteous often do not take their stand against the wicked. The righteous often step aside for the wicked to do whatever they want. Why is it that the wicked are so bold and the righteous are often so fearful?

Be bold and stand against wickedness wherever you see it. If you don't, you are like a muddied spring or a polluted fountain. One great example of one who did this is the great prophet Daniel (See Daniel 6.). He stood his ground even when his life was in danger.

Be bold and take your stand before the wicked.

March 26 - Read Proverbs 26

v. 28 A lying tongue hates its victims and a flattering mouth works ruin.

This verse speaks of two kinds of speech: lying and flattering. Both are deviations from the truth. Lying is very often accepted in our culture, but at the same time, it is very unaccepted. To put lying in perspective, we need to realize that the act of lying is an act of hate. When you lie, you actively hate the one you are lying about or the one you are lying to. He becomes a victim of your lie. Lying is wrong and it is an act of hate, not love.

Flattery is another form of lying. It is just one more way to lie to someone. Flattery literally means smooth like skin without hair, and so it refers to smooth talk. It carries the idea of false praise. It is praising someone falsely just to get something from him or her. So, when used, it is a lie told for selfish reasons. The result of flattery is the ruin or hurt of another.

Lying and flattering are accepted by liars. They legitimize their actions because it gets them what they want. But God does not see it that way. God sees both in terms of those who are hurt by these actions. This is also the way we should see it. When tempted to lie or flatter, remember that they are actions of hate which cause ruin.

Avoid lying and flattering, for when used, your actions are hateful and not loving.

March 27 - Read Proverbs 27

v. 5 Better is open love than hidden rebuke.
v. 6 Faithful are the wounds of a friend; profuse are the kisses of an enemy.
v. 9 Oil and perfume make the heart glad, and the sweetness of a friend comes from his earnest counsel.

Someone once wrote, "I love not my friend, if I do not offend him." A true friend is willing to rebuke and does rebuke and help correct the faults of his friends (v. 5). He does it in love, and with the right heart attitude, in order to help his friend be what God wants him to be and do. Far too many people are living in a dream world that makes them think that a true friend only praises them all of the time and continually tells them how perfect they are (v. 6). These are the kind of people who only want "yes men" around them. When this happens, the end result is hardly ever good.

Do you want a whole bunch of friends who, like the mirror on the wall, only tell you that you are the most beautiful of all? Good friends are willing to tell you what you need to hear so that you can become a better person and honor God (v. 9). They tell us when we do well and rebuke us when we don't. These are the kinds of friends we all need, but these are the kinds of friends some push away to their own peril. Real friends are willing to tell you what you need to hear, even if it costs your friendship.

Seek friends who are truthful and be a truthful friend.

March 28 - Read Proverbs 28

v. 23 Whoever rebukes a man will afterward find more favor than he who flatters with his tongue.

Verse 23 takes two opposite things, rebuke and flattery, and compares their ultimate end. Rebuke simply means to confront someone's wrong actions, attitude or words. Flattery means to falsely heap compliments on someone for selfish reasons. A biblical rebuke is honest and loving (Proverbs 27:5-6), while flattery is selfish and deceitful (Proverbs 26:28). While flattery may work in the short term, rebuke has better long-term results.

The person who has been flattered may turn his affections towards the flatterer immediately, but in the long term, he will see through it. On the other hand, a person may not respond well to a rebuke immediately, but in the end they will come to see the value of it (Unless, of course, they are the "fool" mentioned in Proverbs.). We should be careful of those who only speak well of us but who never seem to see our flaws. These kinds of people can become one of two problems. They are either a flatterer or a "yes man." Either person is not good for our own health.

We also need to be willing to be honest and forthright with our friends. We should be friends who are willing to be open and honest with our friends, even sometimes rebuking them, but certainly never flattering them.

Be honest and loving in your speech. Beware of those who flatter you.

March 29 - Read Proverbs 29

v. 18 Where there is no prophetic vision the people cast off restraint, but blessed is he who keeps the law"

I have heard this verse used so often, totally missing what it means and really missing the opportunity to show the importance of God's Word in lives. It has been used to mean the vision of a leader or pastor to look toward the future and plan. For example, this would mean to have a future plan of some sort for the church. But that is not the idea of this verse, and I am so glad for the way the ESV has translated it to correct this confusion.

The idea of this verse is that of having a prophetic vision or revelation from God. It means to have the Word of God in the midst of the people. First Samuel 3:1 tells us that the Word of the Lord was rare in that time. In Amos 8:11-12, we see the same thing. So it refers to the Word of God being present and available to a group of people. The second part of this statement states the result: People cast off restraint. This phrase is all one word in the Hebrew and means to throw forcefully in a direction away from something. Here the people are being cast away from the Word of God. When a pastor or someone is not instructing people in God's truth, people tend to turn away from God's Word. When people don't come to church on a regular basis, they do not become better Christians. On the other hand, those who live according to God's Word are blessed.

Keep God's Word ever before you so that you don't turn away from obeying God.

March 30 - Read Proverbs 30

v. 5 Every word of God proves true; he is a shield to those who take refuge in him.
v. 6 Do not add to his words, lest he rebuke you and you be found a liar.

The Bible makes clear that it is not just the thoughts of God that matter, but "every word of God" that matters. They matter because every word is true (Psalms 18:30), and every word is true because it is God's Word. His words have gone through the refiner's fire and have shown themselves to be true (Psalms 12:6). They have proved themselves true in the lives of men and women (Psalms 119:140). Therefore, all who go to Him can take refuge in them.

No one should add to His "true" words, or, for that matter, take away from them or God will rebuke him (Deuteronomy 4:2; 12:32; Revelation 22:18). God's Words are all we need (2 Timothy 3:16-17). They are all sufficient for life. Unfortunately, people often read book after book, even books about the Bible, but they hardly ever read the Bible. It is the Bible (God's Word), which changes and transforms lives. It is the Bible which prepares us for life here and in the hereafter. So it would be a shame to even read this devotional without first reading the chapter in Proverbs represented by each day. Therefore, read the chapter of the day, then the verse of Scripture and then the thought of the day.

Trust God's Word. It is true and is continually proven true in those who live by it.

March 31 - Read Proverbs 31

v. 30 Charm is deceitful, and beauty is vain, but a woman who fears the Lord is to be praised.

What should a guy look for in a woman? More than that, what should a woman look for in herself? That is, when a woman looks in a mirror and asks the question, "Who is the most beautiful of them all?" - What answer is the right one? I'm afraid the answer is far too often way too wrong. And, even worse, moms are far too often teaching their daughters the wrong thing about beauty.

What should the answer be? "Charm is deceitful and beauty is vain, but a woman who fears the Lord is to be praised." Beauty is not determined by how a woman looks on the outside. And you're wrong, too! Beauty is not determined by what is on the inside. Beauty is determined by a woman's relationship to God. It is the woman who "fears the Lord" who is truly beautiful. This is the verse I used to find my wife, and it has proved true as God's Word always does.

Ladies, seek to be this kind of woman, and Men who have yet to marry, seek only this kind of woman for a wife. Ladies, beware of the kind of clothes you allow your daughters to wear. You may be sending them the wrong message about beauty.

It's not charm or beauty. It's your relationship to God that matters.

April 1 - Read Proverbs 1

v. 28 They will call upon me, but I will not answer; they will seek me diligently but will not find me.

It is so interesting that the truths repeated over and over in the Bible are stated here in the Book of Proverbs. This book, which deals with everyday wisdom and life-living, restates the truths of the rest of the Bible. In other words, Bible doctrine contains the truth needed to live a wise life.

We see in Proverbs 1:24-32 the principles of rejection. There is a point in life where continually rejecting God could bring us to a point of no return. Fear of the Lord is the beginning of knowledge, which is also where the wise person begins. God's call to men, His call for all men to become wise, goes out continually before mankind (Psalm 19; Romans 1). When people reject God's call to them, they can reach a point where God quits calling, and when they call to Him it may be too late (Isaiah 55:6). There could be a time, usually when trouble strikes, when people call out to God but He does not respond. In times like that, people may reap the result of a life of rejecting God.

Don't reject God's call (Romans 10:10-13). People can do so while being so close to the answer to their needs. For example, there was Judas who was so near Jesus but rejected Him. Many churchgoers will be in Hell despite having claimed religion because they never truly came to God. The same will be true for many who claim to be spiritual but don't go to church. Solomon said in Ecclesiastes 12:12-14 that people search all over the place for knowledge, but the answer is simple: They must fear God and obey Him.

Respond to God's gracious call before it is too late.

April 2 - Read Proverbs 2

v. 6 For the Lord gives wisdom from his mouth come knowledge and understanding

I think that most people would agree that all of us could use more wisdom, knowledge and understanding. What most people would not agree with is the place where we get that wisdom, knowledge and understanding. I think, if asked, most people would have a variety of answers. Some may say the school of hard knocks. Others might respond by saying a good college education will work.

This verse tells us that these three things come from God. To this many would retort that religion is foolish and certainly not the place to find wisdom. To be sure, God's wisdom is different from the world's wisdom as is stated in 1 Corinthians 1:18-30. But, in this, the Bible is clear. Wisdom comes from God. James 1:5 tells us that if we want wisdom, we should ask God and He will give it to us. The Psalmist tells us in Psalms 119:97-104 that God's Word makes him wiser than those around him.

In this, we must understand that wisdom does come from God. In fact, wisdom begins with a right relationship to God, according to Proverbs 1:7. If you want to be wise, you must understand the source of wisdom. If you ignore that source, reject that source, or seek it in some other source, you will come up short. If you want to be wise you must go to the source of wisdom – God. Make sure your relationship with Him is right. Daily ask Him for wisdom as you make decisions. Spend much time in His Word, reading, meditating, applying and obeying it.

Do you want wisdom? Go to the right source – God!

April 3 - Read Proverbs 3

v. 5 Trust in the Lord will all of heart, and lean not on your own understanding.
v. 6 In all of your ways acknowledge him, and he will make straight your paths.

These two verses lay down a basic truth, which says that God will guide us through life. But there are three conditions that make this truth possible. First, we must trust God with all of our heart. This is not so easy a task. There are many times in life when we do not see the hand of God at work and wonder where God is. Or even worse, life throws us some curves, like sickness, and we are sure that God does not love us. Just look at the story of Job and how, as you read the book, it became so hard for Job to trust God. Yet if we want God's guidance, we must trust him. So we must understand that no matter what happens in life, God is always trustworthy.

Second, we must lean not on our own understanding. We love to ask "why?" when we do not understand. Most of us want to understand everything in life, especially when it comes to our own life. Yet, it is not necessary for us to understand everything. 'Lean not" means "to trust." Don't trust your own understanding of what is happening in your life. Proverbs 20:24 says, "A man's steps are from the Lord. How then can man understand his way?"

Third, we must acknowledge God in all of our ways. It means more than to simply talk about God. "Acknowledge" means to "show that you know Him." In all of our conduct, we must show that we know God. How do we do that? We do that by doing what Jesus did (1 John 2:3-6). We do that by being obedient to God in all we do.

Obey the first three commands and God will do the fourth.

April 4 - Read Proverbs 4

v. 24 Put away from you crooked speech and put devious talk far from you.

Verse 24 talks about two things that should never be a part of our speech: "crooked speech" and "devious talk." What are they? "Crooked" means bent or twisted out of shape. When applied to speech, "crooked" means deceitful speech. "Devious" means speech that deviates from God's moral standard or speech that is perverse (See: Eph. 5:5). So this is the kind of speech that God does not want on our lips.

Far too many people lie as a matter of fact. Lying is just part of the way they talk. They often do not even consider it wrong to lie. In fact, many people think there are times when lying is the right thing to do. There are even times when people would rather be lied to than to hear the truth. As the lyrics of one song says, "tell me lies, tell me sweet little lies."

The same is true of speech that is immoral. Take immoral jokes and immoral words out of the mouths of some and they would have nothing to say. But, for the believer, this must never be true.

God wants the speech that comes out of our mouths to be honest and moral. He wants our speech to build other people up and not tear them down. He wants our speech to be gracious and becoming. See Colossians 4:6 and Ephesians 4:15.

Speak to others the way Jesus spoke.

April 5 - Read Proverbs 5

v. 5 My son, be attentive to my wisdom; incline your ear to my understanding.

Proverbs 5 is all about avoiding sexual sin. If men (and also women) would listen to this chapter of Proverbs, they could avoid so much trouble. Here is the recipe of how to avoid adultery:

1. Get wisdom. – v. 1-2
   -It is the person who lacks judgment that commits adultery.
2. Avoid the adulteress. – v. 3-8
   -Keeping your wife close and other woman at a distance is wise.
3. Grasp the results of sexual sin. – v. 9-14
   -The promise of sexual sin does not equal the results, which affect you physically, financially, emotionally and socially.
4. Find satisfaction with your spouse. – v. 14-20
   -A person who is satisfied will not tend to look elsewhere.
5. Remember God is watching you. – v. 21
   -Nothing is beyond the eyes of God, even actions done in darkness.
6. Be aware of the power of sin. – v. 22
   -Sin is powerful and enslaves greatly.
7. Discipline yourself. – v. 23
   -Without discipline, a person is open to danger. -1 Corinthians 9:24-27

Please don't read this and not heed the advice. Please don't walk away and walk into sin. The wisest man who ever lived did. In fact, he wrote these words. It was Solomon! At the end of his life, he walked away from everything he knew was right. The women in his life turned him away from God and from moral activity.

Stay away from adultery!

April 6 - Read Proverbs 6

v. 30 People do not despise a thief if he steals to satisfy his appetite when he is hungry.
v. 32 He who commits adultery lacks sense; he who does it destroys himself.

There are some sins that are clearly wrong, yet people have some understanding as to why people have committed such sins. For example, when someone steals because he is hungry, people can sympathize with the act (v. 30). However, an understandable motive still does not make it right. People will be punished for their crimes/sins (v. 31). When people hear about the starving stealing so they can eat, there is a sense of understanding towards it even though it is wrong. It will be punished.

However, the sin of adultery is not looked on with the same latitude. This is especially true of the spouse who has been sinned against by such actions (v. 33-35). The one who commits adultery "lacks sense" and "destroys himself" as stated in v. 32. There is no argument that can be made to make sense out of the sin of adultery. It is wrong no matter how you look at it. There is simply no way to justify that kind of sinful activity. Though adultery is often committed, there is still a stigma attached to it, and rightfully so. God has no tolerance for it and neither should we.

This being true, it is amazing how many people try to justify and excuse the sin of adultery. Yet God is very clear on this issue as can be seen by a reading Ephesians 5:1-7 and 1 Thessalonians 4:1-8.

Be wise! Don't sin sexually!

April 7 – Read Proverbs 7

v. 24 And now, O sons, listen to me, and be attentive to the words of my mouth.
v. 25 Let not your heart turn aside to her ways; do not stray into her paths,

If only people would listen to advice. Pastors, parents, friends and family members pour out their hearts to their loved ones to get them to listen, but their advice is often rejected. They see the ones they care about going in the wrong direction, or they give advice so that they will not one day go the wrong way. They often plead, but their pleas sometimes fall on deaf ears. Oh how we all need to listen to advice and to counsel!

Here there is a warning to avoid the ways and paths of the adulteress. Our heart and our feet can get us into trouble. First, it is our heart that heads in the wrong direction, then the feet move. Once the heart has headed toward her, the feet will follow. This is why the heart must be guarded (4:23).

We must all avoid the ways and paths of the sexual sinner. One of the best ways of doing so is to stay far away physically from those who would lead us into sexual sin. Build a wall of protection in your life, a wall built around your heart and your feet that keeps you from the presence of this kind of person.

Guard your heart and feet from the advances of the sexual sinner.

April 8 – Read Proverbs 8

v. 17 I love those who love me, and those who seek me diligently find me.

Wisdom, in Proverbs 8, speaks to us. It tells us something very important, something worth singing about. It tells us that, "those who seek me find me." What a great truth to behold. It is something that is worth shouting from the housetops.

In Proverbs 1, we are told the main purpose of the book is for gaining wisdom. As people read that, I'm sure some think to themselves and hope it will be true for them. Some may think it is true for everyone but them. Some, maybe a few, even believe that it will happen to them.

But here we are told, eight chapters in, that it is true and that everyone who seeks diligently will find wisdom. I'm so glad it is true for I so want it to be true. I do want to be wise. I need wisdom for the issues that I face in life, and I need wisdom for those who come to me seeking it. Wisdom must be sought eagerly and diligently. Wisdom is available to all, but you don't get it by falling over it in the dark. It must be sought, and sought for in the right places. But if sought, it will be found and I'm so glad this is true.

So no one, I repeat no one, must remain simple or foolish. If you are, it is because you have chosen to remain so, for if you seek wisdom, you will find it.

Search for wisdom in the pages of Proverbs and you will find it.

April 9 - Read Proverbs 9

v. 10 *The fear of the* Lord *is the beginning of wisdom, and the knowledge of the Holy One is insight.*

This world is of the belief that Christians are stupid and simple. This world is of the belief that if you reject evolution you are stupid and simple. This world is of the belief that if you believe in heaven and hell you are stupid and simple. This world is of the belief that if you believe there is a God you are stupid and simple.

This world believes that it is wise to reject God (1 Corinthians 1:20-25). This world makes those who believe in God think they are dumb. But, nothing could be further from the truth. The reality is that wisdom begins with a relationship with God (9:10). Knowing God and fearing God is where wisdom begins and without this you can't be wise. It took the Apostle Paul a while to come to this conclusion but he finally did (Philippians 3:2-12) and it changed his life.

Sometimes it takes people a lifetime to get there, but it is never too late. If you reject God, the creator of the universe, how could you ever become wise?

The wisest thing you could ever do is to love God, and in so doing, you will become even wiser. Knowing this is the place where wisdom starts and the place where it has any chance to grow.

Seek to know and love God through a relationship with His Son.

April 10 - Read Proverbs 10

v. 12 Hatred stirs up strife, but loves covers all offenses.

The thought of this verse is repeated in 1 Peter 4:8 and James 5:20. Hatred and love result in opposite responses for they are opposites. Hatred stirs up strife, but love covers things. Unfortunately, the first is seen more than the second.

Note that "hatred stirs up strife." According to Proverbs 6:12-14, a worthless, wicked man with a perverted heart continually sows discord. Hatred incites man against his fellow man. It arouses or wakes up quarrelling. In other words, where hatred is present, quarrelling will get worse, not better. I think if people were to look deep within their hearts, they may find this ugly emotion far too often. Picture the face of each person you know. Does any face you see cause an ugly emotional response? If so, hatred may be present.

Note that "love covers all offenses." One way to tell how loving you are is to look at how you respond when you are offended. When you are offended, do you cover it up and not let the offense see the light of day? Or, when you are offended do you do any of the following?

1. You repeat the matter to others making sure you let everyone know how bad the offender is.
2. You keep your eye on the offender telling yourself how awful they are.
3. You look for an opportunity to get back at the offender.
4. You grow cold towards the offender.
5. You do not forgive the offender.

Respond in love, not hate, to all offenses.

April 11 – Read Proverbs 11

v. 17 A man who is kind benefits himself, but a cruel man hurts himself.
v. 24 One gives freely, yet grows all the richer; another withholds what he should give, and only suffers want.

There are two ways to live life. One way is to put yourself at the center of your universe and do everything, or at least most things, with yourself in mind or for your benefit. The other way is to put God at the center of your universe and do what He says, which is to put others before yourself. It seems that most people live the first way. Some will admit to living that way, others will not. Just sit back and watch someone for a while and you will learn which way he or she has chosen to live.

It is clear from these two verses that the right way to live life is the first way. The right way to live life is to be kind to others and to give freely. We also can see from these two verses that there is benefit for you from living that way. When you live that way, you don't live with the benefit in mind, but none-the-less, it still comes because God rewards that kind of living.

It is also clear from these two verses that the wrong way of living is the second way. The wrong way of living is to be cruel to others and to withhold what you should give. This way of living also brings a result. Those who live this way hurt themselves and suffer want.

Gain by giving and live by putting others before yourself.

April 12 - Read Proverbs 12

v16 – The Vexation of a fool is known at once, but the prudent ignores an insult.

"Sticks and stones may break my bones but names will never hurt me." I don't fully agree with this old statement, but its meaning does get to the heart of the issue. The thought is that what people say about us can only go so far, and much of what is said can be overlooked. We do not have to go to war over what people say about us and the wise person understands this.

This is the thought of Proverbs 12:16. A fool is at once annoyed, angry or irritated when he is or feels insulted. A fool responds immediately to insults with anything from a facial expression to possibly murder. But a wise person overlooks or covers over an insult. He responds to this kind of thing only when absolutely necessary. He is slow in responding to such things whereas the fool is quick to respond to such things. In cases like this, slowness is best. Unfortunately, the fool does not understand this and often gets himself into trouble by his quick response.

The wise person is slow because he acts in love whereas the fool is motivated by selfishness. It is always wise to do or not do things out of love. This is one of the major distinctions between the fool and the wise person. How do you respond to an insult or perceived insult?

Respond to negatives like the wise person, not the fool.

April 13 - Read Proverbs 13

v. 24 Whoever spares the rod hates his son, but he who loves him is diligent to discipline him.

Proverbs is about wisdom. As I look around, it seems to me that most adults have rejected wisdom, at least when it comes to raising children. Children are a mess these days and if we look at Proverbs, we can see some of the reasons for this. One of them is mentioned in Proverbs 13:24.

Parents have lost sight of what love for their children looks like. Many parents have confused love. They think loving their children is seen in not spanking them, but the opposite is true. A parent who loves their children will spank them because of the long-term benefits. The Bible Knowledge Commentary puts it this way, "A loving parent inflicts temporary discomfort on his children (by spanking with a **rod**) to spare them the long-range disaster of an undisciplined life.[3]" The parent who spares the rod is the one who actually hates his child. All one has to do is to look around and see the results of the two differing ways of raising children and you will see the wisdom of what is stated in Proverbs 13:24. For other verses on this issue see Proverbs 19:18; 22:15; 23:13-14; 29:15, 17.

The rod refers to physical punishment. The rod is not meant to be an iron bar that is used to hurt a child. It simply refers to reinforcing your words with physical punishment. Done with love and control there is great value. Done without love or in anger there can be great harm to a child.

Follow God's wisdom in raising your children, not the World's wisdom.

April 14 - Read Proverbs 14

v. 7 Leave the presence of a fool, for there you do not meet words of knowledge.

Avoid people... Certainly that can't be what God would want, can it? Yes! All throughout the Bible we are told to avoid certain kinds of people. Such is the case in Proverbs 14:7. It says that would should "Stay away from a foolish man." We see this idea of avoiding people in several places in Proverbs. We also see this in several places in the New Testament, such as 1 Corinthians 5:9-13, 2 Thessalonians 3:14 and Titus 3:10-11.

Why should we avoid the foolish man? The reason is that "you will not find knowledge on his lips." The book of Proverbs is all about gaining wisdom and knowledge. I can see Solomon sitting down with his son and saying, "Watch out for this kind of person, for he will not help you with your pursuit of wisdom and knowledge." The more we spend time around people who don't live according to God's wisdom and knowledge, the further we will turn away from God. The more time we spend around people who have God's knowledge and wisdom, the more we will become what God desires for our lives and character. (1 Corinthians 15:33-34)

Choose the words you listen to carefully. When God's wisdom and knowledge begin to sound foreign to you, it may be that you have listened too often to the foolish person on whose lips there is no knowledge or wisdom. Seek to be around the wise where wisdom and knowledge are ever present.

Leave the presence of a fool.

April 15 - Read Proverbs 15

v. 1 A soft answer turns away wrath, but a harsh word stirs up anger.

Do you tend to have a calming effect on tense situations or do you tend to make things worse? Proverbs 15:1 tells us that we could do either by our words. The first part of the verse tells us how to have a calming impact. It says, "A soft answer turns away wrath." The word "soft" means "tender or sensitive." An example of this can be seen in the response of Gideon to the men of Ephraim in Judges 8:1-3.

The second part tells us how to make things worse. It says, "...a harsh word stirs up anger." The word "harsh" means "hurtful." It refers to any statement that produces irritation. For an example of this, see 1 Samuel 25:10-13. Yes, how we act in stressful moments can either help or hinder. Which do your words tend to do, calm anger or stir up anger?

As people get angry and as things get stirred up, people tend to use harsh and hurtful words. Have you ever noticed how as one person gets loud the other tends to match the volume of the first? The longer a quarrel continues, the more people turn away from trying to solve the quarrel and begin attacking each other. As a result, things gets worse, not better. We need to learn to diffuse people's anger in a quarrel, not make it worse. This verse tells us how we may do that very thing.

Lower the heat with wise words. Don't stir anger up when moments are tense.

April 16 – Read Proverbs 16

v. 16 How much better to get wisdom than gold! To get understanding is to be chosen rather than silver.

There are all kinds of things in life we can chase after. If we made a list, it would not be a short one. For sure, one thing that many people chase after is wealth whether seen in money or seen in the things money buys. The Book of Proverbs has much to say about the issue of money and its place in our lives. Maybe it says so much because so many people chase after it. Or, maybe it says so much because it touches our lives in so many ways. Even Jesus talked about money more than Heaven and Hell combined.

If you could have one thing, which would you choose, money or wisdom? Solomon was given the choice of having anything he could want. He chose wisdom.

This verse states that wisdom and understanding are the better choice to chasing after money. What does your life state? Do your life choices show that you value wisdom over money or the other way around? Given the choice, do you choose to make more money on Sunday or to go to church? There is no doubt that money is needed to live in this world, but wisdom has far greater worth than money. This same truth is stated in Proverbs 3:13-18; 8:10-11, 19.

Solomon had both great wisdom and great wealth. Having had both, he concluded that wisdom was far more valuable.

Choose wisdom over money. It's the right choice, for it is more valuable.

April 17 – Read Proverbs 17

v. 15 He who justifies the wicked and he who condemns the righteous are both alike an abomination to the Lord.

People often wonder why the wicked do so well in this world, yet those who seek God don't. The answer to that is deep and far reaching, but maybe at its core the answer is simple. The moment Adam and Eve ate of the fruit everything got mixed up. We often find things are backwards in this world, and so we often see what happens in the verse that is before us.

There are those who do not have the heart and thinking of God. They do the opposite of what God would desire. They "justify the wicked" and they "condemn the righteous." This is not what is just, but this is what happens in a sinful world. This is what happens in a world that has rejected God and God's principles of morality. This all began with the choice Adam and Eve made in disobeying God and eating of the fruit.

These kinds of actions are the exact opposite of what God would do and what God does. Therefore, God looks at these actions, and they are an abomination to Him. "Abomination" is a strong word, which means to "loathe" something. God hates these kinds of actions. They are not only wrong, they are "backwards." Yet we see this very thing happen in life all of the time.

We should condemn the wicked and justify the righteous. This is how life should work. This is what God does.

Treat the wicked and the righteous the way God does and don't get it backwards.

April 18 - Read Proverbs 18

v. 22 He who finds a wife finds a good thing and obtains favor from the LORD.

I have conducted many weddings in over thirty years of pastoring. With every couple I have married, I have conducted premarital counseling. At the first session I have often asked what the friends of the couple have said to them about getting married. The answer comes back in many forms, but in reality it says the same thing. "What, are you nuts?" Unfortunately, marriages, wrecked by sin, often do not do well and many end in divorce. So people think that getting married is not a good thing.

This is so different from what God says about marriage. God sees marriage as a good thing to happen to any person for whom it is God's will. Though I have no verse to back this up, I believe it is God's will that most people get married. The verse that is before us today says that a person who finds a spouse, that is, gets married, finds a good thing. Marriage is good, for God created it when He brought Adam and Eve together. God said that is was not good for Adam to be alone (Genesis 2:18). It was better for him to be married than to be by himself. The institution of marriage is not the problem. It is our actions that often make being married difficult. If we start with the right foundational concept, that marriage is good, it will go a far way in making marriages better.

Know that marriage is good and don't let anyone convince you otherwise.

April 19 - Read Proverbs 19

v. 5 A false witness will not go unpunished, and he who breathes out lies will not escape.

Lying in the Bible general relates to two areas. The first is lying in general, and the second is perjury or lying in a courtroom setting. Proverbs 19:5 speaks of the second. It focuses on the fact that those who lie in a courtroom will not get away with it. They will be punished and not escape. Why do people lie in court? Because, for whatever reason, they think lying is the better choice over telling the truth. This verse tells us that that conclusion is wrong. It is wrong every single time, and those who choose to lie will be punished sooner or later.

The same is true with lying in general. Those who lie think that they can lie and not get caught. But there is a common saying that confirms what the Bible says. It goes like this: "Be sure of this, your lies will catch up with you." You may get away with lying here or there, or maybe even a whole bunch, but sooner or later, your lies will catch up with you. This is what Proverbs 19:5 is saying. If you lie, you will get caught and be punished. In fact, in Revelation 21:8, the Bible says that all liars will be punished in Hell. People lie when they think they can get away with it, but they won't and neither will you. You may lie here or there, but you will get caught and punishment will come.

Don't lie. Ever. You will get caught at some point and be punished.

April 20 - Read Proverbs 20

v. 13 Love not sleep, lest you come to poverty; open your eyes, and you will have plenty of bread.

We are living in a society that does not like to work. People would rather get a check from the government than work. If what a person gets from the government is the same as he would get from working, most people would rather sit home and collect. That is not how America became great, yet this is what America has become.

The Bible has much to say about laziness. Just like Proverbs 20:13, which basically says that if you love sleep you will become poor, but if you work hard you will have what you need. Throughout the Bible, God praises hard work and condemns laziness. Some people, if given the opportunity, would stay in bed or on the couch all day, every day.

God's Word tells us to make sure that we help the needy. Yet, it also says that we should not help the lazy (2 Thessalonians 3:6-12). Which are you? Some people work, but in their hearts they are lazy. What we see in the Bible is that we need to cultivate a work ethic. A work ethic will move us to keep going. I think this is the reason why some self-employed people don't make it; they are just too lazy to do what it takes. A work ethic is that voice inside of us that gets us out of bed in the morning. A work ethic is that belief that moves us to work even if we could make more money sitting home collecting checks from the government.

Don't be lazy. Work hard and you will have what you need.

April 21 - Read Proverbs 21

v. 31 The horse is made ready for the day of battle, but the victory belongs to the LORD.

One of my favorite verses in the book of Proverbs is found in chapter 21. It is the last verse in the chapter. It has helped me to keep my head where it needed to be so many times. It says that victory is in the hands of God. God had to remind Israel of this truth over and over (See Isaiah 31:1). Yet, they forgot it over and over. They kept thinking that their victories were the result of the size of their army.

We trust in all kinds of things for success or victory in life instead of putting our trust where it ought to be. Compare: Psalm 20:7 with 1 Corinthians 15:57. The great people of faith which are found in Hebrews 11 made the list because they trusted God for victories. They are an example for us. Two great examples of choosing to trust God and choosing not to are found in 2 Kings 6-7 and 2 Kings 18. They are well worth reading.

How sad that we are willing to put our trust in everything other than God, the Creator of all things and the only one worthy of our trust. Victory or defeat does not rest in my hand or my enemy's hand. It belongs to God. All of our planning does not do us a lick of good if we are not trusting God.

Trust God to win your battles. Never forget victory is in His hand.

April 22 – Read Proverbs 22

v. 29 Do you see a man skillful in his work? He will stand before kings; he will not stand before obscure men.

I love sitting and watching people who know what they are doing. I have often watched skilled people work on my house, and at other places. I do this not to make sure they are doing what they should, but to learn and because I admire people who have taken the time to learn their trade.

There is value in learning the trade which you find your hand doing. This is true even if you believe you will not continue long in what you are doing. Yet, it is even more true if you think you will do it for years to come. Owners of businesses and managers look for skilled workers, and so skilled workers are valuable to companies. If you become good at what you do, you will stand out from others who are not. When you become skilled at what you do, there are all kinds of good things that will come your way. For example, when layoffs come to a company, the skilled people are usually the ones kept. There is value in having value for those for whom you work.

I am not alone at appreciating skilled workers. Those who are skilled at what they do will stand before important people such as kings. There is great value is taking the time to become skilled at what you do.

Become skilled at what you do. You won't regret it.

April 23 - Read Proverbs 23

v. 31 Do not look at wine when it is red, when it sparkles in the cup and goes down smoothly

What a sad thing it is when we keep going back to those things that are so harmful to us. We run back to those things that hurt us. For example in Proverbs 23:19-35, we are given a list of seven things that happen to drunkards because of their drinking. They are: poverty (19-21), misery (29-30), poison (31-32), hallucinations (33), dizziness (34), numbness (35a), and enslavement (35b). Notice that the sad thing is that with all of these things happening to the drunkard, it ends with them waking up looking for another drink. The drunkard has become enslaved.

This is the sad thing about sin. It does enslave. Alcoholics are hurt by it and yet they seek more of it. You can counsel them time after time and often it only gets worse. Sin enslaves, and, sadly, people think they can dabble in it and not be hurt. Proverbs 5:22, speaking of sexual sin, says, "The iniquities of the wicked ensnare him, and he is held fast in the cords of sin." That is why it is always best to stay as far away from wrongdoing as possible. It is best to stay away from those things that can enslave us. Once enslaved, it becomes hard to stop. Even worse, the person who is enslaved believes he is not. Is there a sin or sinful activity that you are toying with? Run!

Stay as far away from sinful activity, or activity that enslaves, as possible.

April 24 - Read Proverbs 24

v. 27 Prepare your work outside; get everything ready for yourself in the field, and after that build your house.

In life we tend to do the things we want to do first and then we do the things we need to do. This is a general rule for many people. Yet, highly successful people do not tend to follow that pattern. They tend to do the things that need to be done first – first. When those things are finished, then they go play or do whatever. These people tend to be successful because in their actions, knowingly or unknowingly, they are following a principle of wisdom. Proverbs 24:27 tells us to finish our outdoor work first, get the fields ready and then we can build the house.

What it is saying is that you can build your house anytime, but first go do the things that will feed you and or provide an income for you and your family. It is saying to do those things that matter first. They are not always the easy things, but they are the high priority things that must get done first. They may even be the things you least want to do, but they are the things that need to be done first if you are going to be successful. In life, each day, or each week, do you do the most important things first? Do you do things based on priority? Wise people do!

Seek to do the most important things first. Then do the less important.

April 25 - Read Proverbs 25

v. 6 Do not put yourself forward in the king's presence or stand in the place of the great
v. 7 for it is better to be told "Come up here," than to be put lower in the presence of a noble.

Some people seem to want to let everyone know how great they are. It seems like some make a living out of exalting themselves in front of others. Some want to claim a home for themselves among the great. Even society seems to teach that we should promote ourselves if we want to get ahead in life. I have seen this principle put forth so often. Yet, Proverbs teaches the opposite.

Proverbs 25:6-7 tells us that when we are in the presence of important people, it is better to take a back seat and be asked to come forward than to take a front seat and be asked to move backward. Pride claims the seat of importance, but humility is willing to take the seat of least importance. If we claim the important seat, our pride can be humbled, but humility has nowhere to go but up. It reminds me of a mother's request for importance found in Matthew 20:20-28 that did not work out so well for two brothers.

I remember being told in a sales meeting, "If you don't make it, fake it." That statement is wrong in so many ways. As it relates to the topic before us, it is wrong in that we are pretending to be what we are not. When found out, we will certainly be moved lower.

Seek to exalt others, not yourself.

April 26 - Read Proverbs 26

v. 20 For lack of wood the fire goes out, and where there is no whisperer, quarreling ceases.

One of the things I just love to do is to build fires. Oh, not the kind that hurts people, but the kind that one builds at a campsite or in a fireplace. I love sitting around watching a fire at nighttime. I love the sparkling, glowing fire in the darkness of night. I love the smell of the wood burning. I was a camp counselor for a year and often one of my jobs was building the campfires. I have built many fires in my lifetime and loved every minute of it.

I know one thing for sure about fires. When you run out of wood, the fire dies. I know this from experience. The same principle is true of a quarrel. If you stop the whispers (gossipers), a quarrel dies out (Proverbs 26:20). One of the things that is often involved in fighting or dissention between people is gossip. When a gossip is around, quarrels continue. A gossip is a person who goes around slandering others behind their backs (whispering). As much as I love building campfires, I hate gossip. Gossip hurts people and keeps quarrels going. God wants believers to avoid gossip (gossip literally means whispering) and instead wants us to build others up with our speech. See Colossians 4:6.

I once was involved in a bad situation involving many people. I tried to find the cause but could not. Until one day, I learned of a gossip busy at work and then it all became clear.

Avoid the fuel that keeps a quarrel going by neither gossiping nor listening to gossip.

April 27 - Read Proverbs 27

v. 1 Do not boast about tomorrow, for you do not know what a day may bring.

Do you have plans for tomorrow? What are they? A great new business plan? A trip or vacation? A test? Work? Retirement? Maybe you are just looking forward to some down time. Even people who are not considered planners have, at least, some plans for tomorrow. All of this is fine, but do you talk about tomorrow and your plans as if you were in control of tomorrow? This is where the problem comes in. No one but God knows what will happen, as we see in the first verse of Proverbs 27.

We plan tomorrow as if we are sovereign, but there is only One who is. All such planning and boasting and thinking is sinful (James 4:13-17). We should do no such talk or planning without a truth being in the depths of our heart and even squarely on our lips: "If the Lord Wills." Beware! Beware! Beware! This warning is given several times in God's Word – heed the warning. Keep God in the center of your plans and make no plans without considering His sovereignty. Here are some examples: Luke 12:13-20; Matthew 26:31-35; Acts 16; 1 Corinthians 16:5-9.

Knowing that we should not boast about tomorrow does not give us an excuse to not plan. That would just make us unwise; remember the ant (Proverbs 6:6-8). We should prioritize, plan and set goals concerning the future. But, as we do, we must keep in mind that there is only one who is Sovereign, and it is not us.

Plan for tomorrow, but remember, God is sovereign, not you.

April 28 - Read Proverbs 28

v. 27 Whoever gives to the poor will not want, but he who hides his eyes will get many a curse.

All around us are people who are hurting financially. Some are hurting because they have not been wise with their money. Others are hurting because they have been lazy and unwilling to work. Others are out of a job through no fault of their own. They may have lost their job because of the economy. They may have not made enough money to keep up, even with a frugal lifestyle. Still others may be hurting financially for other reasons.

Throughout the Bible, God has made clear that believers are to help the poor. We help in Jesus' name, but we help. We must never close our ears to the cries of the poor. This does not include those who are lazy and unwilling to work (2 Thessalonians 3:6-12). You do not help people who are lazy by paying theirs bills or giving them money. That will only make them lazier. Let their growling stomachs lead them to work. Yet for those who are truly poor and in need of help, everyone should do what he can to help. There is also a promise here to those who help the poor. Their needs will be met. See also Galatians 2:7-10.

Isn't it interesting that in helping others, we are helped? The more we look out for others, the more God looks out for us.

Keep your eyes open to the need of the poor and God will see your needs too.

April 29 - Read Proverbs 29

v. 11 A fool gives full vent to his spirit, but a wise man quietly holds it back.
v. 22 A man of wrath stirs up strife, and one given to anger causes much transgression.

In Proverbs 29, there are two verses that speak to the issue of anger. The first verse tells us the fool lets his anger go beyond the point of self-control. He blows up and his anger reaches the point of "full vent," meaning that the volcano erupts.

If you are wise, you will keep yourself under control. If you get angry, and we all do at times, keep yourself under control and use that emotion to solve the problem instead of lashing out at people.

The second verse speaks of becoming an angry person. This is when you let life or people get the best of you and you become an angry person. You, so to say, walk in anger. God tells us in this verse that the one who walks likes this "stirs up strife" and "causes much transgression." "Strife" refers to quarreling. "Transgression" refers to an offense or a break in a relationship with the emphasis on rebellion or revolt. It also says not just some transgression, but "much" transgression will occur when you walk in anger.

Don't blow up, letting it all out and erupting like a volcano. Don't clam up, holding it in and hiding your displeasure only to let it all out later like a sneak attack on others. Don't bottle it up, becoming a bitter person, mad at the world.

Don't let anger get a grip on your life. Let it go down with the sun.

April 30 – Read Proverbs 30

v. 2 Surely I am too stupid to be a man. I have not the understanding of a man.
v. 3 I have not learned wisdom, nor have I knowledge of the Holy One.

An interesting thing happens in Proverbs 30:1-4. Agur is looking at himself in a mirror and demeaning himself for his lack of wisdom. He must have done something really stupid. He sounds like me when I do something stupid. I yell at myself for being so stupid. I say something like, "Boy, that was stupid." Or, "Man, I'm so dumb." Do you do that? I'm sure you do.

An interesting thing happens in the midst of his statements. If you hadn't been reading Proverbs through every day, you might have missed it. In verse 3, he connects not being wise with not knowing God. We have seen this truth all through Proverbs. Wisdom, true wisdom, is impossible without knowing God. For examples of this, look at Proverbs 1:7; 9:10; 15:33. Certainly this truth has been stated over and over in Proverbs. Wisdom and knowing God always go together. You can't get wisdom devoid of God. A relationship with God is where wisdom starts.

Because people who claim to know God are so lacking in wisdom, our world thinks people who truly know God don't have wisdom. The truth is that people who claim to know God often don't, but people who really do know God do have wisdom, or are at least at the right starting place to gain it. Those who know God and regularly spend time in His Word can't help but become wise.

Wisdom and God always go together.

May 1 – Read Proverbs 1

v. 13 we shall find all precious goods, we shall fill our houses with plunder;

God's Word is very strong with warnings against doing wrong, against sinning. Think about it: we are warned of an eternal lake of fire. Our conscience also warns us when we are about to do wrong. Our eyes warn us every time we look at people and lives that have been destroyed by choosing to sin. Just look at the person who lies in the gutter after wasting a life in making bad choices. It is everywhere before us: lives, families, businesses, communities, governments and nations destroyed by choosing wrong over right. Even nature cries out to make the right choice (Romans 1). So why do we do it? Why do we choose wrong over right, sin over obedience to God?

This verse gives us the reason. When we face the point of choosing to sin or to do the right thing, we are faced with the promise that doing the wrong thing offers so many benefits. Think about it. This offer goes all the way back to the Garden. Satan tricked Eve into eating the fruit by telling her she would gain all kinds of good things by eating it. He even told her the greatest lie of all, "You will be like God" (Genesis 3:3-4). That's the problem with the promise of sin – it is always a lie. When you come to the choice of doing right or wrong, realize that sin's offer of good things is a lie!

Don't buy into the lie of sin. Choose right over wrong.

May 2 – Read Proverbs 2

v. 17 who forsakes the companion of her youth and forgets the covenant of her God;

We are told here what happens when adultery is committed. Two things take place and neither one is good. Notice what the two actions are: forsakes and forgets. They become even worse when we see what is forsaken and what is forgotten.

People sometimes think that adultery is not that big a deal. We know that because there is so much of it. But if we state it in terms of someone being "forsaken" we might think differently about it. When people commit adultery, in that act they have forsaken the companion of their youth. God does not look lightly on this. In Malachi 2:13-16 God strongly rebukes the men of Israel for how they had treated their wives. In Malachi 2:14, wives are called the "wife of your youth," "your companion," and "your wife by covenant."

Another thing that happens when adultery is committed is that the adulterer forgets the covenant made before God. When you get married, you make a covenant or promise before God to be faithful to your spouse. Adultery breaks that promise you made before God.

Adultery is no small thing! We need to protect our marriages from it. We do this by building hedges (walls of protection) in our marriage so that adultery becomes difficult. Notice the hedge mentioned here in Proverbs 2. The hedge is wisdom. Wisdom will keep you from the adulterer.

Never forsake your spouse nor forget the covenant you made to your spouse before God.

May 3 – Read Proverbs 3

v. 3 Let not steadfast love and faithfulness forsake you; bind them around your neck; write them on the tablet of your heart.

v. 4 So you will find favor and good success in the sight of God and man.

How would you like to find favor and success in the sight of both God and man? Can you imagine having both God and man think well of you? Wouldn't it be great if both God and man thought you were a success?

In these two verses, we are told how this can happen. There must be something in our lives that is so strong that it is as if it were bound around our necks. In fact, it must be so strong that it would be figuratively written on the tablets of our hearts. These two things must never be forsaken, that is, they must always be with us. What are the things that will win us favor and success in the sight of God and man? They are steadfast love and faithfulness.

Steadfast love means loyalty to one's commitment. Faithfulness means dependability or trustworthiness. These two characteristics are also seen together in Proverbs 14:22; 16:6; 20:28. There are important characteristics in a person's life. Together they describe a person who keeps his or her word when it is given, which is something which people certainly admire.

Make sure steadfast love (loyalty) and faithfulness (trustworthiness) always describe who you are.

May 4 – Read Proverbs 4

v. 10 Hear, my son, and accept my words, that the years of your life may be many.
v. 11 I have taught you the way of wisdom; I have led you in the paths of uprightness.

I wonder how many fathers can say what is said in these two verses. The first is that a father has taken the time to teach and lead his children. The second is that in doing so, he has led his children in the correct paths. Of course, as is true here, the children must accept the instruction.

Here we learn that Solomon took the time to teach his children about wisdom. We see some of that teaching here in Proverbs. I'm sure there was much more than what is in Proverbs, but here there is a boatload of wisdom for his children. Proverbs is full of topics that he taught his children, topics such as choosing friends, planning, working, issues of morality, family life, fearing the Lord, straight paths, speech, anger, pride/humility, riches, truthfulness, finding a good wife, interpersonal issues, and many more. Dads, have you sat down and taught your children about these issues?

Yet, it did not stop there. Not only did he teach his children, he also led them. He set the example in life of what he taught. He led them in the right paths of life. Amazingly, though, in the end he failed (See 1 Kings 11). Dads, don't fail your children.

Dads, teach and lead your children in the way they should go.

May 5 – Read Proverbs 5

v. 22 The iniquities of the wicked ensnare him, and he is held fast in the cords of his sin.

It is much easier to stop a fire when it is still on a match. When a fire sets the forest ablaze, it becomes hard to put out. It is much easier to avoid sin and sinful lifestyles than to stop sinning. Once sin is invited into our lives, it becomes hard to kick it out the door.

Notice what sin does to a person. It "ensnares" him and he is "held fast in the cords." Both of these describe a person who is enslaved to sin. That is what sin does to us. It promises us all kinds of goodies, but in the end it enslaves us. Paul said in the New Testament that he did not want to be "mastered" by anything. Each person must come to grips with the fact that sin will enslave him. The farther down its road you go, the more you get enslaved by it. The best way to keep from being enslaved is to say, "No!" right from the beginning. In the context of these verses, the sin that enslaves is adultery. People who get involved in sexual sin can be far more enslaved than those who smoke or become drunkards.

Before you walk down a road, it is a good idea to know where it heads. It is good to know where the road leads. The end of the road of sin is slavery.

Avoid that which leads to slavery.

May 6 – Read Proverbs 6

v. 10 A little sleep, a little slumber, a little folding of the hands to rest-

The word "little" is used three times here. There are people who tend to be on one side or the other of this word. If you talk about a "little" rest, some beg for more and will take all they can get. Little for them is ten hours at night or sleeping until noon on Saturday, unless forced to get up. Given the opportunity, they would rather rest than work. They like to sit and watch. They seldom volunteer for anything. If they can hide from work, they take the opportunity. They can't wait for the task to be over with. They would rather stand and talk than help get the task completed.

On the other side are those who hardly ever rest. They are driven. As a friend once said to me, "I work hard and I play hard." A few hours of sleep are all they take, whether they need more or not. They would rather work or do anything other than rest. They feel guilty sitting and doing nothing. These are the kind of people who look for things to get done. They see a task and ask what is not being done and then do it. They don't wait to be asked to help.

Now you may ask, "Which one is right?" I would tend to lean towards the second from all that I read in the Scriptures, except the second also comes with its own set of dangers. However, if you ever sit down and watch that "little" ant, you will find that he tends to stay as busy as a bee.

Beware that your "little" rest does not become "big" rest.

May 7 – Read Proverbs 7

v. 21 With much seductive speech she persuades him; with her smooth talk she compels him.

v. 22 All at once he follows her, as an ox goes to the slaughter, or as a stag is caught fast

v. 23 till an arrow pierces its liver; as a bird rushes into a snare; he does not know that it will cost him his life.

The prostitute was able to persuade this young man to go with her. She was able to overcome all of his morals, his conscience, his views, his parental training, and his beliefs about God. She was able to get through all of the things that might have kept him from committing this sin. But in the end he went along.

Now here is the rest of the story. I know. We are seldom told the rest of the story, but, here it is. The stooge in Proverbs 7 follows along, having been "compelled" into thinking that everything is going to be great, just like the animal that looks at the trap and thinks that the bait looks great and is "compelled" to eat, then his liver is "pierced" and he is caught in the "snare". Now here is where the story really goes downhill, "it will cost him his life." So many people have been killed by the spouse of the adulteress, but, I don't think that this is what is spoken of here. I think verse 23 is talking about the cost being his relationship to God, his eternal life (See Ephesians 5:3-7; 1 Thessalonians 4:1-8).

Don't commit adultery. The price may be your life.

May 8 – Read Proverbs 8

v. 22 "The LORD possessed me at the beginning of his work, the first of his acts of old.

We look around at the world and we see so much stupidity. It seems that everything and almost everyone is messed up. I read an article in the news about a police chief and a fireman who were having a physical relationship with a 15 year old. This world is messed up!

Now when we look around and see how messed up this world is, we are tempted to think it has always been that way, but it has not. When God created the world, wisdom was right there (v. 22-31). Everything God made was made with wisdom from the universe, to the world and to man. Then God put man in charge and told him to watch over what He created (Genesis 1:26-31). When God had finished He said that everything He created was "very good" (Genesis 1:31). Of course it was; it was all made with wisdom. Look around at creation. His wisdom can still be seen.

The problem came when man took of the fruit (Genesis 3). From that point, everything went downhill. It did not take long for us to mess it up. We have really messed things up. Now here is the good news: The same wisdom that God used to create everything is available to us.

Ask God for wisdom and find it in His Word.

May 9 - Read Proverbs 9

v. 13 The woman Folly is loud; she is undisciplined and without knowledge.
v. 16 "Let all who are simple come in here!" she says to those who lack judgment.

There are many who would offer those who are simple wisdom. Since wisdom is such a need, people often are like pails just waiting to be filled and looking for someone to fill them with it. The problem is that not everyone who offers to fill them with wisdom is wise. In fact, many who offer are devoid of wisdom. One such person is the "woman Folly." She offers wisdom but "knows nothing" (v. 13).

Like wisdom, she also has prepared her house (See April 9th). Like wisdom, she also calls to everyone who passes by (v. 14-15). She also offers to make those who come to her wise (v. 16). Yet her wisdom is not wise, but it is the exact opposite (v. 17). The "guests" who accept her offer to come in do not learn wisdom (v. 18). The result of her offer is death. Her house is to be avoided at all costs.

Beware of the offers you accept. Be discerning as you enter houses (v. 1, 14) offering to make you wise. Some will make you wise, but others will lead you far away from that which you seek. We need to test the spirits (1 John 4:1) and make sure that the feet at which we sit do not smell. Listen to those who have walked in righteous paths.

Be discerning as to where you seek to get wisdom.

May 10 – Read Proverbs 10

v. 19 When words are many, transgression is not lacking, but whoever restrains his lips is prudent.

It seems like there are some people who really, really talk a lot. Then there are others who talk very little. It seems like we want those who talk a lot to talk less and those who don't to talk more. But, the general truth is that those who talk little may be at the place we all should be.

This verse tells us that when we talk a lot, sin is often found. The more we talk, the more chance there is that we will say something sinful. Our words can get us into trouble and the more they come out… well, you know. In fact, look at what Jesus said in Matthew 12:36-37, "I tell you, on the day of judgment, people will give account for every careless word they speak, for by your words you will be justified, and by your words you will be condemned."

I would rather talk less and be kept safe than talk more and risk sin. We need to learn to use our words sparingly. It is wise to use restraint since much talk risks sinful talk. James 3 warns us of the power of the tongue and its ability to cause harm, which is the warning we find here. It does not mean that we should never use our mouths, which God gave us to be used, but we should be careful.

Use words with restraint and be careful of talking too much.

May 11 – Read Proverbs 11

v. 14 Where there is no guidance, a people falls, but in an abundance of counselors there is safety.

Countries, states, cities, community groups, churches and families are much better off when there is good wise guidance. The "go it alone" approach is not wise. We all need advisors to help us. There is wisdom when we have "an abundance of counselors." This thought is seen again in Proverbs (Proverbs 15:22, 20:18, and 24:6). Proverbs 15:22 speaks of "success" and Proverbs 20:18 speaks of "victory" by having an "abundance of counselors." They can all agree on something often cementing a wise decision. Or, there may be a divergence of opinion, giving us several sides to consider. Either way, there is value in hearing what others have to say.

It is possible that you can have too many counselors. Some people keep asking everyone they see for guidance on a subject and never come to a decision. That is not wise. It is also understood that the counselors are to be wise people with knowledge on the subject at hand. It is wise to find people to whom a nation can go when the need arises. It is also true for you to have the same. There is safety and victory in such a plan. The opposite is also true. When there is a lack of an "abundance of counselors," a "people falls." I prefer the safe route, and that is the suggestion here.

Be safe. Find guidance in an abundance of wise counselors.

May 12 - Read Proverbs 12

v. 23 A prudent man conceals knowledge, but the heart of fools proclaims folly.

Watch how people act in a group, and it will tell a lot about their maturity level. A younger person wants to answer every single question and this is most definitely true of a fool. A more mature person is ready to try to answer questions, but does not feel the need to answer them all.

Mature people are thoughtful and careful with their answers. They are more willing to think things through. Even when they have the right answer, they often want to hear what others have to say on a given issue before speaking. They are more willing to sit back and listen. Verse 23 says that "a prudent man conceals knowledge." Prudent people have no compulsion to tell everyone everything they know. There is wisdom in being slow to speak or in not speaking at all at times. The wise person wants to speak at the right time, to the right people, in the right way and saying the right thing.

The fool thinks differently. He is ready to rush in and proclaim his knowledge, often showing his ignorance. The fool loves to proclaim his opinions (18:2). According to Proverbs, this is the character of a fool, in contrast to a person of wisdom. A fool jumps without knowing where he will land, and he will suffer for it. The fool often just wants to let everyone know how smart he is or how smart he thinks he is.

Don't feel the need to blurt out all you know.

May 13 - Read Proverbs 13

v. 10 By insolence comes nothing but strife, but with those who take advice is wisdom.

I have seen this verse proven true so many times. Every time I see it, I am saddened. Proverbs says so much about this subject that I could say it is one of the most touched on topics in the book.

Watch the first half of this verse. "By insolence comes nothing but strife." I wondered why the "ESV" version of the Bible used the word "insolence" instead of the word "pride" which many translations use. The word pride would be easier for the average person to understand without having to dig. Here is why I think they did. Insolence literally means to boil. It is used of acting in a proud manner, but it is more than simple pride. It is a pride that includes defiance and even rebelliousness. We find the word used in Proverbs 21:24, where it says, "Scoffer is the name of the arrogant, haughty man who acts with arrogant pride."

When you find a person who is acting or thinking in this manner, you will often find "nothing but strife." That is, you find nothing but quarrelling. This person thinks that his opinion is the only opinion that matters. He is unwilling to listen to, or at least consider, what others have to say. This is sad because the Bible makes clear that wisdom is found in counsel with others. The second part of verse 10 says, 'but with those who take advice is wisdom." This is the contrast to the person who acts with "insolence." The truth is that no matter who you are or what you know, there is value in taking advice. You consider your opinion and the opinion of others and what the Bible says on the subject and you pray, and then you make your decision.

Let me put the verse together so you can see the contrast. Verse 10 says, "By insolence comes nothing but strife **but** with those who take advice there is wisdom." The result of the first is strife, but the result of the second is wisdom. Which result is better "strife" or "wisdom"? Which do you prefer?

Don't be insolent. Always be willing to take advice.

May 14 – Read Proverbs 14

v. 10 The heart knows its own bitterness, and no stranger shares its joy.

Men much wiser than me told me this. They each said it individually, and I heard it over and over. Now thirty years of pastoring has proven it to be true. This, of course, was stated in God's Word many years ago and so did not need me to prove it true. Yet, I have seen it proven true so many times (1 Samuel 1:3-8).

When you are hurting, people may say, "I know how you feel." Others may say, "I have been there before." Still others may love you very much and want to help you with your pain. But the reality is that no one fully knows your own pain but you. No one can fully understand your suffering, but you certainly know it. It sometimes hurts far more than you can ever put into words. In fact, sometimes it hurts so much you don't put it into words and so you deal with it privately.

At the same time, the opposite is true. No one fully knows your joy. The thing that you are excited about and drives you is something only you can know. You try to bring people on board, but the words are hard. Some get it to a point, but only to a point. But in the end, no one will ever fully love the thing you love like you do. Your hobby or job or whatever you are passionate about will remain with you.

Know that sometimes your pain or joy will only be fully understood by you.

May 15 - Read Proverbs 15

v. 3 The eyes of the Lord are in every place, keeping watch on the wicked and the good.

Today is the middle of the month. Take a moment and think about all that you have done in the first half of the month. You may even want to include last month. Are you pleased with your choices? Are you pleased with your actions? Are you pleased with your thoughts? Would you have done anything differently if you knew someone was watching you?

Proverbs 15:3 makes clear that we are being watched. Many Bible passages talk about this truth. This truth should make you think twice about your choices, actions and thoughts. This is especially true if you did something that you should not have done. Did you use your computer to look at pornography? Have you read a novel that you would not allow your child to read? The fact is that you are never alone. God is always watching you.

Yet, this truth can also be a comfort. God is always watching you, and you are never alone. Have you ever wondered, "Does God really know what is happening to me?" Yes, He does! He is always there for you (Psalms 121). God is watching over you, and he cares about you very much.

Knowing that God is watching you may cause distress if you are doing something you shouldn't. Or, it may cause peace because God is keeping His eye on you. Certainly, the fact that God is watching you can either be a concern or a comfort.

Remember, God is watching you!

May 16 – Read Proverbs 16

v. 5 Everyone who is arrogant in heart is an abomination to the Lord; be assured, he will not go unpunished.

This verse is for "everyone" who is arrogant in heart. The word from which we get "arrogant" here is a word that means high or lofty. The idea is that of exalting yourself above others. This verse speaks to everyone who does this or who might think of doing this. The warning against doing this is strong.

What does God say about the person who would do this? They are an abomination to Him. The word "abomination" means that someone is detestable or disgusting to God. It certainly is a strong word. Here is a list of other things that are called an abomination to God in Proverbs: a devious person (3:32), lying (12:22), hypocrisy (15:8), the way of the wicked (15:9), the thoughts of the wicked (15:26), injustice (17:15), and dishonesty in business (20:10). See also Proverbs 6:16-19. This is a list no one should wish to be on.

Now one more thought is added. The "arrogant in heart" needs to know that "he will not go unpunished." So the one who would lift himself up above others must repent or he will be punished by God. James 4:6 tells us that "God opposes the proud." God so hates pride that he will punish it. For an example of this, look at Herod in Acts 12 or Nebuchadnezzar in Daniel 4.

Avoid elevating yourself above others. The consequences are not good.

May 17 – Read Proverbs 17

v. 3 The crucible is for silver, and the furnace is for gold, and the LORD *tests hearts.*

I would imagine that everyone knows that you test metals by heating them up to find out if they are pure, whether silver or gold. Metals are tested to separate the good metal from the junk. The end result is that the value of the tested material is determined.

God uses trials (James 1:2-4; 1 Peter 1:6-7) to test us. He tests the heart, and He knows it well (1 KIngs 8:39). Fire is used to learn about metal, but God alone knows the heart and he tests it continually. People can hide their heart from men, but not from God. We can neither know the heart of a man nor our own hearts very well. God tests the heart and when it comes out on the other side, the heart is better off, just like metal that has been tested.

People sometimes do not like God's testing, but God's testing produces positive results in the one who has been tested. So the test itself, though it is not always easy, is good. Medical tests can tell us what is going on in our body. God's tests not only do that, but they also result in better spiritual health. His tests do both investigation and refinement, so like the testing of metal we have greater value.

Look at God's testing as having value instead of being something that only hurts. Keep your eye on the end result. It will help your attitude as you go through the time of testing.

Embrace God's tests, for they result in a better you.

May 18 – Read Proverbs 18

v. 8 The words of a whisperer are like delicious morsels; they go down into the inner parts of the body.

Oh how we are warned against gossip! It is a dangerous sin that ruins lives, but we are too quick to want to listen to it and so we listen. We see that here. Gossip is like "delicious morsels." It's so delicious that this thought is repeated in 26:22. This verse tells us how good gossip is to the one who listens. People sometimes ask, "Do you want to hear a juicy or a good story?" If it did not taste so good, people would not be so ready to consume it. But that usually it true of sin. At first it tastes good, but in the end it is bitter.

It is at the same time a warning to the one who listens. The best way to deal with a gossiper is not to listen. The best answer to the question is "No, I don't want to hear that story." Gossip does not do one good thing. In fact, it does much harm. It separates close friends (16:28). It keeps a fight going (26:20). It hurts others 100% of the time. Yet, it often tastes so good until you become the story of the gossiper. Maybe that is the answer to gossip. Listen to it as if you are the topic of the gossip. If we listened to gossip that way, we would not listen to it at all.

Gossip is a food that turns sour in the stomach, so don't eat it up.

May 19 - Read Proverbs 19

v. 11 Good sense makes one slow to anger, and it is his glory to overlook an offense.

There are two things that we can do that would go against wisdom and good sense. The first would be to get angry easily or quickly. The second, which is just a further statement of the first, would be to not overlook an offense. Things that might anger us or cause us to be offended will come in this life. In fact, they must come because we live in a sinful world. Whether they come or not is not the issue in life. The real issue is how we respond to these things when they come our way. Is our response one of wisdom or one of foolishness?

Watch how people respond to life and other people. What is their first reaction? Does their first reaction display wisdom or foolishness?

Since offenses will come, how should we react? We should be slow to anger and overlook an offense whenever possible. This is the advice of Proverbs 19:11. The wise do not respond to life like the vast majority. The wise respond wisely to events and to people who might cause anger. They are slow in allowing things or people to anger them. When offended, they most often overlook the offense unless there is more value in dealing with it. "Good sense" keeps one from anger, and one's glory is seen in overlooking an offense.

Don't be easily offended. Respond with love, not anger.

May 20 - Read Proverbs 20

v. 11 Even a child makes himself known by his acts, by whether his conduct is pure and upright.

The truth is that our actions give us away every time. People can profess to be something they are not with all of the vigor possible and may even be believed. But, it is our actions that tell the true story of our heart. I have met some very good liars in my time. I can usually tell when someone is lying, but some people have fooled me. Yet, if you watch people's actions long enough, they will give away their heart.

Actions, more than words, tell the true story of a person's heart. This is even true with children. Children or teenagers who claim to be spiritual but are disrespectful to authority or disobedient to their parents need to examine themselves. Parents who claim for themselves to have children who are saved (born again) but whose actions are far from that need to reconsider. Actions, even for children, tell the story of the heart. This is seen in this verse.

It is our actions that speak the loudest about our character, not our words. We all need to ask, "Do my claims match my actions?"

Our actions give the true portrayal of our character. Believers were first called "Christians" because their actions showed that they were followers of Christ. Forget your words. What do your actions say about who you really are?

Be a Christ follower in both words and actions.

May 21 - Read Proverbs 21

v. 5 The plans of the diligent lead surely to abundance, but everyone who is hasty comes only to poverty.

Some people take pride in their haste. Their lack of planning and preparation almost makes them, in their own eyes, seem righteous. But according to God's Word, in His book of everyday wisdom, it is not wise. This kind of living does not lead to success, but to failure.

God says it better than I can when He says, "The plans of the diligent lead surely to abundance, but everyone who is hasty comes only to poverty" (21:5). The wise are careful and thoughtful and know that doing anything without thorough planning can cause problems in the long run. The word "hasty" means hurrying or running without purpose (Proverbs 19:2; 21:5; 29:20). This is not the same as working hard and fast, but it is hurrying without planning and being thoughtful. The thought found here relates to life (19:2), work (21:5), and words (29:20). Anything done quickly and without thinking can lead to trouble.

I remember an old saying that I have heard since I was a child, "Haste makes waste." It is attributed to Benjamin Franklin. The truth of what Benjamin said can be found here. Proverbs 20:21 also warns of doing things in haste. It is not how quickly we get to the goal, but how long we last once there that matters. Don't be in such a hurry that you ruin the results.

Don't be in a hurry. Think, plan and be careful.

May 22 – Read Proverbs 22

v. 6 Train up a child in the way he should go; even when he is old he will not depart from it.

Don't you wish that the day you came home from the hospital with your child there was an owner's manual waiting for you? It is absolutely scary coming home, putting your child in the house and then saying, "Now what?" Most parents have no idea what to do. Even if you have some idea, it is scary.

Proverbs has much to say about raising children and you would expect that to be the case since its topic is wisdom. Surely, raising children is an area of life where wisdom is greatly needed. This verse gives us a basic truth about raising children that ought to comfort parents. First, we must start with a very important definition. The word "train" means to "inaugurate" or "start." The idea is that if you start children out on the right path they will stay on the right path. Note also that it does not say when he gets older he will come back to the right path. It says that he will stay on the right path. So it is very important that you start your children on the right path and that you don't wait until they get older to get them on the right path. The sooner you start them on the right path, the better.

Get you children started right so that they stay on track.

May 23 – Read Proverbs 23

v. 13 Do not withhold discipline from a child; if you strike him with a rod, he will not die.
v. 14 If you strike him with the rod, you will save his soul from Sheol.

As I look around at children and teenagers and see what they do, it scares me for the next generation. I see girls walking around with hardly any clothes on, and then so many pregnant. I see boys walking around with their pants down to their knees. I see teenagers with no respect for authority. We live in a day when many teens are taking all kinds of illegal drugs. Also, we see far too many children being medicated to correct behavior. People often wonder where the bad behavior finds its source. My answer is it often starts with bad parenting.

Parents need to realize what is at stake when they fail to discipline their children. Note the phrases above: "he will not die" and "you will save his soul from Sheol." Failing to discipline your children is no small matter. Parents must not "withhold discipline" from their children. The consequences of doing so are as great as these verses warn. This failure is epidemic in our society, and we are seeing it in the behavior of our children. Failure to discipline can result in an untimely or premature death in your child, along with other bad things as mentioned above. People who are not ready to do the hard work of disciplining should not have children.

Parents, be wise. Discipline your children or bad things may happen to them.

May 24 - Read Proverbs 24

v. 6 Whoever gives an honest answer kisses the lips.

I don't think people always realize how important honesty is or how good it is. When people teach, they often look for an illustration that explains a truth. Jesus did this with masterful perfection. He often took physical objects and with them explained spirituals truths in such a wonderful way.

So back to our topic, which is the value of honesty or truthfulness. People tend to be willing to lie for anything and about anything. I could not say it better than the way God has said it, and He has said it in Proverbs 24:6 "an honest answer is like a kiss." Don't let the temptation to lie ever succeed in your life. No lie could ever be illustrated like a kiss on the lips. There are many reasons why people may lie in answer to a question. For example, someone may be afraid of getting caught or of hurting the questioner. But none of these reasons could ever be as positive as an honest answer. An honest answer has the same value as a kiss from a loved one. Such an answer is an expression of love and friendship.

My wife tells me that she is willing to ask me anything because she knows I will always tell her the truth. Can you imagine what it is like to answer the question, "How do I look in this dress?" and not worry about getting hit in the head with a frying pan? That is the value of honesty in a relationship.

Always answer people honestly.

May 25 - Read Proverbs 25

v. 16 If you have found honey, eat only enough for you, lest you have your fill of it and vomit it.

v. 17 Let your foot be seldom in your neighbor's house, lest he have his fill of you and hate you.

Have you ever eaten too much of something you love? It does not feel good. You walk away saying, "My eyes were bigger than my stomach." It is like eating too much honey (25:16). The idea is that you have to know when to say when. You have to have some wisdom to know when something is too much.

This is also true in dealing with our neighbors. Some people will go over other people's homes every day, all day long, if they could. On the one hand, that "might" be fine if you are continually invited. But on the other hand, one must be careful. Too much of that and your neighbor may just have eaten too much of a good thing, and you will have worn out your welcome (25:17).

This verse is not to be used as an excuse for never going out of your house. Remember, this is the activity of selfish people who isolate themselves from others (18:1). We ought to visit people and go to their activities when possible. But every person needs wisdom to know when it is too much. Most neighbors are too polite to tell us that they are about to vomit up a really good meal.

Know when you have been at your neighbor's house enough.

May 26 - Read Proverbs 26

v. 13 The Sluggard says, "There is a lion in the road! There is a lion in the streets!"
v. 14 As a door turns on its hinges so a sluggard on his bed.
v. 15 The sluggard buries his hand in the dish; it wears him out to bring it back to his mouth.

Proverbs 26:13-15 is all about lazy people. A lazy person is called a sluggard, which means lazy or sluggish. Swanson defines the word this way: "lazy bones, i.e., a person who is habitually lazy and inactive, suggesting he has no discipline or initiative, as a moral failure (Pr 6:6, 9; 10:26; 13:4; 15:19; 19:24; 20:4; 21:25; 22:13; 26:13, 14, 15, 16+)."[14]

We are told a few things here about this kind of person and many more things in the verses above. He makes up excuses, even outlandish ones, for why he cannot work, but he is just plain lazy. A bed to a sluggard is like hinges to a door; you can't have one without the other. Round and round, he turns on his bed, he is so lazy. The lazy person is seen as someone who can't even pick his head up from his food. If it were up to him to feed himself, he would starve.

America in many ways has become a lazy nation. It is not the nation it used to be. People would rather sit home and collect from the government than go to work. Laziness helps no one.

Don't be a sluggard!

May 27 – Read Proverbs 27

v. 21 The crucible is for silver, and the furnace is for gold, and a man is tested by his praise.

Silver and gold are tested to see how pure they are. For one the crucible is used, and for the other the furnace is used. Proverbs 17:3 is similar and states, "The crucible is for silver, and the furnace is for gold, and the LORD tests hearts. Proverbs 27:19 tells us that we can know a person by his or her heart. The idea of all of these verses is that there are things in a person's life that reveal who he or she is.

One of the ways to find out who a person is beneath his skin would be to look at the praise he receives. The praise someone receives tells a great deal about the person who is in question. To figure out who a person really is, you may want to consider who speaks well of him. The people who praise a person tend to have the same goals, values and heart. We may also consider why he is praised. Why a person is praised tells us what a person does to earn that praise. It would not be far-fetched to even consider who criticizes him and for what he is criticized. A person's reputation is usually earned and often accurate.

In your search of who a person really is, take a look at the praise he receives or the lack thereof. In so doing, we may also want to look at the praise we receive. It may give us a picture of ourselves that we have not thought through.

Take a look at the praise a person receives and you may see beneath their skin.

May 28 - Read Proverbs 28

v. 19 Whoever works his land will have plenty of bread, but he who follows worthless pursuits will have plenty of poverty.

Two things can get all of us into trouble: laziness and foolishness. Over my lifetime, I have seen people be very lazy and very foolish. Either of these pursuits can get us into trouble, but it usually doesn't happen until the trouble is upon us.

When it comes to life, we need to work hard, for hard work usually pays off. Proverbs 28:19a says, "Whoever works his land will have plenty of bread." Hard work pays, whereas laziness harms. We see these two opposite things often played against one another in Proverbs. If you want to be wise, work hard. Far too many people don't want to work hard. They would rather have everything given to them.

But working hard is not enough. You must also work smart. Proverbs 28:19b says, "but he who follows worthless pursuits will have plenty of poverty." "Worthless pursuits" means empty, meaningless goals or plans. Proverbs 14:23 tells us, "In all toil there is profit, but mere talk tends only to poverty." Proverbs 28:19 and 12:11 are almost identical, so this truth is repeated for emphasis. I sometimes see people work very hard but not get ahead because they fail to plan, that is, they fail to think. A hard worker who also thinks can go a long way in this life.

Be wise. Work hard and also work smart.

May 29 - Read Proverbs 29

v. 15 The rod and reproof give wisdom, but a child left to himself brings shame to his mother.

v. 17 Discipline your son, and he will give you rest; he will give delight to your heart.

A while ago I heard a statement that has stuck with me, "Christianity is one generation from extinction." How sad to see so many families falling apart and children heading in the wrong direction. It seems we are growing up in a generation that thinks leaving children to themselves will make better children. But verse 15 says that "a child left to himself brings shame to his mother." On the other hand, when parents are involved in disciplining their children, verse 17 says that such children "will give you rest" and "will give delight to your heart." Raising children is not an easy task, but we all want to raise children who will do what these verses mention.

Verse 15 says, "the rod and reproof give wisdom." The "rod" stands for physical punishment such as spanking. It is mentioned in several spots in the book of Proverbs, such as 13:24; 22:15 and 23:13-14. It is never to be done in anger or to hurt a child, but it is to be a reminder that family rules are to be obeyed. "Reproof" (rebuke) stands for verbal correction. The reality is that children who are allowed to do whatever they want without correction will in the end cause grief to the parents. Proper discipline will have a much better result. A child who is disciplined correctly will become wise.

Use the Bible as your guide for raising your children. There is no better guide.

May 30 – Read Proverbs 30

v. 21 Under three things the earth trembles; under four it cannot bear up:
v. 22 a slave when he becomes king, and a fool when he is filled with food;
v. 23 an unloved woman when she gets a husband, and a maidservant when she displaces her mistress.

Under four things the earth "cannot bear up." Today we will look at the last two, two things that make the earth shake. Both deal with how a wife is treated. Both deal with how a wife should not be treated.

One of the worse things that can happen on this earth of ours is for a woman to be married and not be loved. This earth is full of women who feel this way, and some of it is valid and some of it is not. Yet, when it is true, it is a horrible thing. The main command given to men is that they must love their wives, and when this does not happen, the earth trembles. What men often don't realize is that their love for their wife is supposed to be a picture of Christ's love for the church (Ephesians 5:25-33). So, men need to consider their love for their wife and how it pictures Christ's love. It does not matter if your love is better than the husband's down the street. It must picture Christ's love. This picture in some marriages does not measure up.

The third statement carries the same idea as the first. No wife should ever be so unloved that her maidservant would replace her.

Husbands love your wives as Christ loved the church.

May 31 – Read Proverbs 31

v. 1 The words of King Lemuel. An oracle that his mother taught him:

Much, not all, of what we find in Proverbs is a father teaching his son about wisdom and life. But, not here! Here in this last chapter of Proverbs, we find a mother teaching her son about several topics, but mostly about women. Mothers need to consider very carefully the importance of teaching their sons, specifically teaching them about women. I wonder how many mothers have spent time while their sons were growing up teaching about this topic.

Most of what we find in this chapter is teaching about the kind of a woman her son should marry. She tells him that this kind of woman is not easy to find (v. 10) so he needs to be careful and not just pick any woman that comes along. She tells him that when he finds such a woman he should value and praise her (v. 31). Men should certainly think about this after yesterday's devotional thought. She even warned him to keep the women in his life in proper perspective (v. 2-3).

Mothers have such a great impact on the lives of their children, their sons and daughters. That impact can even be greater if mothers would prepare their sons for relationships with the opposite sex. Mothers need to both warn their sons of the wrong kind of woman (v2-3) and teach them what the right kind of woman looks like (v. 10-31).

Mothers, teach your son(s) about women.

June 1 – Read Proverbs 1

v. 18 but these men lie in wait for their own blood; they set an ambush for their own lives.

In the world of illegal or sinful activity, there is a predator - relationship. There are evil predators looking to seek out and attack prey for their own selfish desires. Their eyes look for prey that is easily attacked and conquered, just like in the animal world.

Sadly, these predators hurt many people. Families and individuals often never recover from what happens to them by those who are willing to hurt them for their own selfish motives. We live in a world that has been affected by sin, and so people reap the results of those who allow sin to control them.

There is something that everyone who decides to do sinful things needs to understand. If you go from beginning to end, the last person who is hurt by this predator-prey relationship is the predator. Men or women who seek to hurt others set out on a path that will in its final tally only hurt themselves. For example, look at what the verse tells us, "for their own blood" and "for their own lives." If you choose a path or make a choice today that you think will benefit you by hurting others, you are going to hurt yourself at the end of your journey. This is what sinful activity does; it promises good things, but in the end it destroys those who choose it.

Those who choose to harm others will face the consequences of their actions. No intentional act of harming others will escape the hand of God.

Don't think you can hurt others and escape unharmed.

June 2 – Read Proverbs 2

v. 7 he stores up sound wisdom for the upright; he is a shield to those who walk in integrity,

God is the one who is mentioned above. He is the one who gives wisdom. What we learn here is that wisdom is not given to everyone and anyone without discrimination. Wisdom is given to a select group of people. God gives wisdom to the "upright" to "those who walk in integrity."

This truth is repeated in the New Testament. We find in Romans 1 that people rejected God, and therefore wisdom, while "claiming to be wise." This action resulted in them becoming foolish. In the first chapter of 1 Corinthians, we find that God made foolish the wisdom of the world through the cross of Christ. And, in 1 Corinthians 2, we learn that God's wisdom is seen as foolishness to this world. So this world thinks that it can be wise without God. In fact, this world thinks that the rejection of God is wisdom. This world thinks that choosing God is the foolish thing to do and that living life in light of what the Bible says is pure foolishness.

This reality leaves every person with a choice. You can choose God and become wise as stated in God's Word. Or, you can reject God and be seen as wise by the world. So do you choose what the world says about wisdom, or do you choose what God says about wisdom in His Word?

Choose today to believe God and become wise.

June 3 – Read Proverbs 3

v. 7 Be not wise in your own eyes; fear the Lord, and turn away from evil.
v. 8 It will be healing to your flesh and refreshment to your bones.

There is great danger in being "wise in your own eyes." It can create all kinds of problems for you. It is a very, very dangerous place to be. Listen to this warning from Proverbs 26:12: "Do you see a man wise in his own eyes? There is more hope for a fool than for him." With what Proverbs says about the fool, you would think that the fool would be the lowest on the totem pole. But, he is not. The one who is "wise in his own eyes" is. He is the one who is in the most danger.

We are warned not to be wise in our own eyes (Proverbs 3:7; Isaiah 5:21). What trouble can come from being wise in our own eyes? We are told in the verses above that this condition can have an impact on our bodies (flesh & bones). We end up like the fool who is unwilling to listen to advice (Proverbs 12:15). Where we are unwilling to listen to advice, there is no way but down for us.

What can make us wise in our own eyes? There can be many culprits on the list. For example, the pride that is found in every one of us can do it. Yet, maybe at the top of the list is our own successes in life. Someone who works hard and becomes rich may fall into it (Proverbs 28:11).

Be not wise in your own eyes!

June 4 – Read Proverbs 4

v. 18 But the path of the righteous is like the light of dawn, which shines brighter and brighter until full day.

v. 19 The way of the wicked is like deep darkness; they do not know over what they stumble.

Life is full of choices. Some choices are easy. Some are hard. One of the choices we face in life is whether to take the path of the righteous or the path of the wicked. This choice is made in a major way at crossroads in life and also in minor ways on a daily basis.

The choice of taking the path of the righteous is not as easy as it may seem. In fact, most people do not take this path (Matthew 7:13-14). This path, most of the time - if not all of the time, is the harder choice because at the beginning of this path, it is the more difficult way. Choosing to do right over wrong begins with difficulty. Yet, this path gets better as it goes. The end of this path is by far better than the other path. This path may not be easy, but it ends in glory (Revelation 21-22).

The other path is the path of the wicked. This path is an easy choice and its beginnings seem full of ease. People on this path often think they have made the right choice. Yet, this path is characterized as "deep darkness", which causes those on it to stumble and not even know why. The end of this path is not good (Revelation 20:11-15; 21:8).

Choose the path of righteousness for it is the right choice.

June 5 - Read Proverbs 5

v. 3 For the lips of a forbidden woman drip honey, and her speech is smoother than oil,
v. 4 But in the end she is bitter as wormwood, sharp as a double edge sword.

In a battle, it helps to know the weapons that will be used against you. In the battle against sexual immorality, one of the weapons that will be used against you is speech. It will be speech that "drips honey" and is "smoother than oil." This is the thing that the forbidden woman would use to draw you in.

The forbidden woman (adulteress) will draw you in with her speech. Therefore you need to avoid listening to her. Both "drip honey" and "smooth as oil" warn us that she is very good at using her speech to draw men in. It can happen at work or where people gather together. The adulteress begins to say things your spouse does not. She listens to you and says the kinds of things that make you feel better. Men find women who are willing to praise them. Women find men who are willing to understand them. Speech leads the way to sin.

But both men and women need to look past what they hear. Both need to understand that in the end, it's not honey or oil you taste. It is wormwood (a shrub with a bitter taste). In the end, it is a sword that gets stuck in your heart.

Beware of sweet, smooth speech for in the end it may lead to suffering and death.

June 6 - Read Proverbs 6

v. 1 My son, if you have put up security for your neighbor, have given your pledge for a stranger,
v. 2 if you are snared in the words of your mouth, caught in the words of your mouth,
v. 3 then do this, my son, and save yourself, for you have come into the hand of your neighbor: go, hasten, and plead urgently with your neighbor.
v. 4 Give your eyes no sleep and your eyelids no slumber;
v. 5 save yourself like a gazelle from the hand of the hunter, like a bird from the hand of the fowler.

Borrowing money is a very serious matter. Yet it happens so often in our society, that most people look at it as being just a natural part of life. This is a matter we need to consider carefully. Borrowing can put us in a dangerous place in life.

Here the case concerns "putting up security" for someone (the borrower) other than yourself. This means that you become a cosigner to the borrower's purchase, thus also incurring his debt and responsibility for payment. If he doesn't pay, you assume the responsibility for that debt. According to these verses, doing this is a very bad idea. If you have already done this, what do you do? Do all you can to get out of the financial mess!

Instead of getting into this mess, you can give the person the money instead of loaning it, if possible. This is another option in dealing with this situation in order to avoid this dangerous scenario.

Don't cosign a loan for a neighbor or a stranger.

June 7 - Read Proverbs 7

v. 27 Her house is the way of Sheol, going down to the chambers of death.

We often make decisions based on looking at things from the front side of the decision. But it is far better to make decisions based on looking at it from the backside. When we look at the decision from the front side, all we see is the good of it. But if we look at it from the backside, then we see what happens after. We see the consequences. We see the results. We see the possible punishment or reward. We see the long-term instead of the short-term things that happen as a result of the decision in question.

How about this issue of sexual sin, of adultery? This is the context of chapter seven. On the front side, as a song once put it, "How can it be so bad if it feels so good?" On this side, the decisions made look like good ones. That is certainly how Hollywood makes it look.

But, what about the other side of the decision, the backside? What truly happens when you choose to commit sexual sin? Would you commit sexual sin if when you walked in the room, you saw a sign that said, "This way to the 'Chambers of Death"? It changes things, doesn't it? Sexual sin is not what this world makes it out to be. It is not a good thing (See Ephesians 5:3-7; 1 Thessalonians 4:1-8).

Reject sexual immorality!

June 8 - Read Proverbs 8

v. 7 for my mouth will utter truth, wickedness is an abomination to my lips.

It is clear from Proverbs that there is a correlation between wisdom and righteous living. People are only wise when they make righteous choices. As soon as you choose to do that which is wicked or sinful, you have departed from wisdom. You came to a "Y" in the road and veered off the wise path. As the verse states, wisdom utters truth, so when you choose to lie, you are no longer wise.

There is no such thing, biblically speaking, of wisdom and wickedness living together. Every time a person chooses to do the wrong thing, he or she chooses an unwise path. For example, people often think it is wise to live with someone outside of marriage so that they can see if the partnership will work. If it doesn't work, it is easier to separate than if they were married. It makes sense, right? If you say, "Yes" you have agreed with the world, but have disagreed with God and have chosen an unwise path, which will be punished by Him (Revelation 21:8).

This world has a hard time understanding why Bible believing Christians don't agree with them and don't buy into the wisdom of such choices (1 Peter 4:3-6). We must keep in mind that it is God's will that we abstain from sexual immorality (1 Thessalonians 4:3). The truth is that believers believe that choosing any path that places you in front of God's judgment is not wise.

Be wise, make choices that are morally righteous, not wicked.

June 9 - Read Proverbs 9

v. 7 Whoever corrects a scoffer gets himself abuse, and he who reproves a wicked man incurs injury.

v. 8 Do not reprove a scoffer, or he will hate you; reprove a wise man, and he will love you.

In life we sometimes find ourselves in situations where other people do not act wisely. In these situations, we find ourselves making the choice to either reprove this person or to say nothing. We often decide what to do based on whether or not we feel it is worth the trouble (v7). Yet there is also another thing to consider, our relationship to the one who has acted unwise (v8).

Rebuking an unwise person can have dramatic effects on the relationship with that person. It can go one of two ways. If the person is wise, he will love you for taking the time to love him enough to rebuke him. If he is unwise, he will hate (grow cold towards) you for having offended him (which is what he thinks you have done).

So in relating to other people, we often have to consider what our actions may have on the relationship. With this being so, some will choose to rarely rebuke anyone. However, this is the wrong choice in life. If we love people, which we should, we should always take actions which we believe will help people, no matter what will happen to us. This can be hard, but it is the right thing to do. Just remember that just because you love people enough to rebuke them, that does not mean that people will understand it.

Love your friends enough to rebuke them, but know that they may misunderstand you.

June 10 - Read Proverbs 10

v. 18 The one who conceals hatred has lying lips, and whoever utters slander is a fool.

Oh, how true it is! Many have hid their hatred with lying lips, for example Cain (Genesis 4), Saul (1 Samuel 18) and Judas (John 13) among others. I have seen it, sad to say, in the church. One person will tell me his dislike for another (not in those words of course) and then turn around and hug that same person. The statement in the first part of verse 18 is so true. Hatred in one's heart is covered up by lying lips. This is the point. I just got it! The point is that since this statement is so true, so is the second statement "whoever utters slander is a fool."

We don't, as polite people, want to call anyone a "fool." Calling someone a "fool" is so strong and impolite that we dare not do it. Yet if you utter slander, you are indeed a fool. Slander is speech that defames, blasphemes or insults another person. Legally speaking, it is speech that makes false or malicious statements damaging to another person. One of the things that makes speech slanderous, biblically speaking, is intent. The one who slanders is looking to cause other people to rise up against or think critically of the one who is being slandered. Why are you a fool? Because the Bible clearly and unmistakably forbids slander (Matthew 15:19; Romans 1:30; Ephesians 4:31; Colossians 3:8; 1 Timothy 3:11; 1 Peter 2:1; James 4:11-12).

Don't slander others. Save slander for fools.

June 11 - Read Proverbs 11

v. 1 A false balance is an abomination to the Lord, but a just weight is his delight.

"Church is for Sunday" is what many believe and say. Many believe that what you do on Sunday, that is, if you go to church, is meant to stay at church. The idea is that Sunday and Monday should never mix. Even many who strongly profess Christ seem to have no time for Christian principles at work. Yet, this is not what God's Word teaches.

The Bible teaches that Sunday should affect Monday through Saturday. What we learn on Sunday at church should impact how we live when we go home and when we go to work. So often when we go to work, we leave what we learned on Sunday at church. We often think, I would assume, that Sunday's teachings should not be considered when we are trying to make money. I guess that some think that we can't be both holy and make money at the same time. But is this the case? Does it matter to God what we do at work?

It does matter to God. God expects us to work and be holy at the same time. He wants us to be both fair and just when we are working. God wants and expects that our Christian principles will affect how we work. As stated, dishonesty at work is an "abomination" to God, but He delights in honesty at work.

Take Christianity to work with you today!

June 12 - Read Proverbs 12

v. 4 An excellent wife is her husbands crown, but she who brings shame is like rottenness in his bones.

It is surprising to me that the most basic and important issues of life are so often left unstudied by believers. Forget digging for gold on some deep theological issue, shall we not even search for the issues that touch life daily? For example, what is an excellent wife? I'm not talking about reading books on the subject. I'm talking about opening a Bible and going to work digging for yourself, especially if you are a wife, on such an issue as being an excellent wife.

My pastoral experience has taught me that most women (and men) have not done the digging. So to get you started, here are some of the main passages that describe what an excellent wife looks like: Genesis 2:18-25; Proverbs 31:10-31; Ephesians 5:22-33; Colossians 3:18-21; 1 Timothy 5:3-16; Titus 2:3-5; 1 Peter 3:1-7. These are just some of the passages that deal with being an excellent wife.

Then there are the passages that deal with being a good Christian that could be added to these. Even verses that deal with what a bad wife looks like (1 Kings 19 & 21; Proverbs 19:31; 21:9; 25:24; 27:15) will help a woman to see what makes an excellent wife.

Now why is it important for a woman to be an excellent wife? The reason is that the one who is not is like "rottenness" to her husband's bones. Rottenness speaks of a decay or inflammation which causes pain. It should be the goal of every married woman to become an excellent wife.

Search God's Word for the characteristics of an excellent wife.

June 13 - Read Proverbs 13

v. 13 Whoever despises the word brings destruction on himself, but he who reveres the commandment will be rewarded.

Both the "word" and the "commandment" refer to divine revelation. So this verse speaks of a person's attitudes toward the Bible. There are two different attitudes mentioned here that you can have toward the Word of God, despising or revering. These attitudes lead to actions, which come from the attitudes.

The first attitude is a negative one towards the Bible. There are those who despise the Bible. To despise the Bible means to scorn or have contempt for it. This kind of an attitude will lead to actions that rebel against God's Word and which will bring God's judgment.

The second attitude is a positive one towards the Bible. There are those who revere the Bible. To revere it means to have reverence for it and therefore tremble before it. This is exactly the kind of attitude that God wants us to have concerning His Word (Isaiah 66:2). This attitude is seen in one who loves and obeys God's Word.

Jesus contrasted these two kinds of attitudes when he said that those who hear and obey are wise and those who hear but don't obey are foolish (Matthew 7:24-27). The New Testament is full of verses that state that those who revere God's Word will be rewarded and those who despise it will be punished (Revelation 20:11-15).

Revere God's Word and so obey it today.

June 14 – Read Proverbs 14

v. 12 There is a way that seems right to a man, but its end is the way to death.

This thought is repeated in Proverbs 16:25, and whenever anything in the Bible is repeated, it is especially worth our time to think it through. This we must do here. Unfortunately, there are many who are on roads that seem so right, but in the end they lead to death (Matthew 7:13-14). Why does this happen? One reason is that people are often not discerning. They do not give proper consideration to their steps. This truth is stated in Proverbs 14:15 when it says, "The simple believes everything, but the prudent gives thought to his way."

Those who are wise use discernment considering all aspects of their choices in life. They not only consider where they are right now, but they also take into account where their path ends up. A path that is fun for today, but will end in misery tomorrow, is not a wise choice. We saw this in Proverbs 7:27 where the house of the adultery leads to death.

Some people are so self-deceived that they think they are right when, in reality, their path leads to death. The end of the road must be considered as it relates to God, when taking a job or even getting married. There must be a guide for us to make sure we do not get on a path that seems right but leads to death. And, of course, the Bible is the best guide.

Let the Bible lead you to the right way, the one that leads to life.

June 15 – Read Proverbs 15

v. 16 Better a little with the fear of the Lord than great wealth with turmoil.
v. 17 Better a meal of vegetables where there is love than a fattened calf with hatred.

This is a "this is better than that" scenario. The problem is that we often have "this" but wish we had "that." Or, we have "this" but think that it is not enough.

Yet here we are told that wealth is not always what it is made up to be. It is not always as good as it looks from afar. In fact, sometimes the closer you get to it, the more you see that it does not measure up to what you had thought it would be.

As we consider this, we find that having little financially with a right relationship with God (the fear of the Lord) and with love is an awfully big thing to have. It is also worthy of praise. I have often seen people who have this very thing and yet still wish they could have wealth. They often think that having more money would be better for their children. They often think that money somehow makes things better.

The fact is if you are rightly related to God and are surrounded by love, there really is not anything you need more in this life. I have seen both sides: the rich without God or love and the poor who have God and love. I would always choose the second every single time.

Realize the wealth of having God and love and look no further

June 16 – Read Proverbs 16

v. 4 The Lord works out everything for his own ends – even the wicked for a day of disaster.

Most people think that the world is man-centered. Maybe that is why so many people are me-centered. Even some theologians look at the Bible and theology from a man-centered perspective. Doing this makes them think that salvation is the central theme of the Bible instead of the Glory of God. But we must come to understand that the Bible, the world and the universe are God-centered. When we mix this up, we really get mixed up.

This world was not created for your happiness or mine. This world is not meant to make us happy and healthy. Who do we think we are, that everything in this world must work out for our happiness? Even more so, who do we think we are, that we can tell God to work out everything for our happiness?

God is the Creator, not man. God is the sovereign in the universe. He has every right to make things work for His glory and for His pleasure. One day we will stand in Heaven and say, "Worthy are you, our Lord and God, to receive glory and power, for you created all things, and by your will they existed and were created." (Revelation 4:11) As our Creator, He has every right to make the world work according to His vast wisdom in such a way as to bring Him glory. He has every right to do with us as He pleases – "Even the wicked for a day of disaster."

Keep in mind that you exist for Him -- not Him for you.

June 17 – Read Proverbs 17

v. 4 An evil doer listens to wicked lips, and a liar gives ear to a mischievous tongue.

What you listen to will tell a great deal about who you are. As stated in our verse for today, the heart of a person listens to conversation that is like his own heart. So we could say that the wicked listen to wickedness, but the righteous have no ear for it (1 Corinthians 13:6).

Those who do not live for God have an ear for those things that go against what God desires. What they listen to will give away their heart. So you can listen to a person's music or watch what he watches on TV or at the movies, and it will tell what is in his heart. Evil words will die without someone listening to them and the wicked love to listen to evil and by doing so give away their hearts. Not only does what one listens to show the wickedness of his heart but Jesus said what he says will do the same (Matthew 15:10-20). So what a person says and what he listens to gives away his heart. How do you learn what is going on in a person's heart? Watch what he says and fills his ears with. The wicked not only delight in doing wrong but they love to listen to the wrong others are doing.

You must turn away from all of this. You must choose from a heart that is right to listen only to that which is right. You must put no evil into your ears.

Keep wicked lips and a mischievous tongue far from your ears.

June 18 – Read Proverbs 18

v. 8 The words of a whisperer are like delicious morsels; they go down into the inner parts of the body.

It happens all too often. Someone starts talking about others for the purpose of putting them down or looking for sympathy. It happens in groups inside and outside of churches. The end result can be devastating to both the group and the people who make up the group.

Those who do this are sometimes people who feel someone has hurt them. It can be someone who has an axe to grind. It can also be someone who is looking to get people to follow him. And, it can be someone who just wants to hurt someone else. It many years of pastoring, I must say, it is most often women. Men have their issues, but this is usually not the one, though it can be.

A whisperer is a gossip. A gossip or whisperer is a person who picks up information here and there and builds it into stories. The gossips do this to hurt others, though they would never admit it. Their goal in "speaking in low tones" is to push their agenda, whatever it may be. They take their garbage about others and hope they can find a can (you or me) to fill up. To your face they talk about others and to your back they talk about you. They can only get away with this if you let them, if you allow yourself to become their garbage can, if you become the can where they can dump their stuff.

Stop gossip by not listening.

June 19 – Read Proverbs 19

v. 14 House and wealth are inherited from fathers, but a prudent wife is from the LORD.

People often joke about having a rich uncle who will leave them all kinds of riches. Yet, most people are not left very much as an inheritance. I once was left some money, along with other relatives, but ended up getting less than stated when a distant relative sued for the money when he was left nothing. Having said that, many who have wealth have gotten it by way of inheritance.

With all of the things that we can be given by way of inheritance, there is something our family cannot leave us. It is a prudent spouse, or as said here, a "prudent wife." This kind of wealth comes from God. The word prudent means "wise" and "understanding." So, a wise and understanding spouse comes from God.

This says a couple of things to us. First, if you are married and have this kind of spouse, it is God who blessed you in this way, and you should be thankful. Second, if you are not married, pray that God would give you this kind of spouse. Third, if you are looking for a spouse and wondering if you will ever get married, don't lose hope and just grab the first person who offers. If God's will for your life is to be married, trust Him to bring the right person for you to you in His timing.

The gift of a great spouse comes from God, ask Him.

June 20 – Read Proverbs 20

v. 1 Wine is a mocker, strong drink a brawler, and whoever is led astray by it is not wise.

Over the years I have seen lives destroyed by alcohol. I have seen families ruined and broken up. I have seen tragedy and unwise acts because of what people drink.

Within the Christian community there has always been debate over whether Christians should drink alcoholic drinks. I would say that there are many other options for us to drink, and since there is a chance that it will cause damage, why drink it?

Here we find one of the verses we must consider in this whole debate. Notice what God calls drinks such as wine and strong drink. Wine is called a "mocker" and strong drink is called a "brawler."

Wine was made from grapes and was sometimes fermented and sometimes not. Beer was made from various things and some people were not allowed to drink it. "It was intoxicating (Isaiah 28:7) and was forbidden for priests (Leviticus 10:9), Nazarites (Numbers 6:1-3), and others (Isaiah 5:11)."

What does all this mean? The word "mocker" means to talk big, making fun of the thing in question or ridiculing it. This indicates that wine can make a mockery of those who drink it. The word "brawler" means one who growls, roars, or makes a loud noise and indicates that it makes those who drink it aggressive or boisterous, resulting in them doing stupid things. And we have the further statement, "whoever is led astray by it is not wise."

With so many options available, don't let what you drink ruin your life.

June 21 – Read Proverbs 21

v. 17 Whoever loves pleasure will be a poor man; he who loves wine and oil will not be rich.

There is an old saying that speaks of people who try to stay even with their neighbors, "Keeping up with the Joneses." Some people look around at their neighbors and try to have all that their neighbors have even if they don't make the same amount of money.

I have seen people with money to spare who are very careful of how they spend. That being said, I have seen far more people who spend way more then they can afford, buying "only the best" of things. They seek the best of this and the best of that and are hardly ever willing to settle for anything less. It is often the poor who live this way, thinking that every person with some money does the same, but it is not true. "Pleasure, wine, oil" all speak of costly indulgences. They speak, in that culture, of living in luxury. What people, many people, do not realize is that living in luxury, generally speaking, will impoverish, not make you rich. It can be seen when people spend more than what they can afford on things they really do not need. Credit card bills keep going up and the stress of financial pressure keeps making people less happy, not more. The old phrase, "He who dies with the most toys wins" is not biblical and is not true. We need to remember the words of Jesus on this issue (Matthew 6:19-21).

Have the wisdom to control your spending.

June 22 – Read Proverbs 22

v. 3 The prudent sees danger and hides himself, but the simple go on and suffer for it.

There are people who love to live on the edge. I have seen some of what they do on TV and I sit back and think they are nuts. I have seen hang gliders fly down mountains at very high speeds flying dangerously close to mountain sides. I could never do what some of them do and maybe some of them could not do what I have done in my life.

In life, there are times when you have to go forward even when there may be danger ahead. As an example, during times of war this may be true. You go forward risking your own life to save others. Sometimes you have no other choice. You may have a business and have to take great risks because to do nothing would cause your business to fail. There are certainly other examples of this in life.

But what we find in this verse is a general truth about life and the simple. The wise and understanding among us see danger and get out of the way. So to say, they know when to come in out of the rain. The simple push forward, not being wise enough to know when it is time to avoid risk. Because of this, they "suffer for it." Wisdom tells us when to move forward and when it's time to take shelter.

Be wise. Know when to know when.

June 23 – Read Proverbs 23

v. 15 My son, if your heart is wise, my heart too will be glad.
v. 16 My inmost being will exult when your lips speak what is right.

We hear so much in our culture of people who blame their bad actions on their parents or their upbringing. They excuse what they have done because of what they feel were bad actions by their parents. And, it is certainly true that our upbringing has an impact on what we do when we grow up. The fact is that we hardly ever hear of the other side of this equation.

In past generations, young adults would say that they wanted to make something of themselves in honor of their parents. Or, they would say that they wanted to make their parents proud of them. People had a desire to honor their family name and to make sure they never did anything that would harm it.

With this in mind, Christians should think about the name they bear when they go out into this world! Christians bear God's name everywhere they go.

Having raised two children with my wife, I have had great moments of healthy pride when I have seen my children do things worthy of honor. This is what we see in these verses. It is a father, a parent, filling with joy because his son, his child, has been wise. This is what ought to make a parent rejoice.

There is great delight in a son or daughter who is wise. Be wise.

June 24 – Read Proverbs 24

v. 1 Be not envious of evil men, nor desire to be with them,
v. 2 for their hearts devise violence, and their lips talk of trouble.

Have you ever been there? The Bible tells us that many have. One good example of this is found in Psalm 73. We live in a world that has been impacted by sin and therefore evil is rampant. People sometimes wonder why bad things happen to good people. Maybe we should wonder why anything good ever happens to people when this world has been so affected by sin.

Since sin has permeated this world, it is no wonder that evil people who have no problem with sinning get ahead. Unfortunately, this world is ripe for that kind of thing to happen. When evil people get ahead and good people do not, they begin to get a "Jones complex" - I want what they have, so how can I get it? While they get it at times through violence and trouble, those who are not evil must reject these kinds of actions.

Those who are "good" must reject evil ways even if it means they will never get ahead in this world. They must do what is right every time and all the time. One step into evil actions can ruin all of the good you have ever done. This has been seen many times in history. Therefore we must "not be envious of evil men, nor desire to be with them." Or, we may choose to do what they did to get where they are. This would ruin everything you have ever done that was good.

Reject evil men and their presence.

June 25 – Read Proverbs 25

v. 2 It is the glory of God to conceal things, but the glory of kings is to search things out.

Do you have questions and no answers? Are there things about life that you do not understand? Do you wish the Bible was twenty times thicker so you could know more about life? Do you sometimes struggle with your lack of knowing which decision is right? Do you have many, many more questions? Welcome to the club! We all do. Life is full of questions.

Yet, this verse gives us some help with our questions. God's glory is seen in the fact that He has not told us everything. He has concealed most things, things we will spend eternity learning. God's glory is seen in His greatness and in His inexhaustible knowledge (Romans 11:33-36). We could never know everything God knows, and the little we do know is because God has chosen to reveal it to us. If we could know all that God knows, than He would not be very much of a God.

Because of this, some would sit back and quit and not seek knowledge. But we must understand that it is the glory of kings, or anyone's glory, to search things out. We must dig and dig to find the knowledge we need to make proper decisions and to do things the right way. It is not that God has left us with no knowledge. He has given us much (2 Timothy 3:16-17).

Seek to know what you must know to live correctly.

June 26 - Read Proverbs 26

v. 7 Like a lame man's legs, which hang useless, is a proverb in the mouth of a fool.

How sad it is when a body part does not work. It affects the entire body. Think of a leg that does not work. It hangs uselessly. It is there, unlike a leg that has been cut off, but it has no value. No matter how well you dress it up, it will never have value to the person whose body cannot make it work. One might say, "I'm glad I have it but it is of no value and never will have any value in helping me walk."

The same is true with a proverb that is found in the mouth of a fool (26:7). Since he is not wise and will not become wise, a proverb is of no value to him. So, this devotional will have no value to you if you have no desire to put into practice the truths which are contained in it. If, like a fool, you think you have learned all you ever need to learn, it will be of no value to you. If, like a fool, what you learn does not affect what you do, it will be of no value to you. If, like a fool, you do not seek wisdom, it will be of no value to you. It has no more value than casting pearls before pigs (Matthew 7:6)

Don't be a fool! Apply these truths, live what you learn, and become who God wants you to be.

June 27 - Read Proverbs 27

v. 17 Iron sharpens iron and one man sharpens another.

We are not meant for solitude, but for community. There is value in being with people. There may be times when you just want to be off by yourself for a while, but there is value in being with people. Being alone for long periods of time is not what God has intended for us. God created us to interact with each other, and through that interaction to make us into something better than we could become by ourselves.

This truth is explained in this verse. As iron is rubbed against iron, it sharpens it. As we interact with good people, we become better people. This interaction can be stimulating and encouraging. It can also be difficult at times. But God uses this interaction to sharpen us. If you constantly seek to avoid interaction with others, you will miss this vital instrument that God uses in our lives. It has been said, "Two things will have an impact on you more than anything else in the next five years: the books you read and the people you meet."

We often hear a lot about making sure that we do not hang around the bad crowd. Yet, there is something just as important that is hardly ever said to us. It is the great benefit we receive from hanging around the right kind of people.

Understand the value of being with the right kind of people.

June 28 – Read Proverbs 28

v. 4 Those who forsake the law praise the wicked, but those who keep the law strive against them.

There are many things in life that, if watched closely enough, will give away a person's heart. One of them is the way a person talks about those who don't follow God and those who do. Listen to what a person says about the wicked and you may learn what is really in their heart.

Those who do not obey God's Word, the Law, praise the wicked. Their disobedience of God may be hidden, but in the language of the wicked their disobedience comes to light. In Romans 1:32 it says, "Though they know God's righteous decree that those who practice such things deserve to die, they not only do them but give approval to those who practice them." In Acts 8:1, we find Saul giving approval to the stoning of Stephen. It revealed his heart.

On the other hand, those who obey God stand against the wicked. Those who obey God do not speak well of the wicked. Instead, they confront the wicked. This can be seen in John the Baptist (Matthew 3:7) or even Jesus (Matthew 23).

The truth is that one's attitude towards God's Word will determine one's attitude towards the wicked or the righteous. Thus, in hearing how a person speaks of the wicked or righteous it will tell us what is in his or her heart. Watch how a person talks about the pastor of her church and you will see into her heart (1 John 4:4-6).

Listen to what a person says about others and you will see into their heart.

June 29 - Read Proverbs 29

v. 1 He who is often reproved yet stiffens his neck, will suddenly be broken beyond healing.

How do you respond when you are rebuked for doing something wrong? There are basically two ways. One is to be grateful to the one who rebukes you and to repent of your sin. The second is to turn cold towards the one who rebuked you and even begin to attack him with gossip, criticism or worse. In this second way you also do not change your actions. Seeing yourself as a victim, you continue in your ways. The first is the right response. The second is the wrong response, according to a host of verses in Proverbs.

Now, here is the problem. The more you choose the second way, the more you become entrenched in your ways and the harder it becomes for you to turn from your sin (Jeremiah 13:23). You reach a point where you feel you will always be like you are. Now, here is where it gets really bad. If this continues, you may suddenly be "broken beyond healing." If you want to read about an example of this very thing, look at the example of Pharaoh (Exodus 5-14).

It may be that God has worked in the heart of the person who has rebuked you, so that he or she would come to you in love to help you. For most people, it is extremely hard to rebuke someone. Love must overcome fear. So beware of a hard, unrepentant heart.

Beware of a hard unrepentant heart (Hebrews 3:13).

June 30 – Read Proverbs 30

v. 4 Who has ascended to heaven and come down? Who has gathered the wind in his fists? Who has wrapped up the waters in a garment? Who has established all the ends of the earth? What is his name, and what is his son's name? Surely you know!

The answer to these questions is an easy one. It is God and His son's name is Jesus. We find the answer in the Word of God in Psalm 19; Job 42; Isaiah 40; John 1; Colossians 1; and Hebrews 1. God is the creator of the universe. The universe did not happen by chance as evolutionists would tell you. He put the work of creation into the hands of the second person of the Trinity, Jesus.

Since God is the creator, we must answer to God. I remember hearing a report that an evolutionist had said there are only two options: evolution or God. He chose evolution, not because of science, but because he did not want to live knowing he would have to answer to God for what he did in his life. What a poor choice! To deny the truth does not make the truth disappear.

You will have to answer to God. Keep in mind that He sent Jesus to the earth to die on the cross so that when you stand at the judgment, things may go well for you. You must repent of your sin and place your faith in the provision of God (the cross of Christ) to take away your sin. This is the only way.

Trust in Jesus to be your Savior and begin to live for Him.

July 1 – Read Proverbs 1

v. 19 Such are the ways of everyone who is greedy for unjust gain, it takes away the life of its possessors.

There are two ways to get ahead in life. One way is to do it the right way, the honest and just way. The other way is to do it the wrong way, the dishonest and unjust way.

We are living in a day when many people feel that anyone who has gotten ahead in this life must have done it the dishonest way. But this simply is not true. I know many people who have done well for themselves and have done it in a way that honors God. You can be honest and just and also rich. Robin Hood's way of robbing from the rich and giving it to the poor gives the impression that everyone who is rich deserves to lose what they have. Riches are not evil or unjust and neither is being poor. Proverbs clearly tells us that hard work and wisdom can get you ahead in life.

Yet, there is the other side of the coin. There are those who are "greedy" and search after "unjust" gain. They want to get ahead in life but for greedy and selfish reasons, and they are willing to do it in an unjust way. This is the characterization of the people in Proverbs chapter one who set an ambush for the innocent (v. 11). They are willing to break the rules of morality and hurt others to get ahead, but the last step of the road will be their own destruction.

Beware of greed and unjust gain. Have integrity at work.

July 2 – Read Proverbs 2

v. 11 discretion will watch over you, understanding will guard you,

How do you protect yourself from evil and those who would do evil? Some would hope that somehow they could just sit back and enjoy the ride of protection, thinking that God will do it all for them. Others look to people to watch over them, and certainly some have that responsibility, such as pastors, but not total responsibility. The reality is that we must make wise decisions.

The words "discretion" and "understanding" in context refer to wisdom. "Discretion" is "the ability to make proper decisions"[5] and "Understanding" is "the capacity for discerning a right course of action."[6] Life must be lived. As we go along in life, we must look at situations and circumstances and discern right from wrong. As we do this we will be protected, watched over and guarded, from those who seek evil.

We are not left on our own to do it all. God gives us His Word (Hebrews 5:11-14). We can go to God in prayer (James 1:5). We can also learn from having a multitude of counselors (Proverbs 24:6). God also brings us through faith testing events (James 1:1-3). With the help of all of these things, we then look at the places we find ourselves and make wise decisions. Decisions must be made and they must be wise or all protection is lost. No one can go through life without the benefit of wisdom and expect to do well.

Get wisdom, for it will watch over you and guard your life.

July 3 - Read Proverbs 3

v. 11 My son, do not despise the Lord's discipline or be weary of his reproof,
v. 12 for the Lord reproves him whom he loves, as a father the son in whom he delights.

These verses are referenced in Hebrews 12:5-11. There we find a commentary on these two verses. There we learn what these verses mean.

Here are its truths: God disciplines believers as a father does his children (Proverbs 3:11-12). You should not despise or be weary of this discipline (Proverbs 3:11-12). Lack of discipline by God demonstrates that you are not His child (Hebrews 12:7-8). Your respect for God must not weaken while being disciplined by Him (Hebrews 12:9). The purpose of God's discipline is that you might share in His holiness (Hebrews 12:10). When disciplined it seems painful, but it yields the fruit of righteousness in your life (Hebrews 12:11). All of these truths must be kept in mind when you are being disciplined by God.

What is the discipline of which these verses speak? It is the work of God that brings you back to Him. It is the punishment and correction that comes from God into your life that helps you toward maturity. It may be times of hardship and suffering (Psalm 119:67-71). It may be trials (James 1:3). The issue you must keep in mind is that God is working for your good out of love and therefore you must not despise His work in your life (Job 5:17).

When hurting, trust the hand of God.

July 4 - Read Proverbs 4

v. 24 Put away from you crooked speech, and put devious talk far from you.

When I was little I often heard people say to me and to others, "Watch what you say." Adults would tell young people this whenever they heard them say something they should not have said. Why? Because there is a right way to talk and a wrong way to talk. For example, God tells us to speak the truth in love (Ephesians 4:15) and that we should let our speech always be gracious, seasoned with salt (Colossians 4:6). This is the right way to talk.

There is also a wrong way to talk. For example, God says that we should not let sexual, immoral or impure speech be used, nor filthiness and crude joking. There is speech that is wrong. We may add two more categories of wrong speech to this list: "crooked" and "devious." "Crooked" means to twist, such as in a woman's braided hair, and in this case, refers to morally perverse speech. Much like the speech mentioned above, "devious" describes words that deviate from a moral standard.

Those who claim to be wise must not use words that are not wise. Ephesians 4:29 puts it this way, "Let no corrupting talk come out of your mouths, but only such as is good for building up, as fits the occasion, that it may give grace to those who hear." Our words ought to raise the moral standard, not lower it. Words that are immoral lower the standard and must not come from a believer.

Reject speech that is crooked and devious.

July 5 - Read Proverbs 5

v. 6 she does not ponder the path of life; her ways wander, and she know does not it.

The adulteress or prostitute does not think about the "path of life." She has not kept God's Word in her heart (4:20-21). She is living life without God's Word and the further she goes, the more she wanders from it. The sad thing is that she does not even know it. She got involved in adultery and did not even realize that her actions were not in line with the truth. Proverbs 9:13 says she "knows nothing." Proverbs 30:20 says that when she is finished, she says, 'I have done no wrong." One hundred fingers could be pointed at her face, and she would swear that her actions are not wrong.

You might wonder how this could be. But, if you do not consistently keep God's Word in front of you by being in church and by reading it, the same can happen to you. Can people do wrong and not know it? Sure, if they sear their conscience and if they do not have the Truth (God's Word) ever before them. People tend to forget and they forget God's Word rather quickly. That is why in 2 Peter 1:12-14, Peter said he would remind people of God's truth.

I have seen this very thing happen in people's lives. They get away from church, and they begin to think differently and live differently, but still believe that they are pleasing God and doing what is right. Don't be so fooled.

Unlike the adulteress, ponder the truth and your way for God does (Proverbs 5:21).

July 6 - Read Proverbs 6

v. 24 to preserve you from the evil woman, from the smooth tongue of the adulteress.

The context here speaks of parental instruction, which will help keep children from sexual sin as they grow. The lips of parents are used to keep their children from evil people who would invite them to sin sexually. This verse tells us that there is value in the wise words of parents warning their children away from sexual sin. Here, it is a case of a father warning his son against immoral women.

The warning is definitely needed for there are women who will use their words to lead men into sin and they are good at it. Such is the case of the "evil woman" and the "adulteress." The first woman here is probably single and the second is married, but both seek to lead the unsuspecting man into sexual sin. Notice that their words are smooth, which refers to speech which flatters or seduces. In others words, her speech is inviting and she uses words well.

This could also be said of men who would lead unsuspecting women into sexual sin. This could very easily be a mother talking to her daughter. There is danger as children grow into adulthood of being lured into sexual sin in a society that seems to think almost any kind of sex is not sin. Parents must talk to their children about this topic which is so difficult for parents to discuss. If they do not, there will be others who will be willing to do so, and not with their children's best interest in mind.

Parents talk with your children about God's moral standard.

July 7 - Read Proverbs 7

v. 14 "I had to offer sacrifices, and today I have paid my vows;

How sad it is when people claim religion and speak religiously, yet live as if they had no religion! Statistics often tell us that the religious are no different than the non-religious. The only real difference is that one claims religion and morality. The difference is that one is a hypocrite and the other is not.

This section of chapter seven is all about a young man who was foolish. He went where he should not have gone and met a woman who invited him into sexual sin. In this verse we read part of what she says to him to get him to go along with her. Here her invitation is that she has already made her offering to God. This offering was a peace offering where the meat had to be eaten by the end of the day. So in essence she is saying to him, "I have a lot of meat in my house for you to eat." She is trying to win him over through his belly. She states the invitation to sin in terms of religion.

This woman uses the pretext of religion to invite this man to sex. It is bad enough that she is rebelling against God, but she then uses religion as the context of inviting this man to sin. Maybe we can understand this in terms of those who would strap bombs to their bodies and kill innocent people in the name of God. Religion is used as an excuse making the sin justifiable.

Make sure your religion is real right down to your bones.

July 8 - Read Proverbs 8

v. 34 Blessed is the one who listens to me, watching daily at my gates, waiting beside my doors.

"Blessed" is a word that is with us throughout the Bible. It means happy or fortunate. Christians often talk about wanting to be a blessed person. They even often say things like, "I feel so blessed." In this verse it tells us one of the things that makes a person blessed.

The context here is that of wisdom. The thought is that the blessed person is the one who has his ears and eyes looking daily for wisdom. Wisdom, according to this chapter, is there for the gaining, but one must be receptive to it. Wisdom is not gained by accident, but by looking and searching for it. And, if one is willing to do this, it is there for the taking.

Now there are places for which we can gain wisdom, such as life experience, but the greatest place to wait, listen and watch is at the feet of God. This is done in two ways. The first is prayer. God said that if we will ask for wisdom, He will give it and give it in abundance (James 1:5). The second is His Word: the Bible. The Psalmist said that God's Word made him wiser than those around him (Psalm 119:97-100).

Most Christians, if not all, would admit that they need more wisdom. It seems that while admitting this, much fewer Christians are waiting, listening and watching daily in God's Word in order to gain it.

Don't be kept from God's wisdom today!

July 9 - Read Proverbs 9

v. 9 Give instruction to a wise man, and he will be still wiser; teach a righteous man, and he will increase in learning

There are many differences between a wise person and a foolish person, and one of those differences is given here. A wise person is always learning more. A wise person realizes that if he is not moving forward, he is moving backward. A wise person knows that he can always become wiser.

Not so the fool. The foolish person reaches a point where he thinks he knows it all. It is funny how so often those who are so young believe they have reached this point. Yet it is not just the young. It is any person who thinks that his learning in any area of life has come to a conclusion. Every so often I see this kind of person and I think of Proverbs 26:12 which says, "Do you see a man wise in his own eyes? There is more hope for a fool than for him."

This is a characteristic of the wise – they never stop learning. They always want to grow and understand more. They know that God and life itself are far beyond them and so there is always more to learn. They are always ready for more truth. They know that there is always more for them to learn. Yet in the midst of their growing and learning there is still a simple truth that will always stand out for them and it is found in Ecclesiastes 12:11-14.

Don't ever stop learning and growing.

July 10 - Read Proverbs 10

v. 27 The fear of the Lord prolongs life, but the years of the wicked will be short.

We often wonder why the wicked seem so blessed and the righteous seem to get so little of this world. But there is another side of this whole equation and it is found here. It is that righteousness prolongs life and wickedness cuts life short. This does not mean that the righteous live longer than the wicked. We know this is not the case. Yet, the truth is that when you live righteously your life will be longer than it might have been, and when you live wickedly your life will be shorter than it would have been.

Now, only God knows the facts of how long or short. There is no way you or I could know the details of this. Still we do know when you give your life to such things as drugs, alcohol, immorality (sexually transmitted diseases), or even a criminal life-style, your life tends to get cut short. When you live the way God intended, your life will be extended (3:2, 16; 4:10; 9:11; 19:23; 22:4). This is a general truth of life and can be seen played out in life.

The "fear of the Lord" is a life-style of righteousness. To fear the Lord basically means that you understand God's greatness and love Him dearly. Living in obedience to him and turning from wickedness is the result. Certainly the "fear of the Lord" and "wickedness" stand out as opposites and opposite ways of living (8:13; 16:6).

Walk today in the "fear of the Lord."

July 11 - Read Proverbs 11

v. 5 The righteousness of the blameless keeps his way straight, but the wicked falls by his own wickedness.

What is guiding your way? Is your path staying on the straight and narrow? Righteousness or wickedness leads people down their paths in life. A life-style of righteousness will keep your path straight (Proverbs 3:5-6). A life-style of wickedness will cause you to fall (v. 3). These two paths are found contrasted throughout the Bible.

When you are characterized by righteousness which comes from Christ, it will guide your decisions. When you do what is right, it directs you and keeps you on the straight path. This kind of person leads a life that begins with the heart and works itself through every part of his being. Then when issues in life confront him, he makes the right decisions which keep him on the right path (for example: Joseph in Genesis 39). Today you will be faced with various choices, and it is your character, your relationship with God, that will help you make the right choices.

Not so for the wicked! When a person is characterized by wickedness, that very wickedness will destroy them. We see this truth very clearly stated in Psalm 73. The wicked (unrighteous) are not to be envied. Their way is not better than the righteous. Wickedness will destroy all who choose that path (Proverbs 1:18-19). There is no gold at the end of the rainbow for those who would choose a path which rebels against a holy God only judgment (Romans 1).

Today let character guide your choices. May your character be righteous.

July 12 - Read Proverbs 12

v. 13 An evil man is ensnared by the transgression of his lips, but the righteous escapes trouble.

It is true that if you listen to someone long enough he will tell you what is in his heart. It is also true that an evil man will, sooner or later, get himself into trouble by what he says. He will get ensnared, that is, his lips will lead him to disaster or ruin. His words will get him into trouble. Notice that it is the wicked person himself that will cause his own trouble.

This is exactly what Jesus said, "I tell you, on the day of judgment people will give account for every careless word they speak, for by your words you will be justified, and by your words you will be condemned" (Matthew 12:36-37). Our words will either help us or hurt us, and for the evil person, his words will hurt him. His words only reveal what is in his heart and sooner or later the heart always comes out in one's words. The Bible is riddled with people who have destroyed themselves by their lips and history is also.

Now, for the righteous it is a different story. The righteous are not perfect in their words, but their words do not lead them into trouble. Rather, through their words they often escape trouble. Because their heart is right with God, their words reveal a pure heart.

Your words will either lead you toward trouble or keep you from it, so watch your words.

July 13 - Read Proverbs 13

v. 13 Whoever despises the word brings destruction on himself, but he who reveres the commandment will be rewarded.

Two opposite actions toward one thing bring two opposite results. That one thing is the Word. It is obvious that the term "word" in this verse means teachings, and in the context here it refers to the Word of God. The issue here is how a person views and responds to the Word of God. Many different words are used to refer to the Word of God in the Bible. Yet, they all have reference to the breathed out Word of God (2 Timothy 3:16-17). It is the Word of God given to the prophets and apostles, and it still stands today. It is the same Word with the same value and authority for us who are living years after it was originally given.

Let's look at the first one, which is the negative side. The person who despises the teachings of Proverbs or any portion of the Bible will bring destruction on himself. The word "despises" means to hold in contempt or to treat as insignificant. The idea being that a person would be careless with or, even worse, reject the teachings of Proverbs and/or the rest of the Bible. Such a person is in danger of destruction.

On the opposite side, the one who reveres the Bible will be rewarded. The term "revere" means to respect or to be in awe of. The one who reveres the Bible is the one who hears and obeys it. This is the person who will be rewarded for having done so. As I think all would agree, being rewarded is far better than being destroyed.

Revere the teachings of Proverbs and the rest of the Bible and don't despise them.

July 14 – Read Proverbs 14

v. 5 A faithful witness does not lie, but a false witness breathes out lies.
v. 25 A truthful witness saves lives, but one who breathes out lies is deceitful.

There is a contrast here, but there always is when it comes to integrity and deceitfulness. Truth and deceit are on the opposite sides of life and death. They neither go together nor are in the same arena.

Truth has no lies in it. Truth is always on the side of what is right. Truth always is the right way and not just the best way. Truth always produces justice. In the end, truth saves lives.

Lying, on the other hand, does not save lives. Lying only destroys lives. It makes me think of the days of Jeremiah. The people wanted Jeremiah to lie about the coming judgment. They wanted to hide from the truth. But no matter how much the prophets lied, the truth was that God's judgment was coming because of the sinfulness of the people. The only hope they had was to hear the truth so that they could recognize their sin and repent so that the judgment would not come. In spite of very difficult times, Jeremiah remained a faithful witness and told the people the truth.

The only hope for people is to hear the truth, whether in court or in life, in general. It is the truth which will always win over deceitfulness when it comes to saving lives.

Be committed to telling the truth, for in telling the truth, lives can be saved.

July15 – Read Proverbs 15

v. 31 The ear that listens to life-giving reproof will dwell among the wise.

[1]There is great power in being teachable. Once you reach a point in life where you are no longer teachable, you are in danger. Once your ears are shut to the help of others, even if it is a rebuke, you have reached a danger point.

There are all sorts of reasons why you may be unwilling to listen to a rebuke, such as pride. Yet, there is not one legitimate reason in the entire world. The rebuke mentioned here is "life-giving." Therefore this rebuke is one of great value, but the inference is that some are unwilling to listen. For whatever reason, they have reached a point where they are not teachable, to their own peril. They have missed out on what could be "life-giving." It is true that some people are unwilling to listen when someone must confront them for wrong in their lives. They have fooled themselves into thinking that nothing negative is ever good for them and they only want to hear pleasant thoughts.

Nonetheless, the truth is that a rebuke may hold "life-giving" thoughts for us that could get us off a dangerous road. A wise person understands that he sometimes needs confrontation to stay where he needs to be. A wise person knows that a "reproof", which means words that show disapproval or a rebuke, can have untold value. A wise person knows that when we put ourselves above being reproved or rebuked, we have raised ourselves too high.

Be teachable and open to being rebuked and you will be among the wise.

1

July 16 – Read Proverbs 16

v. 32 Whoever is slow to anger is better than the mighty, and he who rules his spirit than he who takes a city.

There are three ways we can respond with anger towards others. We can blow up (unleash wrath). We can clam up (hold it inside). We can hold on (hold on to our anger for weeks, months or years). Yet there is something that we need to know about anger. The one who can control his anger is "better than the mighty."

We need to be slow to anger. We need to be able to keep our emotions under control. This is not the same as not getting angry. Some people never get angry, and it makes me wonder if they have any passion about anything. God gave us the emotion of anger to accomplish tasks. Anger should cause us to accomplish things, but not hurt others. The energy it releases in us should be used for good.

The problem arises when we have no control over this emotion. A person who is "slow to anger" is slow to anger because he "rules his spirit." We must have control of every part of our being or we will get ourselves into trouble (Proverbs 5:23; 1 Corinthians 9:27). Our lives must be full of discipline. One can be mighty and have no self-control. An example of this would be Samson, who may have been the strongest man who ever lived, but who messed up his life because he could not control himself.

Have control of your spirit today and be slow to anger.

July 17 – Read Proverbs 17

v. 1 Better is a dry morsel with quiet than a house full of feasting with strife.

It is not that one is good and the other is bad, necessarily. It is a comparison showing that one is better than the other. The first is better than the second. You are better off having the first than having the second. Other examples of this can be found in Proverbs 12:9; 15:16-17; 16:19, 32. Having little food with peace is better than a house full of feasting (full of meat from sacrificed animals).

The first equates to having a home where there is little food (dry morsel refers to bread without butter), a poor home, but where there is harmony. People often complain about their poverty, wishing they had more money. They look over the fence at the "Joneses" and wish they had the stuff the Joneses have. What they don't realize is that the quiet (peace, quietness, ease) in their home is worth far more than all of the material wealth that others have.

On the other hand, the 2nd family here has money. They are wealthy (full of sacrifice) But, they also have strife (unrest). It has often been said by those who learned it too late, "All I ever wanted was riches, now all I want is my family." While it is not always true that the rich do not have a good family life, it is true that riches tend to mess things up.

Don't complain about your lack of money when you have a house full of peace.

July 18 – Read Proverbs 18

v. 14 A man's spirit will endure sickness, but a crushed spirit who can bear?

Sickness can be very difficult to endure. But the drive within you can keep you going. You have much to help you during these times. Friends are a great source of help. Certainly your relationship to God will help you. You also have the Word of God. There are many passages to help and give strength during times of sickness, such at these: Psalm 119:50; 71, 92; Romans 8:18-24; 2 Corinthians 1:3-11; 4:7-18; 12:7-11; Philippians 4:10-13.

Our body can be ripped out from under us by sickness and we can go on. But, how many can keep going after our heart has been ripped out? It is a question of great depth before us. The question is "a crushed spirit who can bear?" It lays stress on our spirit, that is, our inner self. When a man's spirit is broken it is hard to keep going. Look at people whose spirit has been crushed by the lost of a spouse or child or by some other traumatic event (Proverbs 15:13). Stress can also cause the spirit to be crushed (Proverbs 12:25). When a spirit has been crushed, people often lose the reason for living.

From this we learn several things. One, you must guard your spirit from that which might crush it (Philippians 4:6-7). Two, you must be careful not to crush another's spirit. Three, the spirit within you is far more important than your body.

Above all else, guard your heart, for everything you do flows from it. Proverbs 4:23

July 19 – Read Proverbs 19

v. 28 A false witness will not go unpunished, and he who pours out lies will be punished.

Last night there was a big bang on front door of my house. I went to check it out and found that someone had thrown something at it. There were four people who were standing just past my house. I asked them what was going on. One of them began to talk for the group, and it became clear that he was the one who did the throwing.

This kid blamed the act on others whom he said ran the opposite way, of course. I looked around the house and in the direction he said they went – nothing, of course. I then got into the car and went looking. The only people I came across that could possibly have done it were the original teens and particularly this one boy. I stopped and talked with them again. He lied some more. Even the kids with him walked away, knowing his story was a lie. I drove off having listened to the entire story, knowing he was lying.

I went, once again, in the direction he had said the offenders went, but found no one, of course. As I drove home, I knew I was lied to, but I was not angry. I remember saying to myself that God will punish those who lie and I would leave it in His hands.

Then I read this verse this morning and it reminded me of everything that happened last night. And I prayed for the young man, again, that he would be saved.

Don't lie or you will be punished.

July 20 – Read Proverbs 20

v. The sluggard does not plow in the autumn; he will seek at harvest and have nothing.

It is a sad state of affairs for the sluggard, the lazy person. He seeks his crop at harvest, but he finds nothing. There is nothing he can bring home. There is no bacon to put in the frying pan, so to speak. He has nothing to share with his family. All of the praying and weeping will do him no good at this point, for it is all too late.

What is the problem? The sluggard procrastinated. The sluggard may not have even worked at all. When he should have been out in the fields, which would have been during October or November in Israel, he was not there. The sluggard was unwilling to work at a time when he should have been working. This is his problem and this often is the same problem with so many today. It boils down to laziness. It is an unwillingness to be like the lowly ant (Proverbs 6:6-11).

God condemns laziness here and in many places in the book of Proverbs. This is not just an Old Testament issue either. God also condemns it in the New Testament in such places as 2 Thessalonians 3:6-12. When God created man, He gave him work to do. Man's job was to take care of the garden. Even in Heaven we are not going to sit around and do nothing for all eternity. We will be busy serving God and doing other things as well.

When it is time to work – work, so that when it is time to reap you will have something.

July 21 – Read Proverbs 21

v. 19 It is better to live in a desert land than with a quarrelsome and fretful woman.

Proverbs is very clear on telling men that finding a wife is a good thing. Proverbs 31 extols the value of an excellent wife. At the same time, there are also warnings in Proverbs about the kinds of women men ought to stay away from. This verse contains one of those warnings.

Can you imagine it being better to live in the dessert than anywhere else? It would seem that living in the dessert would be the last place most people would want to live. Yet, there is a worse place. It would be worse to live with a "quarrelsome and fretful" woman. Since this is true, we should determine what kind of woman this is.

"Quarrelsome" refers to a person, in this case a wife, who is argumentative or even possibly nagging. In v. 9 it says that it would be better to live on the corner of a roof than with this kind of woman (see also 19:13; 25:24; 27:15). The word "fretful" means to "stir up to anger" or "easily provoked." The thought is that living with a quarrelsome and angry wife is not something to be desired. A man should look at this and realize that he must go beyond what he sees in choosing a wife. A woman looking at this should make sure that she could not be categorized as being this kind of woman.

Stay far away from a woman who is quarrelsome and easily angered.

July 22 – Read Proverbs 22

v. 7 The rich rules over the poor, and the borrower is the slave of the lender.

v. 26 Be not one of those who give pledges, who put up security for debts.

v. 27 If you have nothing with which to pay, why should your bed be taken from under you?

What is borrowing? It is taking money from someone else to pay for something that you do not have the money to buy. People borrow for all sorts of reasons such as cars, homes and other such things. When you borrow money you agree to pay the lender more money back than what you have borrowed. On top of this, you agree to pay any fees which are incurred.

There are some dangers in doing so. The borrower becomes a slave to the lender. The lender determines how much interest you will pay, how much you will pay each month and how soon you must pay all of the money back. The lender could come and take all you have if you can't pay the debt. If you have borrowed for your home and can't pay the debt, you could be out in the streets. So, depending on the loan, the lender has a great deal of control over the borrower. In those days, the lender could also send you and your family into slavery to pay the debt.

Depending on the borrowing, the risks can be great. So one may ask these questions before getting into such an arrangement: Do I really need this? Can I afford it plus interest?

Before you borrow, give great thought and prayer to your actions.

July 23 – Read Proverbs 23

v. 12 Apply your heart to instruction and your ear to words of knowledge.

It amazes me how many people do not mind living in ignorance. That is, they live without the knowledge they need on so many issues. I just watched a video of people who voted for the president of the United States. Three people were surveyed, and they could not answer basic questions about people in government. Remember, their vote affected who would be president of the United States.

As bad as that is, it is even worse when it comes to knowing the Word of God. Many, many believers are ignorant of God's Word. In Hosea 4:6 God said of the Israelites, "My people are destroyed for lack of knowledge; ..." and so they did not live according to God's will. This is also true of believers today. It is sad that believers today are afraid to talk to people in cults because they know the Bible better than believers. In fact, many believers cannot even find their way around the books of the Bible.

As believers, Christ-followers, we need to apply our hearts to instruction and we need to listen to knowledge. We need to be busy gaining the knowledge we need to live according to God's Word. Second Timothy 2:15 tells us, "Do your best to present yourself to God as one approved, a worker who has no need to be ashamed, rightly handling the word of truth.

Seek and listen to truth.

July 24 – Read Proverbs 24

v. 11 Rescue those who are being taken away to death; hold back those who are stumbling to the slaughter.

v. 12 If you say, "Behold, we did not know this," does not he who weighs the heart perceive it? Does not he who keeps watch over your soul know it, and will he not repay man according to his work?

There are those who would want to define all sin as "selfishness" but I do not think that it describes all types of sin or all sin. They want to do so because so much of sin can be tied to selfishness. We tend to be selfish. We tend to do that which is in our own best interest. There is a saying, "Look out for yourself for no one else will." There is a lot of selfishness in that statement.

Selfishness often causes us to not reach out to others. We often see our own pain and not the pain of others. We often see our own needs and not the needs of others. We need to do so much better. We need to look beyond ourselves and reach out and take time for other people, even if no one would do so for us. That is Christianity! This is especially true for those who are headed towards disaster like death and slaughter (v. 11).

Some will try to plead ignorance, but God does not allow this plea (v. 12). Christians need to be outward focused and not self-focused. We need to think about others and sometimes, if not often, even before ourselves (See Philippians 2:5-11).

Get busy helping others.

July 25 - Read Proverbs 25

v. 8 What your eyes have seen do not hastily bring into court, for what will you do in the end, when your neighbor puts you to shame?

Benjamin Franklin once said, "Believe none of what you hear and half of what you see." This may not be totally true, but it does have merit and is a warning against running with what you have heard or seen. We must be careful not to rush to judgment. Someone may say, "But I saw it with my own eyes." This does not necessarily make it true.

We can get things wrong. I know... most people believe that only the other person can get things wrong. We all can get things wrong even things we see with our own eyes. We can be mistaken about what we have seen or the context of what we have seen. One time I watched an illusionist do amazing stuff, but before he began his tricks he said that everything he did was just that, a trick. When he was finished performing, he gave one of the best presentations of the gospel I have ever witnessed.

The call here is for carefulness. We need to be careful when we accuse another of anything. This verse describes a court case. Yet it does not matter the situation, whether it is in court or life in general. Accusations against another person can destroy a life, so we must be correct. We must be careful when lives are involved. This is why courts would like more than one eyewitness.

Don't rush to accuse others with what your eyes have seen.

July 26 – Read Proverbs 26

v. 12 Do you see a man who is wise in his own eyes? There is more hope for a fool than for him.

There can be great danger in how you view yourself. There is danger in what you think about yourself, even in the things you never tell anyone else about how you feel about yourself. The statement here is clear that a person who is "wise in their own eyes" is in the place of great danger. The reason is stated quite loudly in what follows, "there is more hope for a fool than for him." But, it gets even louder when you read what precedes this statement.

In the verses that precede this statement, it tells us how little hope the fool has. In verse 7, we are told that a proverb in the mouth of a fool is like a lame man's legs. In verse 8, it is stated that giving honor to a fool is basically a senseless act. In verse 9, a proverb in the mouth of a fool is like a thorn in a drunk's hand. In verse 10, we are told that hiring a fool is like going out and killing everyone in sight. In verse 11, it states that a fool continually repeats being a fool. All of these statement point to the fact that a fool has little hope, very little. This now shows how grave it is to be "wise in your own sight." Pride is a killer!

Don't be wise in your own sight, have enough wisdom to know how foolish that is.

July 27 – Read Proverbs 27

v. 15 A continual dripping on a rainy day and a quarrelsome wife are alike;
v. 16 to restrain her is to restrain the wind or to grasp oil in one's right hand.

I am reminded of a torture that has been used in China. They would take a person, restrain his head so he could not move it, and put a constant drip of water right on his forehead. I have heard that this simple little thing could drive a person insane at its worst. I have seen it tested on a TV show, and it does work.

Have you ever tried to grab the wind in your hand and hold it? Probably not because you know it is impossible. Or, have you ever gotten oil in your hand and tried to stop it from running down your arm. It can be very difficult.

I know numerous women who have a real desire to be godly women and wives. They search books and read the Bible seeking great truths that will get them there. The desire is real and sincere.

I would like to point out one very simple and easy to understand truth that will help a wife to be on her way toward being a great one. It is that she must avoid being quarrelsome. A woman who is constantly arguing or being contentious is like torture to her husband.

It is no little issue in many homes. In fact, this issue is mentioned several times in Proverbs. I have even had ladies quarrel with me about this verse when I have taught on it.

Ladies, do not be quarrelsome.

July 28 – Read Proverbs 28

v. 25 A greedy man stirs up strife, but the one who trusts in the LORD will be enriched.
v. 26 Whoever trusts in his own mind is a fool, but he who walks in wisdom will be delivered.

Trust! It is a great issue of our time and of every time. Who do you trust? What do you trust? There are many things in our world vying for our trust. But it often comes down to two: the Lord or ourselves.

A number of years ago I heard a man who ran for political office telling why he was not a Christian. He basically said he did not need to trust in anything outside of himself. He said that he didn't need to lean on anything as a crutch because he could deal with life on his own. For him, he trusted in himself. The Bible says the one who does this is a fool.

The Christian places his trust in God. He knows that there is One greater than himself for whom all things bow. He knows that the Creator of the universe is in charge and not him. The Christian knows that there are greater things in this world, far mightier than himself, for which he needs help. He knows that the Creator of the universe is greater than all and worthy of our trust.

Sometimes God reminds us of this truth. Paul said that God brought him through difficult circumstances, so great, that he was taught to rely on God and not himself (2 Corinthians 1:8-9). Everyone will learn this truth someday. The wise ones learn it before it is too late.

Be wise, trust in the one who is worthy of your trust – The Lord God Almighty.

July 29 – Read Proverbs 29

v. 10 Bloodthirsty men hate one who is blameless and seek the life of the upright.

People often wonder why "good" people are attacked and hurt by "bad" people. They wonder why people would want to hurt those who are only seeking to do good. For example, recently the American Ambassador to Libya was killed. By all accounts, he was a good man who loved the people of Libya. Why would anyone want to kill such a good man?

Here is where reality must set in for those who seek righteousness. They think the rest of the world is just like them. They think that everyone wants to do what is right and seeks the same things they seek. They think that man is basically good. But, they are wrong!

Let's look at this issue in the life of Jesus. He loved everyone equally. He had no hidden motives of selfishness. He healed everyone he came into contact with. He never, not once, did anything to hurt anyone. Yet, the people of His day hated Him and killed Him. Even more, the ones who led the charge to kill him were the most religious people of the day. Those who do evil hate those who seek to do right. Jesus warned of this in John 15:1. Just look at the apostles: Every one was killed but one. Look down through the ages at righteous people who only sought the welfare of others and see what has happened to them.

Beware. Righteousness does not make people love you. Some will hate you for it.

July 30 – Read Proverbs 30

v. 32 If you have been foolish, exalting yourself, or if you have been devising evil, put your hand on your mouth.

"If you have been foolish…" If we stopped right there we would all be laughing knowing that we all have been foolish. There are things I have done that I still cringe about for having been so foolish. We all have been foolish in many ways. Whether we are willing to admit it or not is a different issue.

Here Proverbs speaks about two specific ways that people can be foolish. The second one is being foolish in devising evil." I am not going to talk about that one today for I want to zero in on the first one. The first one is being foolish in "exalting yourself."

We must begin by understanding the word "foolish," which means to lack understanding, or to be senseless, or we can even use the stronger word, "stupid." So the first thing we understand here is that exalting yourself is not wise. To exalt means to lift up. If someone is exalted it means that they have been lifted up in front of others. There is nothing wrong with that, if God or others praise you and lift you up. The foolishness comes in when you lift yourself up. God's Word has examples of men who did this very thing such as Adonijah (1 Kings 1) and it never worked out well. Proverbs 25:6-7 and 27:22 also warn against doing this.

Don't be so foolish as to exalt yourself in front of others.

July 31 – Read Proverbs 31

v. 4 It is not for kings, O Lemuel, it is not for kings to drink wine, or for rulers to take strong drink,

v. 5 lest they drink and forget what has been decreed and pervert the rights of all the afflicted.

v. 6 Give strong drink to the one who is perishing, and wine to those in bitter distress;

v. 7 let them drink and forget their poverty and remember their misery no more.

There is much debate in America about the use of alcohol amongst Christians. As stated earlier in this devotional, I fall on the side of those who believe that Christians should avoid it. There is not enough room to go into the reasons here, but these four verses do help us with this whole issue.

Notice that his mother warns this king to avoid drinking alcohol. The reason given here, which is one of many that could be given, is that alcohol causes people to forget things and the use of it may pervert justice. This being true, certainly anyone in a position of authority, such as a king, should avoid it. Those in positions of authority must always, like a parent, at all times, maintain their ability to think and reason. It is hard enough to lead people with a clear mind, why make it worse with a drunken mind?

That being said, there may be times when alcohol may have some benefit. Notice when someone is near death and in great distress, alcohol can help medicate him or her and make his or her death peaceful. Yes, notice that alcohol was used for medicinal purposes, but today we have medicine to do the same thing and it is much more effective.

Wisely consider whether drinking alcohol is proper for you.

August 1 – Read Proverbs 1

v. 22 "How long, O simple ones, will you love being simple? How long will scoffers delight in their scoffing and fools hate knowledge?

What great questions! What great frustration! What great sadness! Great question: How long will you remain where you are, which is so far from where God would like you? Great frustration: For those who care about you enough to sacrifice for you and still see you unwilling to move from your position. Great sadness: For those who so badly want to see you become wise and live the right way and for those whose hearts break because you are unwilling.

I see all of these things in this verse. I have felt all of these as a pastor, so much wanting people to be what God desires for them. Jeremiah preached God's Word to Israel for 40 years and still the people remained unwilling to listen. They even beat him, threw him in jail and forced him to leave his homeland. What will it take for those who are not where they should be to get right with God? If you are not right with God, what will it take for you to get where you should be? I think of Jesus' words over Jerusalem in Matthew 23:37, "…How often would I have gathered your children together as a hen gathers her brood under her wings, and you would not!" It is God's desire to have a right relationship with you. That is why he sent His Son.

"Seek the Lord while He may be found; call upon Him while he is near." Isaiah 55:6

August 2 – Read Proverbs 2

v. 11 discretion will watch over you, understanding will guard you,

People, generally speaking, want to know they are safe. They feel better when there are police around. They feel better when someone is watching over them or at least when they know they are safe. It is good when you are being watched over and are being guarded.

Here we find that this is a reality when we have two things in our life, "discretion" and "understanding." When we have these two things they will watch over us and guard us. Discretion and understanding refer to understanding righteousness and justice (v. 9). They do this by delivering us from the way of evil and from evil men (v. 12).

All of this speaks of the result of gaining wisdom. It speaks of the hard work (v. 4) of seeking to become wise and doing what is wise, which seems like something that everyone would be willing to do. Yet, so often this is not the case. People often give themselves over to sleep or some other thing rather than digging into God's Word to find the wisdom that gives the benefit spoken of here. The TV, or book, or activity, or hobby, or whatever takes up your time so that you find no time for the work of seeking silver and hidden treasure. Your Bible may collect dust while you busy yourself with so much other stuff as mentioned above.

Don't be found among those who gave up the important for that which has so little value.

August 3 - Read Proverbs 3

v. 13 Blessed is the one who finds wisdom, and the one who gets understanding,
v. 14 for the gain from her is better than gain from silver and her profit better than gold.
v. 15 She is more precious than jewels, and nothing you desire can compare with her.

Consider the value of wisdom. First, the one who finds it is blessed. Second, it is worth more than silver or gold. Third, it is worth more than precious jewels. The truth is that it is worth more than anything you can think of in this world.

As you think about this, realize that the wisdom spoken of here is not the wisdom the world offers (See 1 Corinthians 1:18-31.). Keep in mind that the wisdom spoken of here begins with having a right relationship with God (Proverbs 1:7; Romans 1:21-23). It is wisdom that God gives (James 1). This truth is summarized in Ecclesiastes 12:13-14, which was written by the same author as Proverbs, Solomon.

There is a certain amount of wisdom you can gain by living life. Having said that, understand that God's wisdom goes well beyond that kind of wisdom.

So many people live their lives almost immune to gaining wisdom. They do not seek it, and some even do not desire it. That is why God chose to tell us repeatedly in Proverbs of the value of gaining wisdom. If you would go to God's Word and just find one pearl of wisdom this week, you would be much further ahead than the average person.

Seek to be wise for there is great value in doing so.

August 4 - Read Proverbs 4

v. 27 Do not swerve to the right or to the left; turn your foot away from evil.

When I was younger, I remember riding down the hill on sleds next to my house with a friend. I don't know why, but that night neither he nor I could keep our sleds straight. No matter how hard we tried, we would swerve left or right. It happened so much that we finally decided to go home for the night.

When it comes to living life, some people feel that this describes their life. They are always falling off the right path and heading for trouble. This verse tells us that we have control over whether we stay on the right path or fall off it. It is not out of our control; doing right is within our control. We need to listen to this command and stay on the right path and keep our feet from evil.

Where we will be and how we will get there is determined by the choices we make. Sure, some things can happen to us in life and things can get out of control. But, for the most part, our life is a result of the choices we make. We can choose to stay on the right path or we can chose to head towards evil.

I know a person who does not want that ability. He just wants to be hit over the head and wake up in the right place on the right path. Life just does not work that way.

Choose not to swerve but to stay on the right path.

August 5 - Read Proverbs 5

v. 18 Let your fountain be blessed, and rejoice in the wife of your youth,

Our world is full of evil, and one of those evils in sexual immorality. Adultery is one of the great causes of divorce. I have heard many men say, "I am married, but not dead." I have also heard men say, "It is OK to look as long as I don't touch." But I have never heard men say these things to their wives. They know better.

Yet, it is this kind of thinking that gets people into trouble. They live so close to the edge that it is just one short step into adultery. This verse gives us one of the hedges that can keep a man or woman far from sexual immorality. It may be said this way, "Love your spouse and find satisfaction in your spouse." Here it speaks of a man towards his wife, but the same may be said of a wife towards her husband. TV shows, movies, magazines, books and society in general all push the thought that our spouse will not complete us. They tell us in many different ways that we must seek pleasure in other people to truly be happy. It is a lie!!!

God created marriage (Genesis 2). God created it to be the place where we can find true fullness and pleasure. If your marriage is not up to that, the institution of marriage is not what has failed. Don't look for fulfillment outside of your marriage. Put forth the effort to make your marriage everything that God created it to be.

Find fulfillment in your spouse and let everyone know that is the only place you will seek it.

August 6 - Read Proverbs 6

v. 25 Do not desire her beauty in your heart, and do not let her capture you with her eyelashes;

As we saw yesterday, too many look outside of the marriage union for fulfillment. We see it all around us. Yet for the believer, he must find it in his spouse and nowhere else.

Wandering eyes can be a very real danger, especially when they come across the adulterous. They may land on the person who is every bit willing to return the favor. You must keep a tight control on your eyes. They must never be allowed to tug at your heart. The old story is that you may see things that you should not, but you don't have to stare. Your eyes may take your heart places where it should not go. The end result may be that your heart begins to desire not your spouse, but someone else.

Such is the story of King David. He saw Bathsheba bathing, and she was very beautiful (2 Samuel 11:2). From there he felt the tug of his heart pushing him in the wrong direction. Instead of stopping it, he followed it. He allowed it to come to full bloom and he sinned. Your eyes should only be found desiring your spouse. Besides, outward beauty only has some value. Proverbs 11:22 and 31:30 warn us of the limited value of outward beauty. We need to keep a tight reign on our hearts and make sure they do not desire what they should not have.

Guard where your eyes go and guard what you heart desires.

August 7 - Read Proverbs 7

v. 5 to keep you from the forbidden woman, from the adulteress with her smooth words.

When I was in my mid to late 40s I heard of several big-name pastors committing adultery in their 50s. A pastor friend and I discussed this issue. It was cause for concern since we were both around the same age. We were both heading into our 50s. We wondered what might cause these pastors to do such a thing after years of faithful marriage. Were they phonies? I did not think so. Did they just give into temptation? If so, why several in their 50s?

This was a cause of concern for me and for him. We did not want to become disqualified for serving God (1 Corinthians 9:24-27). The very last thing I would ever want to happen in my life is that I would do something that would dishonor my Savior and cause me to never again be able to preach the gospel.

I am now in my early 50s and have been faithful to my Lord and my wife. I do not know the answer to the above questions. I do know I would do anything to avoid the "forbidden woman." I have put hedges in my life since I was first married to protect my marriage and myself. I want to be careful that I'm not fooled by the "smooth words" of the forbidden woman. This I know, that no believer, no matter how mature, is above giving into sin, even sexual sin. Its victims are "mighty" and 'many" (Proverbs 7:26).

Do whatever it takes to keep from sin.

August 8 - Read Proverbs 8

v. 35 For whoever finds me finds life and obtains favor from the LORD,
v. 36 but he who fails to find me injures himself; all who hate me love death."

Again we see the value of wisdom in the book of Proverbs, in the writing of Solomon, the writing of the wisest man who ever lived besides Jesus. He was the one who was told by God that he could have whatever he wanted. His choice was to ask for wisdom (1 Kings 3). Most people probably would not have asked for that given all of the possibilities, but he did. Most would have asked for money, or power, or fame. Yet, because he asked for wisdom, God gave him all of the other things. If the story ended there it would be a great story, but it did not. To be sure, it was not just a "story", but real life.

Solomon tells us in the Book of Ecclesiastes that wisdom by itself without a right relationship with God falls short (Ecclesiastes 12:13-14). We also find in Proverbs, Solomon telling his son to make sure he did not forget the words of his (Solomon's) mouth.

Not only must we attain wisdom, but also we must maintain wisdom. Life is lived one day at a time. If we do not continue in a life lived wisely, we will swerve off the right path. We must choose to be right and stay right every day, all of the way. This reminds us of the apostle Paul who did that very thing once he came to Christ (2 Timothy 4:6-8). Solomon, sadly, did not (1 Kings 11)!

Do what is right one day at a time all the way to your last day.

August 9 - Read Proverbs 9

v. 11 For by me your days will be multiplied, and years will be added to your life.

Here we also see the value of wisdom. Having wisdom has value compared to being foolish. Here we are told that it is the fountain of youth. By it, we will live longer. Certainly, wisdom will help make wise choices and by those choices days, and maybe years, will be added to our lives. Why would anyone reject wisdom?

All throughout Proverbs, we see Solomon teaching his son. He encourages him to get wisdom and to do what God would have him do. We see it in the first verse of chapter two through chapter six and it is in the eighth verse of chapter one. The son being taught is Rehoboam (1 Kings 11). Sadly, Rehoboam rejected his father's teachings (1 Kings 12:6-11). So if we look at this situation from a distance, we see the wisest man and his son both ultimately turn away from wisdom and all that it offers. What happened? Did wisdom fail? Should we look at these teachings and turn from them because these men did not live up to them?

God's Word never ever fails. With all of its benefits and all of its wealth, why would anyone not do all that it tells us to do? What is wrong with people? The answer is that it shows how unwise we really are and how much we really do need these teachings.

Let God's Word dwell in you richly and do not turn from it all the days of your life.

August 10 - Read Proverbs 10

v. 9 Whoever walks in integrity walks securely, but he who makes his ways crooked will be found out.

To walk securely means to walk in safety and free of danger. This is something that most people would want for their lives. This is something that people can have in their lives. Notice the word "Whoever", which tells us that all or anyone can have what follows. So what is needed to get it?

This verse tells us that we can have it if we are willing to "walk in integrity" which speaks of moral goodness. We used to be able to speak of men and women who had great integrity, but those days seem to be passing. I hope they do not pass. I hope you and others will choose to have integrity.

As we look around us all we see is corruption. It rises from within families and goes all the way to the government. People today often do not trust the court system or people in places of high authority in the government because integrity has been left behind by many, many people. The Bible tells us that moral goodness will be left behind as we get closer to the Lord's return (2 Timothy 3:1-9).

But – this does not have to be true of you! You can choose to have integrity. You can choose to be honest and moral. You can choose to be and do all that is in line with integrity.

Choose to walk with integrity and be secure!

August 11 - Read Proverbs 11

v. 12 Whoever belittles his neighbor lacks sense, but a man of understanding remains silent.

Proverbs and the rest of the Bible are full of comparisons between the righteous and the wicked. They also, often in the same vein as Proverbs, compare the wise and the foolish. This is what we see here. In seeing this, we should ask ourselves which category fits us. Which of the two activities mentioned above describes your lifestyle?

Let's begin with the one who lacks sense. Notice that his lifestyle is one of belittling his neighbor. You can find him slandering, gossiping and beating up his neighbor with his mouth. This is the one who often fills his conversation with how bad other people are or have been to him. And, when you are not in his presence, he is doing the same to you. This is the one who if he did not say at least one bad thing about someone he would not have much to say. He is the one who accuses everyone else of doing this when in fact he is the perpetrator. His actions show that he is not wise, for God continually condemns this action in His Word (See Proverbs 14:21).

I find it interesting that the wise are often seen as not talking. They are often spoken of as being silent. Proverbs tells us that even a fool can be thought wise if he is silent. A person often shows who he is when he opens his mouth. As has been said, "If you have nothing good to say don't say anything."

Don't sin by belittling people. It is better to be silent.

August 12 - Read Proverbs 12

v. 26 One who is righteous is a guide to his neighbor, but the way of the wicked leads them astray.

The Hebrew behind this verse can be translated two different ways. In this case I believe the alternative, as seen in the ESV footnote, is the better way to translate it. The alternative says, "The righteous chooses his friends carefully." It literally says, "The righteous investigates his neighbor."

So the issue is: does the righteous person investigate for his neighbor so that he becomes a good guide for his neighbor? Or, does he investigate his neighbor making sure that he is the kind of person that should be chosen as a friend? The second option, I believe, is the better choice and is chosen by other reputable translations.

With this in mind, Proverbs is full of truth concerning the choices we make in choosing friends. Here is a list from Proverbs of the people you should not consider as close friends: People who entice you to sin – 1:10-19; 24:1-2, Fools – 13:20, Gossips – 20:19, Adulteresses – 5:1-14, Those Easily Angered – 22:24-25, Drunks and Gluttons – 23:19-21. From the New Testament we can also add these to the list: False Teachers – 2 John 7-11, Idle/Busybodies – 2 Thessalonians 3:6-15, Divisive People – Titus 3:10-11; Romans 16:17-18, and Professed Believers who persist in sin – 1 Corinthians 5:11-13.

In 1 Corinthians 15:33, we learn that the wrong choice of friends can have a detrimental effect on our morals. So, choosing with whom we would make friends is no small matter. In fact, it is vitally important.

Be careful and prayerful in your choice of friends.

August 13 - Read Proverbs 13

v. 14 The teaching of the wise is a fountain of life, that one may turn away from the snares of death.

The "fountain of life" is the source of spiritual vitality. It reminds me of a show I saw on the history channel where they showed the search throughout history for the "Fountain of Youth" which involved many different people. The fountain of life was thought to be found in several different places all over the earth. Of course, no one ever found it.

The fountain of life has only once source, God, as seen in Psalm 36:9 and John 4:10; 7:38-39. He is the vine, we are the branches, and the branches get all of their nourishment from the vine (John 15). Without the vine, the branches die. So we do not have to waste our whole lives looking for the fountain of life as so many did looking for the Fountain of Youth. Life, true life, vitality of life, can be found in no other source (John 10:10) for God is the one and only source.

We tap into the "fountain of life" as we listen to righteous and wise people (Proverbs 10:11; 13:14) as they teach us from the Word of God and tell us about life. We also drink from it as we learn to fear God as we see in Proverbs 14:27. As we learn from these, we gain wisdom, which becomes a "fountain of life" for us (Proverbs 16:22). Therefore, we should not turn away from the teaching of the righteous and wise for that path leads to death.

How you respond to the righteous and wise will either lead you toward life or death.

August 14 - Read Proverbs 14

v. 32 The wicked is overthrown through his evildoing, but the righteous finds refuge in his death.

The wicked person gets himself in trouble. He is overthrown by his own choice to be and do evil. It is sad that there are wicked people in this world. As Proverbs 1:18 states, these people "lie in wait for their own blood." They set an ambush for their own lives." On the one hand, the righteous rejoice when the wicked are brought down. Yet, on the other hand, the righteous are full of sadness when the wicked are brought down. The feelings of the righteous are mixed for they are glad that evil has been stopped, but they also are saddened that another life has been destroyed.

The wicked often consider that the worst thing that could ever happen is death. But not so the righteous; they have refuge even in death. Even if the worst thing happens, death, the righteous know that everything will only get better. They know that after death they will meet their Lord. They look forward to seeing loved ones who died in Christ. They can't wait to walk on the streets of gold and drink from the water of life (Revelation 22:1-4). What the wicked fear is no fear at all for the righteous.

When you think about it, as is stated in Psalm 73 and other places, the wicked who seemed to have so much in this world really do have so little. All they will ever have is what they have now in this sin-stained world.

Even in death, believers have a refuge so don't be discouraged with what life offers you.

August 15 - Read Proverbs 15

v. 29 The LORD is far from the wicked, but he hears the prayer of the righteous.

The righteous have what the wicked could never have, and it is worth far more than anything the wicked could ever own. The righteous have the ear of God. Think about it! Everyone, or at least most, talk about praying to God, but it is only the righteous who have God's ear (Psalm 34:17; 1 Peter 3:12).

As verse 29 states, "The Lord is far from the wicked." God detests the wicked. Their sin has caused God to not listen to them (Isaiah 59:2). The wicked have no time for God. They want to use God like a spare tire and only pull Him out in times of need. But often God's response is to not listen, so that they call out, but He does not answer them as seen in Psalm 18:41. The prayer of the wicked is an abomination to God (Proverbs 28:9). The wicked throw away their opportunity to commune with the Almighty Creator of the universe.

Not so for the Righteous! The righteous have a privilege that is worth all of the gold the world has to offer. The privilege they have is to lay their burdens before the throne of God and commune with their Savior. They have the honor of talking to God.

The righteous are those who have put their trust in what Jesus did for them on the cross. They have been given His righteousness and have been forgiven of their sin. They can talk to God, and even more, God wants to listen (John 9:31; Matthew 7:7-11).

Follower of Christ, talk to God today because He wants to hear from you.

August 16 – Read Proverbs 16

v. 8 Better a little with righteousness than great revenues with injustice.

Oh how this world has rejected God's ways in so many ways! One of these ways is a willingness to do just about anything to get rich. The willingness is there because of the belief that life will be better with more money. In some ways this may be true, but it is also true that money can't, and never will, buy happiness.

God's view is that we are better off having little and living God's way than gaining much by means of injustice. Living life God's way is the right way for one simple truth; in the end we will answer to Him and be judged by Him. This truth can be seen in Ecclesiastes 12:13-14. Since God is the one we must answer to, we must live in a way that pleases Him so that all will go well for us at the Judgment. Furthermore, how could we do anything else since He has loved us so much?

Injustice can include lying, cheating, stealing, trickery and so much more. These are the things one might do at work, not church. These are the things one might do from Monday through Friday. So we are told that our relationship to God is not just for Sunday morning but ought to impact what we do when we go to work. Having learned God's truth on Sunday, we should be taking it with us to work on Monday.

Righteous living is not just for the worship hour; take it to work with you.

August 17 - Read Proverbs 17

v. 7 Fine speech is not becoming to a fool; still less is false speech to a prince.

In this verse we find statements concerning speech that are not fitting to two different kinds of people. The first is the fool for whom "fine speech" is not fitting. The second is a prince for whom "false speech" is not fitting.

Let's begin with the fool. Much has been said about him in the book of Proverbs. Here we learn that "fine speech" does not fit him. What is "fine speech?" It is speech that is in excess or left over which could mean either to talk too much or to use words which are above the level of a fool. A fool should not talk too much for he has nothing good, nothing of value, to say. Or, a fool should not use words beyond his ability (for example arrogant words) for they are not fitting. In 19:10 and 26:1 we learn that luxury and honor are also not fitting for a fool.

Now we take this thought to a prince. Like the fool, there are words that don't fit those who are leaders of people. "False speech" should never be found on the lips of those who lead others, such as a prince. This truth would also be true of any kind of political leader or spiritual leader. We should expect honesty from those who lead us. How can we trust a leader who is dishonest?

Make sure you speech is fitting for a child of God, if you are a child of God.

August 18 - Read Proverbs 18

v. 1 Whoever isolates himself seeks his own desire; he breaks out against all sound judgment.

Have you ever met a person who is considered a loner? In life we often find people who do not want to be around others so they stick to themselves. There may be various reasons for that, but here we are told that it comes down to selfishness. It could be said this way; "A person who isolates themselves from others is selfish."

Now if you are this person, you may have various reasons why you choose not to be around others. For example, you may have a hard time making friends. Or, you may be shy. Or, there may be various other reasons. But ultimately, the isolator is a selfish person.

Isolators seek their own desires. They are happier doing what they want to do and it is easier for them to do it if they are by themselves. There is no need for a vote or to compromise or to do what others may like to keep people happy. By themselves, it is easier to keep happy, so they choose that life-style, isolating themselves sometimes even from their own families.

This choice defies "sound judgment." They forget that long ago God said, "It is not good that the man should be alone." (Genesis 2:18). God created us not to be an island unto ourselves. He created us for community. He created us to interact with each other.

Don't be selfish and isolate yourself from others for it defies sound judgment.

August 19 - Read Proverbs 19

v. 1 Better is a poor person who walks in his integrity than one who is crooked in speech and is a fool.

Comparisons of people are often made. Sometimes we ask questions like, "Which would you rather be this person or that one?" Sometimes we make statements like, "This person is better than that person."

Here, there is no question given to us. It just states that integrity is more important or is of greater value than wealth. Getting rich by lying or being "crooked" is not worth it. In fact, the proverb states that this person, the rich liar, is a fool. He is a fool because one day his actions will catch up with him. His crookedness will get caught either by man or by God. The punishment will not be worth the wealth that he got from his actions.

Integrity is of great value. Integrity in its simplest definition is honesty. It is healthy moral character. God puts great value on it. The Bible says much, and not only in Proverbs, to make integrity attractive. It also says much to denigrate dishonesty. The first sin tackled in the church In Acts was one of dishonesty both in word and in pretense. Here in Proverbs we have the same. It states that honesty is far better than gaining what most people in this world desire, wealth. God puts a higher value on what any person could have "integrity," whether rich or poor, than on what only some have, but many desire "wealth."

Choose integrity instead of gaining riches by lying, for it is of greater value.

August 20 - Read Proverbs 20

v. 9 Who can say, "I have made my heart pure; I am clean from my sin"?

Have you ever been asked one of those questions where the answer is so obvious that you do not need to even answer? I'm sure you have. We all have. This is one of those questions. It clearly states the obvious, which is the impossibility of sinless perfection.

First Kings 8:46 tells us that "there is no one who does not sin." First John 1:8 says, "if we say we have no sin, we deceive ourselves, and the truth is not in us." In Matthew 19:16-26, the rich young ruler who came to Jesus tried to pull one over on Jesus, but God knows men's hearts. This is also true of many people today, though some will admit it and some will not.

We are often told of the goodness of mankind in our society, so much so that we would wonder if there is anyone who is truly sinful. In fact, even those who are truly evil are often said to really only be sick and not evil at all. We are sold the bill of goods that they just need medicine and they will be fine. It is mankind's belief that man is basically good and not evil. I believe that often keeps people from seeing their real need for God and the salvation that He offers mankind. There are even many Christians who believe they can reach a state of sinless perfection. Yet I wonder how anyone who reads the Bible could come to this conclusion when they read such passages as Isaiah 6 and Romans 7.

Have a healthy understanding of your sin.

August 21 – Read Proverbs 21

v. 6 The getting of treasures by a lying tongue is a fleeting vapor and a snare of death.

We are often told that the only way to make money in this world is by lying. Whether this is true or not, and I believe it is not, we must consider the consequences of getting rich by lying. There are consequences to everything we do in life, whether what we do is good or bad. In this case, the actions are bad and the consequences are negative.

Two consequences are mentioned in this verse. First, getting treasures by lying is "a fleeting vapor." A fleeting vapor carries the idea that money gained by lying will vanish into thin air. So, money gained by lying will not last.

The second consequence of getting treasure by lying is that it is a "snare of death." The teachings of the wise will keep one from the snares of death, according to Proverbs 13:14; 14:27. Here we see one of those snares. It is lying to gain money. I have sat in sales meetings where people taught others to lie in order to make sales. But one must understand, whether you make more sales or not, the consequence of lying to gain treasure is most grave. Revelation 21:8 says that all liars will have a portion in the lake of fire, which is the "second death."

At work you may be taught to lie or you may be enticed to lie. Keep in mind the consequences of such actions. The consequences are not worth the risk, in fact, the consequences are much worse than anything gained by lying.

Don't lie to gain treasure for it is not worth it!

August 22 – Read Proverbs 22

v. 26 Be not one of those who give pledges, who put up security for debts.
v. 27 If you have nothing with which to pay, why should your bed be taken from under you?

There are some things in life we ought to avoid due to the danger that is involved. One of them is cosigning or signing for another's loan. Yet, people often do this very thing. The Book of Proverbs mentions this subject a number of times (See 6:1-5; 11:15; 17:18; 22:26).

Proverbs tells us several things about making yourself responsible for another's loans or debts. Refusing to do so is wise. If you have done it, try to get out of it as soon as you can. There is a very real danger that your bed can be taken right out from under you because of your inability to pay the debt when the other person is no longer paying the loan.

You might say, "I want to be helpful to others and not be seen as a stingy person." Or, "Are there any other alternatives to helping people in need?" The answer is, yes! You can give it to them as it is stated in Proverbs 19:17. Or, you can lend it to them without interest as stated in Proverbs 28:8. However, if you lend without interest, in the back of your mind, you must think of it as giving it away. But, you might say, "I can't afford to do either of these." Wisdom would say that if you can't do either of them, you can't afford to place yourself at risk for another's debt.

Do not put yourself at risk for another's debt.

August 23- Read Proverbs 23

v. 1 When you sit down to eat with a ruler, observe carefully what is before you,
v. 2 and put a knife to your throat if you are given to appetite.
v. 3 Do not desire his delicacies, for they are deceptive food.

There is an old saying, "If you have never had a steak you will not crave it." I like steak and I crave it often. But there are things that I have never had, so they pose no allurement to me. If I had tasted them, then they may have drawn me back a second time.

Sometimes those with much lure those with little by throwing a feast of goodies. The goodies are meant to soften you up and prepare you for what they want from you. This can be seen in Daniel 1, but Daniel did not buy into it. So when you are thrown such an event you should be careful of what may lie before you. With this kind of event, the ruler is basically saying if you do what I want you to do you can have this stuff on a regular basis.

There is another issue I can see in these verses. Just as in life in general, when you are in the presence of those wIth much more than you could ever afford, be careful your heart is not drawn away after the goodies that they have. Keep your heart within the blessings God has given you and rejoice with others over the blessings God has given them.

Be careful that another's delicacies do not mess up your heart.

August 24 – Read Proverbs 24

v. 19 Fret not yourself because of evildoers, and be not envious of the wicked,
v. 20 for the evil man has no future; the lamp of the wicked will be put out.

This whole issue of how the righteous view and think about the wicked has been around for a long, long time. As far back as the Old Testament, we see people in the Bible thinking about the life of the wicked in the world compared to the life of the righteous. With this in mind, two issues usually arise as we see in this verse: fretting and envy.

The word "fret" means to cause to burn with anger. It means to be really angry. When the righteous hear and see what the wicked do it often causes anger to flare up. This is especially true when the wicked directly attack the righteous (See Psalm 37:1, 8). Seeing the actions of the wicked, for example on the evening news, can be hard for the righteous to bear. Yet, often another emotion arises in the righteous as they look at the wicked. This emotion tends to be the opposite of being angry, that of envy.

Sometimes the righteous (Christ-followers) become envious of the wicked, thinking that they have a better life then the righteous (See Psalm 73). They often get confused and see the wicked as having peace, power and popularity. This is a very dangerous place to be in life. One must keep in mind that the wicked do not have the same hope as the righteous (v. 20).

As you consider your life and the lives of the wicked always keep in mind the final chapter.

August 25 – Read Proverbs 25

v. 24 It is better to live in a corner of the housetop than in a house shared with a quarrelsome wife.

If there is one thing that a man really desires, it is to have peace in his home. Men deal with the world and with difficulties all day long. When they come home, they want peace and quiet. They want their homes to be a place surrounded by walls where calamity is kept out.

One thing that might disrupt this desire is a wife who is quarrelsome. This is such a trouble to married men that it is mentioned at least three times in Proverbs (See 21:9, 19). Generally speaking, men do not like to quarrel and certainly do not like women who are quarrelsome, especially when they are their wives. Here God states that you would be better off living on the corner of the roof than with such a woman. Most men would say "Amen" to that.

This verse becomes a warning to young men as they look for a perspective wife. On their list of disqualifications of a would-be wife, this one should be at or near the top. But, it is also a warning to women as they consider the kind of woman they are going to become. Being quarrelsome should be on their list of what they should never become. This truth can be seen in 1 Peter 3:4. It is also something a wife should consider if she might be having trouble in her marriage.

Ladies, remove "quarrelsome" from your resume.

August 26 – Read Proverbs 26

v. 17 Whoever meddles in a quarrel not his own is like one who takes a passing dog by the ears.

Most people want nothing to do with quarrels. They want to avoid them like the plague. Quarrels can cause trouble and pain. But others delight in getting involved in quarrels, even ones they have no business in. Then there are those who should have had more wisdom than to do so.

To "meddle" literally means to be angry or even furious, and carries the idea of being a busybody in someone's affairs. In this case, the issue is not yours and belongs to another person, but you have involved yourself in it and so have been affected by it. This is not a wise thing to do. It is much wiser to stay out of something that does not involve you, unless you are invited in, for example as seen in Matthew 18:15-17.

How unwise it is to do this? In those days, in the ancient Near East, dogs were not domesticated. They were more like a pack of jackals. Grabbing onto one puts you in danger. Grabbing onto one of their ears made it worse. And so, getting involved in a quarrel that you have no part in does the very same thing. It is far wiser to stay out of it than to put yourself into a bad situation like that. Unless invited in, there is no reason to get involved and so become a busybody.

Be wise and don't get involved in quarrels that you are not part of.

August 27 – Read Proverbs 27

v. 4 Wrath is cruel, anger is overwhelming, but who can stand before jealousy?

Wrath, anger and jealousy are all emotions. "Wrath" is used of the poisonous venom of a snake and refers to a very strong feeling of rage or hostility. "Anger" is used of any part of the nose and refers to anger that changes the color of the nose area. An example of this would be when you see a person's face turn red because he is angry. Jealousy or envy refers to a strong desire to have something, or for others not to have it, because you can't obtain it.

All three of these emotions can be very strong, but according to this verse, jealousy is the strongest of the three. It indicates that no one can stand before it. We can see the strength of jealousy by looking at Proverbs 6:34-35, which says, "For jealousy makes a man furious, and he will not spare when he takes revenge. He will accept no compensation; he will refuse though you multiply gifts." The idea is that jealousy can be so strong that nothing can soothe it. We see this also in Song of Solomon 8:6, which says, "Set me as a seal upon your heart, as a seal upon your arm, for love is strong as death, jealousy is fierce as the grave. Its flashes are flashes of fire, the very flame of the LORD."

What does all of this tell us? Jealousy is a dangerous emotion. It is not good to have in your own life for it may destroy you. It is also not good if someone is jealous of you for they may set out to destroy you because of it.

Beware of jealousy for it hurts everyone with whom it comes in contact.

August 28 – Read Proverbs 28

v. 6 Better is a poor who man walks in his integrity, than a rich man who is crooked in his ways.

Who is better a rich man or a poor man? Which is better, to be rich or to be poor? These questions are often pondered by people. Often people fall on the side of one or the other, perhaps, most saying that it is better to be rich. God, I believe, would answer that generally one is not better than the other, but there are circumstances when one is.

In the Bible we have examples of rich people who loved God. Phoebe would be one such example. Job would be another example of this. At the same time, riches come with their own set of difficulties. For example, Jesus said it is harder for a rich man to enter Heaven.

It seems that poor people often do not like the rich yet wish that they were one of them. It seems the poor think that the rich have a better and easier life. They think that the rich do not have any difficulties. They think that the grass is much better on that side of the fence.

Here, God does not say that one is better than the other. What He does say is that you are better off being poor than being rich, if you walk with integrity instead of being crooked. The idea is this: it matters not how strong your bank account is but how strong your character and walk are.

Integrity is more valuable than money, walk with it today.

August 29 – Read Proverbs 29

v. 27 An unjust man is an abomination to the righteous, but one whose way is straight is an abomination to the wicked.

Have you ever noticed that light and darkness just can't get along? You just can't have both at the same time. This is also true of the righteous and the wicked. The righteous and the wicked just come from opposite ends of the spectrum. What they love and hate are opposite from each other. Their hearts and lives are just not in agreement.

The righteous and wicked hate opposite things because they love opposite things. The righteous hate that which is "unjust" which means unrighteous, wicked, perverse or wrong. The wicked, on the other hand, hate that which is "straight", a word which means not crooked, and so, morally upright.

Righteousness and wickedness have two separate paths, just like light and darkness. You cannot choose to be righteous and walk on the path of the wicked and vise versa. The two are mutually exclusive (2 Corinthians 6:14-18). Is it clear yet?

It is clear from Proverbs 25-29 (The Proverbs of Solomon copied by Hezekiah's men) that the path of the righteous is the right choice. The path of the righteous is a path that must be chosen. You must choose to take that path and so choose to reject the path of the wicked. Most will not choose the path of the righteous, but still, it is a path that you must choose.

Walk in the path of the righteous and hate what they hate.

August 30 – Read Proverbs 30

v. 11 There are those who curse their fathers and do not bless their mothers.
v. 12 There are those who are clean in their own eyes but are not washed of their filth.
v. 13 There are those—how lofty are their eyes, how high their eyelids lift!
v. 14 There are those whose teeth are swords, whose fangs are knives, to devour the poor from off the earth, the needy from among mankind.

In these four verses we have a description of four different kinds of people. It is a list of people in which our names should never be included. This is a list of people who do not live the way that God would want us to live.

The first on the list are the people who are disrespectful, as seen in how they treat their parents. The second on the list belongs to those who are self-deceived. They think they are clean, but they do not see themselves correctly. Their dirt (sin) is hidden from their own eyes. Take notice of the words "in their own eyes." These people do not see themselves correctly, maybe even hiding their own hypocrisy. The third on the list are the proud people, who lift their eyes high as though they are above everyone else. They see themselves as being better than others. The fourth on the list are those who plunder the poor, like wild animals who attack and destroy their vulnerable prey.

All four of these types of people walk not in wisdom, but in wickedness. They are as common in our day as in that day. Disrespectful, self-deceived, proud, and preying on the needy, these people can be seen everywhere we go.

Don't ever let your name be included on this list.

August 31 - Read Proverbs 31

v. 8 Open your mouth for the mute, for the rights of all who are destitute.
v. 9 Open your mouth, judge righteously, defend the rights of the poor and needy.

All through the book of Proverbs we have been told that we are better off keeping our mouth closed. Yet here we are told to open our mouths. So we learn there is a right time to open our mouths and a right time to keep our mouths closed.

Here we are encouraged to open our mouths for those who can't. We are encouraged to defend those who can't defend themselves. We are told that there are people in this world who need help, and if we can, we should help them. Note the list of people who sometimes need help: the mute, destitute, poor and needy. There are others. This list is not exhaustive. The idea is that we should reach out to those who are needy and help them. At times some people need the help of others, and when that is true people should expect that Christians would be there to help them. In doing these kinds of things we are doing the kinds of things that Jesus expects of us. This world should see believers being busy doing what is right for those who are in need. The New Testament tells us to do so and even the Old Testament does, too. Do you open your mouth for those who can't?

Help those who can't help themselves.

September 1 – Read Proverbs 1

v. 23 If you turn at my reproof, behold, I will pour out my spirit to you; I will make my words known to you.
v. 25 because you have ignored all my counsel and would have none of my reproof,

In this section of Proverbs, we have wisdom being spoken of as a woman. Wisdom is calling out, but the scoffer is not listening. A scoffer is someone who is proud and arrogant. As it states here, a scoffer is someone who is just unwilling to listen, unwilling to respond to wisdom.

If you want to be wise, you must always be willing to listen to what others have to say, especially when wisdom speaks. Once you close your mind to wisdom, you're in a dangerous place. There are many reasons why some people may close their ears to what others have to say. One reason would be pride. Being closed-minded is a very dangerous place to be in your life.

Those who are wise are those who are always open to listen to what others have to say. What they hear may be wise or may be foolish. But a wise person takes the time to listen; he takes the time to determine the value of what he hears. A foolish person is unwilling to listen. A foolish person determines the value of what others have to say before he ever hears what they say. Doing this causes one to fall short of being wise.

Always be ready to listen.

September 2 – Read Proverbs 2

v. 13 who forsake the paths of uprightness to walk in the ways of darkness,
v. 14 who rejoice in doing evil and delight in the perverseness of evil,
v. 15 men whose paths are crooked, and who are devious in their ways.

What is described in these verses is evil people. Verse nine tells us that wisdom will protect us from these kinds of people. So in effect, verse nine is telling us that these kinds of people are evil. Being wise will keep us from them.

While this is not an exhaustive list of the characteristics of wicked people, it does give us some information about what wicked people look like. It speaks of the kind that we are to stay away from. Notice that wicked people forsake the path of uprightness and prefer to walk in ways of darkness. In the Bible, darkness refers to sin. Wicked people choose to live a lifestyle of sinfulness rather than uprightness. If fact, notice verse 14 tells us that they delight in this. These are people whose paths are wicked and whose ways are devious.

If these are the kinds of people that wisdom would keep us from, then we also learn of the kind of person we should not be. Consider where you're at in life today. Do these verses describe you? Are you the kind of person that wisdom would help us avoid? As we look at these verses, there are two issues to consider. The first issue would be the kind of people we ought to avoid, and the second issue would be the kind of person we ought not to be.

Be different than the kind of person who is described here.

September 3 - Read Proverbs 3

v. 31 Do not envy a man of violence and do not choose any of his ways,
v. 32 for the devious person is an abomination to the LORD, but the upright are in his confidence.

Be careful what you set your heart on. Be careful what you choose to envy. There's a great danger in looking at what people have, and wanting what they have and ultimately wanting to be like them. So this proverb begins with a warning about not envying a man of violence.

We may look at a man of violence and see his accumulated goods and set our heart on them. In this world, those who choose to do evil and be evil sometimes get much further ahead than those who choose to do what is right. We must always consider things in light of our relationship with God and in light of eternity. Notice that this man is considered an abomination by God. Also, notice that the Lord's curse is upon him, as we see in verse 33. This spot reminds me so much of what the Psalmist said in Psalm 73. He said that he had almost messed up his life because he had envied those who go against God's Word. He envied them because he saw their prosperity. And the only reason he didn't mess up his life is because he went into the sanctuary of God and considered his life in light of eternity. We must do the same.

Be very careful in your life that you don't envy the wrong things. Be very careful that you keep your desires in line with the Word of God.

Do not envy the wicked or choose their ways.

September 4 - Read Proverbs 4

v. 27 Do not swerve to the right or to the left; turn your foot away from evil.

According to verse 20, this section, verse 20-27, like so many places in Proverbs, is a father talking to his son about life. In it, he talks to his son about his heart, speech and path. In the last verse of this section the issue is his path (v. 26).

The encouragement is to get on the right path and stay there: "Do not swerve to the right or the left". Which path is he referring to in this verse? The last part tells us when he says, "turn your foot from evil." The right path is the one that is the opposite of the evil path (4:14). The right path is the righteous path (2:20). It is the path that acknowledges God in all of your ways (3:5-6). It is the path that avoids immorality (5:8). It is the path of obedience to God's Word.

God warned Israel not to turn off this path (Deuteronomy 5:32), and he also warned Joshua of this (Joshua 1:1:7). Here a dad is warning his son of the same.

Jesus said that there are two paths: one leads to Heaven and one leads to Hell. It is obvious which one we should make sure we are on, and the way we live our lives will show which path we are on.

Walk on the path that leads to Heaven, which is demonstrated by a biblically moral life.

September 5 - Read Proverbs 5

v. 20 Why should you be intoxicated, my son, with a forbidden woman and embrace the bosom of an adulteress?

Wow what a question! This could be asked of so many in our world today. This could be asked of so many throughout history. In many cultures, being involved with more than one spouse, more than one person, is considered normal.

The answer to this question is given in this chapter. Why would one want to do be intoxicated with someone other than his spouse when the following is true? The results of doing so are grave, including physical, financial, emotional and possible public disgrace. Also, there is the possible danger of having to share your children with other people. Then, there is the reality that God is watching everything you do, including the immoral behavior that is mentioned here. Finally, there is the very real truth that sexual sin is very addictive and much more so than the average person realizes. With all of these things being true, one would wonder why anyone would be intoxicated with anyone other than his spouse.

This then brings up an unstated truth, nevertheless a real truth, that we ought to be intoxicated with our spouses. When you make a vow to spend the rest of your life with your spouse, you should spend every day becoming more intoxicated with the one you married. Sure relationships have their difficulties, but you should work hard at loving the person you have vowed to love.

Be intoxicated with your spouse and no one else.

September 6 - Read Proverbs 6

v. 26 for the price of a prostitute is only a loaf of bread, but a married woman hunts down a precious life.

Sexual immorality... At what cost? Here the prostitute looks at a man's value as equal to a loaf of bread. She sees him only as a way of earning bread, or whatever she needs, and nothing more. He is a "meal ticket." Proverbs 28:21 tells us that a person will do wrong for a piece of bread. People are willing to do just about anything if it will earn them money and possessions. Yet, for him, the end result is squandered wealth (29:3).

The second half of this verse refers to a "married woman." This woman is not his wife but the wife of another man (v. 29). She is after a life which is so precious. Going into her will cost him all he has (v. 34-35). Adultery is a sin that can bankrupt a man or woman (5:10). Married men have lost fortunes to this type of sin buying gifts and food, and paying for hotels. They have been blackmailed by those who threatened to bring their affairs to light. Then there is the cost of divorce that takes even more money.

Make no mistake, the price of sin, the price of immorality, can be great. This leads us to verse 32 which says, "He who commits adultery lacks sense; he who does it destroys himself." Money is not the only price to be paid either; there is so much more, even his life.

Beware and take every precaution for the price of sexual immorality is steep.

September 7 - Read Proverbs 7

v. 19 for my husband is not at home; he is gone on a long journey;

We see here what is so often true of sin. The vast majority of people who sin think they will not get caught. By far, those who do wrong think they will get away with it. This thinking is wrong.

The context of this verse is that of the adulteress who thinks she can get away with committing adultery. Her invitation to sin is based on the fact that she thinks her husband will not be back for a while. She thinks that because he will be gone for a while she will get away with her sinful deed, and so she invites this young man to join her in her sin.

This is true of most people who sin, of most who do wrong. It is true of the crook who thinks he can steal and not get caught. It is true of the murderer who kills and thinks no one will find out. It is true of anyone who sins, or of anyone who lures someone else into sinning, and thinks he will get away with it.

You must remember that there's a very real chance that you will get caught. One must remember that most people get caught. One must remember that even if no human being ever catches you in your sin, God always does. Remember the truth of Proverbs 5:21 which says, "For a man's ways are before the eyes of the Lord and he ponders all his paths." God sees everything you're doing. There is nothing that you can do that God will not catch.

Don't sin because you think you can avoid getting caught.

September 8 - Read Proverbs 8

v. 10 take my instruction instead of silver, and knowledge rather than choice gold,
v. 11 for wisdom is better than jewels, and all that you may desire cannot compare with her.

What do you teach your children is of the most value in this life? What do you tell your children is worth getting over everything else? Sadly, many parents teach the children that silver gold and jewels are far more important, far more valuable, than anything else in this world. Parents do this in a variety of ways. They do by example and they do it by their teaching.

Here we see Solomon giving wisdom human qualities. Wisdom is given the ability to talk. With that, wisdom cries out for people to listen. It tells us that all the money in the world is not as valuable as wisdom.

I see it all of the time - people chasing after money. I see people working themselves to death just to get a little more. Some are willing to sell their souls for a dollar bill. Many are willing to work themselves to death just to have a little more of what this world has to offer.

These verses remind us that money and wisdom do not go hand-in-hand. You can have a lot of money without wisdom, and you can have a lot of wisdom without money. Yes, it is possible to have both, but given the choice wisdom is of far greater value than money. Without wisdom, money has very little value. So how much time in a day do you spend seeking to gain wisdom, as opposed to seeking to gain money?

Be wise and understand that wisdom is of far greater value than silver, or gold, or jewels.

September 9 - Read Proverbs 9

v. 12 if you are wise, you are wise for yourself; if you scoff, you alone will bear it.

Every one of us has choices in life and the choices we make reap results. We each choose for ourselves what will happen with our lives. We are each responsible for the choices we make.

In life we can choose to be wise. We can make every effort to read, to learn, to grow, to listen with the purpose of growing wiser. Wisdom cries out for us to listen to it. It is there for everyone who wishes to choose it. No one who seeks it will ever be kept from it. But, the choice must be made to become wise. It will not happen by accident. If you choose it you can have it, but you must choose it.

On the other hand, you can also choose to scoff, but you alone will bear it. To scoff means to boast or to be arrogant. It is not the activity of someone who is wise. It is the activity of a fool.

This verse speaks of individual responsibility. Each person can choose to be wise or to choose to be a scoffer, and each person will bear the responsibility for his choice. You cannot blame others for the choices you make, for they are your responsibility. If your life is messed up, it is your responsibility. You are where you are in life because of the choices you have made, either good or bad. The sooner we each take responsibility for our choices, the sooner our choices will begin to head in the right direction, as long as we combine wisdom with our choices.

Know that you are responsible for the choices you make and don't blame others.

September 10 - Read Proverbs 10

v. 32 the lips of the righteous know what is acceptable, but the mouth of the wicked, what is perverse.

I was listening to a radio program a while back and heard the announcer say that four letter words do not lower moral values and do not hurt society. This is not true. How we speak and what we say definitively has an impact on people around us. Certainly the righteous and the wicked don't talk the same.

Our verse today makes this contrast, and it continues the thought of the previous verse. The mouth of the righteous "brings forth wisdom" and it "knows what is acceptable." What comes out of the mouth comes from what is in the heart. This is what Jesus said (Matthew 15:18-20). Jesus said that this will defile a person, and let me add, a society. The righteous are careful and slow in what they say, knowing that their words have great impact. They also have a desire to make sure that the impact they have is positive and helps the hearer. They make sure that they speak the truth and they do so in love. They make sure that their words are ones of reproof, rebuke and exhortation and they speak them with patience and teaching (2 Timothy 4:2).

This is not true of the wicked. They speak what is "perverse", which means to turn away from what is morally correct. The wicked do not care how their words affect others. Their main concern is for themselves, but in the end, their speech will only hurt themselves.

Speak what is acceptable, not what is perverse.

September 11 - Read Proverbs 11

v. 13 Whoever goes about slandering reveals secrets, but he who is trustworthy in spirit keeps a thing covered.

In our verse for today there is a contrast between a slanderer and a faithful friend. Slandering and revealing secrets certainly do not come from the mouth of a faithful friend. They come from a wicked mouth. They come from a mouth bent on hurting others. The mouth of the righteous speaks only those things which will benefit others. Even in rebuking someone, the righteous do so only for the benefit of the one rebuked.

The slanderers run around looking to harm the one being slandered. In so doing, they reveal secrets they may have been told or information that they have for the purpose of hurting. The wicked not only are evil with their words, but they also do not know how to keep a secret. They cannot be trusted. They will use anything in order to harm the person they are seeking to destroy with their words. They go from place to place revealing anything they know to the public in order to hurt. Someone who is trustworthy is different than this. You can trust them with private information. You don't have to worry about what they might do with your inner secrets.

You should consider what kinds of friends you have and what kind of friend you are. What do you do with the private information of your friends or former friends? Is it kept in a lock box?

Be a faithful friend who can be trusted, not a slanderer who reveals secrets.

September 12 - Read Proverbs 12

v. 18 There is one whose rash words are like sword trusts, but the tongue of the wise brings healing.

Words can be used for good or evil. They can be used to help or to hurt. The Bible often contrasts the words of the wicked and the righteous. This verse contrasts words that are unwise with words that are wise. One hurts; the other heals.

The first part of our verse speaks of a person whose words are characterized by two things. The first is that they are rash words. "Rash" describes thoughtless or reckless words. It can even describe words that are nonsense. The second characterization is that this person's words are like sword thrusts, that is, they hurt or kill. So, this person speaks with quick, unthinking, and uncaring words which hurt people. This is an unwise way of speaking and is never right.

This is not true of the second person, the wise person. The wise person speaks words that bring healing. The wise speak words that are thoughtful and caring, as opposed to the first person in our verse.

Before you speak today, you may want to ask a couple of questions. Are my words thoughtful? Are my words caring? Will my words bring healing or will they hurt? It is so easy to talk without thinking. However, the wise often think without talking so that when they do talk, their words will heal and not hurt.

Use only words that are healing, not hurtful, words that are thoughtful and caring.

September 13 - Read Proverbs 13

v. 4 The soul of the sluggard craves and gets nothing, while the soul of the diligent is richly supplied.

There are a number of reoccurring themes of comparison and contrast in Proverbs, such as: wisdom vs. foolishness, riches vs. poverty, good speech vs. bad speech, morality vs. immorality, etc. Included in these is laziness vs. hard work. This is the topic of this verse.

It starts with the issue of laziness, here called "the soul of the sluggard." The lazy person has no fewer cravings than the one who is willing to work hard, but the difference is that he is unwilling to work to fulfill them. He is full of excuses for why he does not work. He will take every opportunity to do nothing. He is willing to sit by while others do all of the work. And, the height of his laziness is that he is not even willing to work to get what he wants, or as said here, to satisfy his craving. He craves, but gets nothing, because he is unwilling to do anything to attain what he craves.

The soul of the diligent, on the other hand, is willing to work to get what he wants. He is willing to put the time in, and to sweat and do whatever it takes to get the job done. He does not shy away from work. This is the ethic that built America. This is the ethic of men and women, in the home and outside the home, which has done so much good for America and the world.

Don't be characterized by laziness; hard work supplies.

September 14 – Read Proverbs 14

v. 26 In the fear of the Lord one has strong confidence, and his children will have a refuge.

v. 27 The fear the Lord is a fountain of life that one may turn away from the snares of death.

The fear of the Lord as a subject is spoken of many times in the book of Proverbs. Proverbs chapter 1 tells us that the fear the Lord is the beginning of knowledge. The fear of the Lord begins with a proper understanding of who God is and an understanding of who we are in light of that. Basically, the fear of the Lord means having reverence for God. These two verses tell us of some of the benefits of fearing the Lord.

Let's begin with the first benefit mentioned in verse 26. When one fears God there is security, not only for the one who fears God, but also for the children of one who does. There is security in fearing God because there is security in a right relationship with God. This security is passed on to the children in at least two ways. First, they have it because they are part of a family of one who chooses to fear God. Second, it is demonstrated by the one who chooses to fear God so that he chooses the same for his life.

Notice that secondly, the fear of the Lord is a "fountain of life" which protects a person against the snares of death. It protects a person by causing them to turn away from those things that lead to death. The fear of the Lord gives them the wisdom they need to make the right choices.

Choose "the fear of the Lord" knowing there are many benefits.

September 15 – Read Proverbs 15

v. 27 whoever is greedy for unjust gain troubles his own household, but he who hates bribes will live.

The choices we make have an effect on our families. If we make right and good choices, our families benefit. If we make bad choices, our families are hurt. If we choose the fear the Lord there is benefit to our families. But if we are greedy for unjust gain our families are hurt.

First Timothy 6:10 tells us that, "For the love of money is a root of all kinds of evils…." If you are greedy then you always want more. Greed often ends up causing a person to look for "unjust gain." Greed can often lead to one taking a bribe to get what one wants or what others want. Your greed can affect everyone in your family and not in good ways. Your greed can bring trouble upon your home. Your greed can cause you to take a bribe.

On the other hand, if you hate bribes or hate unjust gain, and if you are not greedy, you can keep yourself and your family out of trouble. A bribe threatens your own soul and threatens your home, and so it is a danger to both you and your family. There is no bribe or gift worth the trouble that it brings to you and your family.

Keep a tight reign on your heart. Watch out that it does not become full of greed. Continually ask God for a heart that keeps things in proper perspective. And, remember the prayer of Agur in Proverbs 30:7-9.

Beware of a greedy heart that is willing to take a bribe; it will hurt your family.

September 16 – Read Proverbs 16

v. 2 All of the ways of a man are pure in his own eyes, but the Lord weighs his spirit.

Is it not true that we all wish we could tell if someone was lying to us? We all wish we had the power to discern the truthfulness of those we talk to. We wish there were some trick or gimmick we could figure out that would work. But maybe, just maybe, we are looking in the wrong direction. Maybe we should be looking and desiring to know when we are lying to ourselves.

It seems that we often lie to ourselves and get away with it. This verse tells us that we are able to convince ourselves that all our ways are pure. It tells us that we are able to convince ourselves that what we are about to do is right. We are able to do this even when it is clear what we are about to do is wrong. We are often able to convince ourselves that our actions are just. I have seen people do this over and over, and I'm sure I've done the very same thing.

God knows this and God is able to see through this. God looks past our self-deception and goes to the heart of the matter to our spirit. He sees when we lie to ourselves and He knows the truth. We must learn to do the same. We must weigh everything we do by His Word. We must ask God for wisdom and a clear understanding of ourselves.

Saturate your ways in prayer and in God's Word, and don't lie to yourself.

September 17 – Read Proverbs 17

v. 27 Whoever restrains his words has knowledge, and he who has a cool spirit is a man of understanding.

Here is the truth. Mark it down. Your words and how you use them tell others whether you are wise or not. Those who use their words loosely, without restraint, do not have the mark of wisdom. People who say whatever they want, however they want, are not wise. This is what Proverbs says over and over.

Wise people use their words carefully and they use them with great restraint. In fact, having read Proverbs many times, the impression that I get is that wise people tend to talk less than others. Wise people have learned to control their tongue. The following verses back up this thought: 10:14, 19; 11:12; 14:23; 17:28; 21:23; 29:20.

Wise people also tend to control their anger by having a "cool spirit." Just like with their use of words, they also have control over their emotions. In particular they have learned to control their anger. The following verses back this up: 12:16; 14:29; 15:18; 16:32.

The lesson here is one we all need to learn in our path towards wisdom. Wise people have control over themselves and unwise people do not. Wise people are disciplined people and unwise people are undisciplined. So in the path of wisdom, there is self-control. Loose lips and uncontrolled anger both have been the cause of many people displaying foolishness. Gaining control, not of the world, but of yourself, shows that you belong among the wise.

Be disciplined in your words and emotions.

September 18 – Read Proverbs 18

v. 24 A man of many companions may come to ruin, but there is a friend who sticks closer than a brother.

Over the years many people will come and go in your life. Some will be considered companions and some will be considered friends. There is a difference between the two, and even within each group there are differences.

Let's begin with the first, companions. Companions are people we hang around with and spend time with, maybe in a group setting. We may have many such people as this in our life. We may even consider some of the people in this group to be friends. The issue with this group is that they are not necessarily close friends. We can have many such people, but when trouble hits they are not there for us. They are not so close as to be willing to stick with us.

But, there are people who may come into our lives who are considered such friends that they stick no matter what. Sometimes we find a friend who is closer to us than even our own siblings. This kind of friend is of great value and is a rare and precious jewel.

This kind of friend is the kind of friend you should be to your friends. You should be the kind of friend who cares so much for your friends that they can count on you no matter what. You should be the kind of friend who readily accepts your friend. Be the kind of friend that stays even when you have disagreements. We all need friends like this.

Be the kind of friend who is closer than a brother.

September 19 – Read Proverbs 19

v. 4 Wealth brings many new friends, but a poor man is deserted by his friend.

As we saw yesterday, real true friends are few and far between. Sometimes the friends we have are not those kinds of friends. Sometimes the friends we have are false friends. This lesson is sometimes not learned until it is too late.

This verse tells us that not all friends are really friends. When I was growing up all of the kids on our block or in the circle of people I knew were always at the house of the kid with the pool. Later, it was the kid with the car. Then, it was the kid who was popular. We often see people who are rich having many friends. I have heard people who are rich wondering if their friends were real friends. Are they their friends because of their money, or are they real? If you have what everybody is after you will get friends, but are they real friends?

Now, the poor man may be deserted by his friends. He has nothing to hold them to him. He does not have the money of the rich guy or gal. He will often look at the rich, or popular, or whatever and wish he had as many friends as the rich guy or gal. But in reality, the rich guy has no more than the poor guy and they both often have no real friends. Everyone wants real friends but few really have them.

Be a friend whose friendship is not based on what a person has or doesn't have.

September 20 – Read Proverbs 20

v. 23 Unequal weights are an abomination to the LORD, and false scales are not good.

This verse is much the same as verse 10 which states, "Unequal weights and unequal measures are both alike an abomination to the Lord." With this stated at least twice, it emphasizes the point of the verse. I find it interesting that so many people go to church on Sunday but do not feel it has any relationship to Monday. All we learn on Sunday should affect what we do at work on Monday and the rest of the week.

So, what we do in the workplace and the marketplace is watched by God. And, God does not like certain practices, practices which include lying, cheating and anything which is deceptive are wrong. We can put all kinds of names to it, but if it is deceptive in any way, God does not approve of it. So our worship should affect our workmanship. If you are at work reading this or getting ready to go to work, ask yourself, "How does what I learned on Sunday impact me now?" Or, you may ask, "How does my relationship to God impact what I do at work?"

Both "unequal weights" and "false scales" are ways of cheating people out of fair practices and are done purely for selfish reasons. Instead of treating people fairly those who do these things cheat and lie for their own personal benefit with no care for the impact on the people they cheat. This is no way for a person who claims to follow Jesus to ever act.

Be honest at work and make no excuses for dishonesty.

September 21 – Read Proverbs 21

v. 30 No wisdom, no understanding, no counsel can avail against the Lord.

God is sovereign and all-powerful. How could anyone ever hope to win a fight with God? In fact, who would ever even consider fighting against God? Yet, it happens far more than you might think.

The Book of Revelation tells us that at the end of time Satan will try to fight against God (Revelation 20:7-15). He will attempt to do this even though God had locked him up for 1,000 years. He will attempt to do this even with all of his knowledge of God and he knows God well. And, he will not do it alone. We are told that he will deceive many thousands of people to follow him in his quest. But, they will lose. In Psalm 2, we are also informed that the nations and the rulers of the earth set themselves against God, but He laughs at them.

How about you, do you ever set yourself against God? Verse 30 speaks of fighting against God and verse 31 speaks of fighting without God. Either one is doomed to failure. Some people think they can do their own thing and go against the will and word of God and not face the consequences. They are wrong, and so are you if you think like that. No one can ever oppose God and expect to win. God's plans will "carry the day."

If you live your life in opposition to God, the outcome will not be good. If you set yourself against the plans of God, you will lose. If you want your plans to succeed, don't be found in opposition to God.

Don't set yourself against God; you will lose.

September 22 - Read Proverbs 22

v. 24 make no friendship with a man given to anger, nor with a wrathful man,
v. 25 lest you learn his ways and entangle yourself in a snare.

There is an old truth that goes like this, "If you run with the wolves, you will learn to howl." There are many more sayings just like it. These kinds of sayings inform us that we often become like those we spend time with. This is true in both a positive and negative way. Here we are warned of making friends with a person who is characterized by anger.

If we spend much time with such a person, two things can or will happen. Number one: we will learn his ways and so become like him. Often people think that they are too strong to become like their friends. But, seldom is anyone that strong. No, we tend to become like the people we spend time with. A person given to anger or to wrath is a person who is controlled by it. A person controlled by anger is a dangerous person, both to himself and those around him.

Number two: we will fall into the same troubles that happen to anyone given to anger. Have you ever seen someone drive like a nut to catch up with a person who has pulled in front of him? Have you ever seen a person so enraged by something that they have lost control of themselves and done something stupid? If you have seen these kinds of things, they will also be seen in you if you spend too much time with a person controlled by anger.

Be cautious in friendships, especially with those given to anger.

September 23 - Read Proverbs 23

v. 31 Do not look at wine when it is red, when it sparkles in the cup and goes down smoothly.

Often that which can do much harm on the surface can look very inviting. Here the look and taste of wine is put forth as such a thing. The problem is what wine or an alcoholic beverage can do to you if you are given to it (drunk – enslaved, v. 32-35).

In this verse we have the warning. In the following verses explain what happens to a person who has gotten drunk by it. I can say it this way, what is seen here is the bait that is put into the trap to attract the unsuspecting mouse whose neck is later broken. There are many things in life that seem good up-front, but on the back-end hurt us. The reality is that those things that can do harm often look good up front, and that is why people try them or do them. The easiest way to avoid danger is to stop before you have begun. We all know of many issues in our world that hold danger. One such issue is wine and/or strong drink. The best way to never become a drunk is to never touch the stuff. It is to avoid it, and not even look at it, or especially not to taste it.

Looking at it might cause you to think the worse will never happen to you since it looks so good and harmless. Tasting it may be the thing that sends a message from your taste buds to your brain that tells you more would be better. Don't fall into that trap.

The best way to avoid drunkenness is to avoid that which would make you drunk.

September 24 – Read Proverbs 24

v. 29 Do not say, "I will do to him as he has done to me; I will pay the man back for what he has done."

There is an old saying that I first heard from a friend of mine who had spent much time in jail. It goes like this, "What goes around comes around." The meaning is that whatever you do to others will come around to you at some point. With this in mind, the question becomes, "Who has a right to seek revenge?"

There are many people who feel they have a right to seek revenge. They believe that having been hurt, they have a right to hurt back. They believe they can do what is said in this verse, but our verse says that we do not have that right. This truth is stated over and over and over in the Word of God. For example, we find it stated in Proverbs 20:22; Matthew 5:38-42 and Romans 12:17-21.

As Christians we have no right to retaliate against those who would do evil to us. God desires that we leave things in His hands. On the contrary, when people do evil towards us we are to respond with love. We see this example when Jesus and Stephen prayed for those who were killing them. It is a very hard example to follow because our sinful human response is to want to retaliate, but we must not. In fact, if we do, God will turn His anger away from that person and towards us (Proverbs 24:17-18).

Rather than repaying evil with evil, respond with love.

September 25 – Read Proverbs 25

v. 9 Argue your case with your neighbor himself, and do not reveal another's secret,
v. 10 lest he who hears you bring shame upon you, and your ill repute have no end.

How important is it that you keep someone's confidence? Or, to put it another way, at what point can you reveal what someone has said to you in private, "another's secret?" Would you be willing to lose an argument that you could easily win, but only if you used what was said to you in private? These are questions that some struggle with while others do not give the issue a second thought. Some have no problem taking a private thing and making it a public thing.

God's Word is pretty clear, no, very clear on this issue. A confidence is a confidence. What is told to you in private must remain private. I hate it when someone comes and tells me something and then says, "But you can't tell anyone I told you this." They have given me critical information about something that needs to be dealt with without giving the permission to deal with it. I would rather not know, than know, and not be able to use the information to fix it.

I have found myself in many circumstances where I could have easily won an argument, or proven someone was lying to me, or fixed an issue, but only if I betrayed a confidence. I have often walked away knowing this, but not being able to do anything about it knowing that I cannot betray a confidence.

Keep what is private, private, unless you get permission to do otherwise.

September 26 – Read Proverbs 26

v. 23 Like the glaze covering an earthen vessel are fervent lips with an evil heart.
v. 24 Whoever hates disguises himself with his lips and harbors deceit in his heart;
v. 25 when he speaks graciously, believe him not, for there are seven abominations in his heart;
v. 26 though his hatred be covered with deception, his wickedness will be exposed in the assembly.

It is scary when I see so many people done in by what people say. By that I mean people are fooled because deceptive, even wicked, people do so well at covering up their hearts with their words. People tend to be taken in by people who talk well.

Beware! An evil heart can be covered up with fervent (zealous) lips. It is like a jar with a beautiful glaze covering which hides cracks on the inside. The inside of a person can be covered by how they speak and what they say. We are fooled too easily.

Someone who "hates" and "harbors deceit" in their heart can cover it up with gracious words. This person can even have "seven abominations" in his heart and still cover it up with his speech. We need to learn to be careful and perceptive. I think of all of the false teachers in Jeremiah's day who only told the people good things, while Jeremiah told the truth. The people listened to the false teachers.

Let your ears hear more than just words. Let them hear the actions of a person for they are much louder if you listen.

Be discerning for evil people are very good at deception.

September 27 – Read Proverbs 27

v. 10 Do not forsake your friend and your father's friend, and do not go to your brother's house in the day of your calamity. Better is a neighbor who is near than a brother who is far away.

True friendships are hard to find. What is a true friendship? It is one that is based on mutual respect and honesty. It is one that is mutually caring. It is one where both friends are each unselfish and loving. It is one where each friend seeks the best for his or her friend. I often say that you don't have that kind of friendship until you have had a disagreement and the friendship holds. Disagreements test the quality of a friendship and real ones are not pulled apart by them.

When you have this kind of friendship, you need to hang on to it and uphold it. When trouble strikes, it is better to go to a friend like this who is near, than to run to a family member who is far away. This does not belittle family relationships, but uplifts long-term, true friendships. At the same time, true friendships often prove stronger than bloodlines.

There is great value in friendships and God in His Word speaks to it in many places. Make sure your friendships are built and based on God's Word. Make sure that your friendships are mutual edifying. Satan also knows the value of friendships in our lives and will seek to destroy these ties. Don't let him! We need to make sure that we do not forsake the friends that God has guided into our lives.

Don't forsake your friends for when disaster strikes friends can be valuable.

September 28 – Read Proverbs 28

v. 7 The one who keeps the law is a son with understanding, but a companion of gluttons shames his father.

These two, "one who obeys the law" and "one who a companion of gluttons" stand in opposition to one another. The first is good and the second is bad.

Let's look at the first, first. A son who keeps the law, the Law of God, is a wise son. This kind of son honors his father. This is the kind of son any father who follows God would want.

The second one is an unwise son and so shames his father. A son who joins with gluttons will sooner or later create problems for his father. When you read the many passages in the Bible about "gluttons", you can easily see why one who would choose them as companions would shame his father. Proverbs 23:20-21 is one such example of what happens to gluttons.

Sons who seek to honor or make their father proud of them would do well to choose to follow the Word of God instead of following those who live in opposition to God's Word. The son who makes such a choice shows that he is discerning or wise. The second son chooses to live in opposition to the Word of God by choosing to live with those who do not follow it.

We all know that parents' choices affect their children, but it is also true that children's choices affect their parents. That is what we see happen here. Children should keep that in mind when they choose either to do what is right, or choose to head down the wrong path.

Your choices affect those around you; make right choices so the impact will be good.

September 29 – Read Proverbs 29

v. 26 Many seek the face of a ruler, but it is from the Lord that a man gets justice.

When a person seeks justice, he seeks those in charge, or those with the authority to help him get justice. Sometimes this works and sometimes it does not. It may work if the person has the authority and desire to give justice, but this is not always the case. Some may want to help, but cannot. Others may not want to help for a variety of reasons, one being that they do not care about justice. They may, in fact, be the one who is behind the scene robbing the person of justice, which makes the whole process more difficult.

But with God, all of this is different. God has both the authority and power to give any person justice. God also has the desire and ability to give them justice. God is just and always does what is just. He is the one you should seek if you desire justice. As the prior verse (29:25) states, you are much better off in life when you put your trust in God.

Even the ruler's heart is in God's hand. So you may run to one who is in authority, but never do so without first knowing and trusting that it is from the Lord that one gets justice. It is from the Lord that you will get what you seek, and He is sovereign.

Whatever steps you take to get justice, know where it comes from and trust Him.

September 30 – Read Proverbs 30

v. 17 The eye that mocks a father and scorns to obey a mother will be picked out by the ravens of the valley and eaten by the vultures.

What a horrible picture lies before us: eyes picked out by ravens and eaten by vultures. It sounds like something out of a horror picture. It certainly is not something I would prefer to see with my eyes. It is not something a child would choose for her end.

The warning here is to children who would do such things as these. Children who mock or scorn their parents open themselves up to the punishment of God. Children who have no respect for parental authority will face the supreme authority, God. Yet as we get closer to the return of the Lord, the Bible predicts this kind of thing happening in families more and more. It is nothing new.

We see all through the Bible children acting in such ways. One such example would be that of the sons of Eli as found in 1 Samuel. They did not obey their father, and were punished by God. They died at the hands of the Philistines. That family serves both as an example of bad parenting and children who reject parental authority.

Children must not mock their father or scorn their mother. This is the warning found here and in many biblical passages. Children who do so will face a <u>certain</u> future which includes God's judgment. Sadly, parents themselves often teach their children to do such things by their own actions. But, what each one of us does is our own responsibility for which we will have to give an answer to God.

Respect your parents by not mocking or scorning them.

October 1 – Read Proverbs 1

v. 28 Then they will call upon me, but I will not answer; they will seek me diligently but will not find me.

There is a point at which we can seek but not find. Someone may say that could never happen with God for He is so gracious. While it is true that God's graciousness goes beyond what we can fathom, this statement is still true.

Here, it is wisdom that has called out (v20) but has been rejected. It has called out continuously (v. 22), but has continuously been rejected. Now those who have rejected it will seek it but not find it. They will even be "diligent" in their search, but it is too late. I have seen it so often, far too many times in my ministry. Wisdom calls out, and God's truth is being put right in front of people, but it is rejected.

It reminds me of parents who have been taught and warned about how to raise their young children but have not listened. Now their children are teenagers or older, and their life is a mess, and their relationship with mom and dad is a mess. At this point, parents come running and say, "Fix my teen." Sadly, they still do not realize that the teen, though a problem, is not the real one who needs help.

When God's wisdom comes knocking at your door - don't reject it. When God's truth is preached and taught - don't fall asleep. The wisdom you need may be right before your eyes many times, but if you reject it, you may reach a point where it will pass you by and you will no longer be able to find it.

Listen to the wisdom of God today, for tomorrow may be too late.

October 2 – Read Proverbs 2

v. 18 for her house sinks down to death, and her paths to the departed;
v. 19 none who go to her come back, nor do they regain the paths of life.

Have you ever thought of it this way? What I mean is this, have you ever thought of the result of adultery in these terms? The context of these verses is adultery. The context of chapter two is seeking wisdom so that it will save you from the "forbidden woman," or man, for that matter. Here it is "woman" because he is talking to his son about avoiding adultery, but the same is true for women who would commit adultery with married men.

Hollywood often makes adultery and immorality look good, like something you would want to be involved in doing. But, this is not the case here. Look how ugly and how dangerous it can be: "her house sinks down to death," "her paths to the departed," "none who go to her come back," "nor do they regain the paths of life." It is clear that death waits for those who commit adultery. As we have seen people often die physically because of adultery - from diseases to someone killing them because of their actions. Spiritually, it may also lead to death. God expresses, in no uncertain terms, that He hates and will judge the sexual immoral.

People in our day have taken a light view of sexual immorality. God does not! The Bible is full of passages like the ones for today that express His view of immorality.

Run from immorality! Run fast! Run far!

October 3 - Read Proverbs 3

v. 27 Do not withhold good from those to whom it is due, when it is in your power to do it.

v. 28 Do not say to your neighbor, "Go, and come again, tomorrow I will give it"— when you have it with you.

Why is it that we are often ready to "give it" (v. 29-30) to someone, but so slow to "do good" for someone? When it is within our power to give someone something good who deserves it, why is it that so often people don't do it? Believers who have been the recipients of God's grace and mercy should not have to be told to go and do good.

We should be excited every time we have an opportunity to help someone. There is no just cause to withhold something good especially from someone who deserves it. God calls us to a generous walk with our neighbors. One of the problems we may face with this issue is that of selfishness. Sometimes people think things like, "Why should they get it when I can't get it?" We need to learn to take ourselves out of the picture. We need to learn to be others - focused. No matter what has come our way, we need to live life looking for ways we can bring good into other people's lives. Far too often we look for whatever everyone can do for us instead of what we can do for them.

In fact, this thought is so strong that God tells us to do it today and don't wait till tomorrow (v. 28). How would our world change if every believer prayed, "Lord, don't let my eyes touch my pillow tonight without having done something good for someone today."

Find something good you can do for someone today and do it.

October 4 - Read Proverbs 4

v. 7 The beginning of wisdom is this: Get wisdom, and whatever you get, get insight.

If you are on a journey, there is a starting place and an ending place. There is the place you take your first step and the place you take your last step. This father makes it easy for his sons (v. 1) for their journey towards wisdom. He starts with the first step: "...Get wisdom... get insight."

If you want to be wise, you must you must make up your mind to go get it. If you want to be wise, you must strive to acquire it. It is clear from Proverbs that though people talk of wanting to be wise, many people just don't do what it takes to get it. The assumption we can take from this is that they really don't want it or are unwilling to pay the price to get it. The very next verse tells us to prize her highly but it would seem that many people just don't do that. We are told so much about wisdom's availability in this book. In fact, we are told that over and over in the rest of God's Word. God tells us to ask Him for it and He will give it generously. He tells us that His Word will make us wise, wiser than most people. Yet, so few people pray and so few people regularly spend time in His Word.

The first step of our journey on the path toward wisdom is to want it. It is there for you, do you really want it?

Get wisdom: pray, dig into His Word and learn from the trials He brings you through.

October 5 - Read Proverbs 5

v. 23 He dies for lack of discipline, and because of his great folly he is led astray.

It is interesting to learn what destroys a life, for by learning it we can avoid the same pitfall. Examples are either good or bad. They say to us, "Come here, follow me." Or, they are a warning to us and say, "Run as fast as you can the other way and don't do what I did."

Here we see a man who committed adultery. He left the wife of his youth having neglected the commitment he made before God when he married. The temptation to do this is all over this world, inviting both men and women to do that which God condemns. This world sees nothing wrong with it, but God says that His judgment will come because of it (Ephesians 5:1-7).

The interesting thing is seeing what caused this man to mess up so badly. God says that it came because of his lack of self-control. In other words, when temptation came, he did not have the discipline to say, "No!" If you do a study of God's Word on this subject you will see that lack of discipline is at the root of mankind's sins. The reality is that in this world temptation will come. There is no way to avoid every temptation. So we need to learn to be able to have the discipline to say no. If you look at your life and see yourself as undisciplined, you are in a dangerous position (Proverbs 25:28). You must turn to God for help or you may fall prey to all sorts of sin.

Discipline yourself and keep yourself under control (1 Corinthians 9:24-27)

October 6 - Read Proverbs 6

v. 26 for the price of a prostitute is only a loaf of bread, but a married woman hunts down a precious life.

This verse is a warning against becoming involved in adultery or involved with a prostitute. There are many warnings against this activity. This adds to all of those. With so many warnings, one would wonder why so many do not listen and head straight into danger. The context of this warning deals with the issue of lust (v. 20-35).

This warning speaks of being brought down to nothing including the loss of one's wealth. With adultery, even prostitution, comes divorce, lawsuits, sexually transmitted diseases and all sorts of negative consequences including public disgrace (5:14). Everything a person has can be lost in a moment of undisciplined insanity. While, upfront, sin may seem very inviting, the end result does not deliver what was promised in the beginning. The adulterer is risking his wealth. This warning is no small warning. It is a warning that shouts, "Stop in your tracks! Don't take another step! Run as fast as you can in the opposite direction!"

Even with this warning, some will brush it off as of little consequence. They will run forward, willing to take the risk, maybe not even believing the warning. Yet, the result will still be the same. There are many examples in history and more will come in the future of the stupidity of not heeding the warning. Hopefully those who read this warning today will not be among the mighty throng (7:25-27) of those who were unwilling to listen.

Heed the warning; don't put your wealth and life at risk in this way.

October 7 - Read Proverbs 7

v. 23 till an arrow pierces its liver; as a bird rushes into a snare; he does not know that it will cost him his life.

Having been a hunter, I know what happens when something pierces the liver. It kills, but it does so in a slow agonizing way. No hunter ever wants to shoot any animal in the liver. Even the bird that gets caught in a snare is going to die. So the man who gets involved in adultery is risking his very life.

The context here is that of adultery. It brings the warning of yesterday to an even stronger height: It warns that adultery risks not only one's wealth but one's very life. This very warning is found throughout the book of Proverbs and the rest of God's Word. One may ask how death is possible from adultery. There is the risk of disease. There is also the risk of jealousy (6:34-35). I once even heard of an adulterer being run over by his own wife for his actions. In fact, she ran over him seven times if I remember correctly. Then, there is the possibility of the direct judgment of God. Even worse is the judgment of God that can come for all eternity (1 Corinthians 6:9-10).

Warnings come in all sorts of ways. None can be stronger than the warning that says your very life could be in danger. Why would anyone want to risk their life for something that does not deliver what was promised?

Don't risk your life for that which is not worth your life.

October 8 - Read Proverbs 8

v. 20 I walk in the way of righteousness, in the paths of justice,

One may ask, "What are the characteristics of wisdom?" Or, "What does wisdom look like?' People often make claims of wisdom, but does the reality prove the claim?

Here wisdom is personified as speaking. It is telling us what its path looks like. It is giving us two characteristics of what is true of the path of wisdom. Let's look at the first one – righteousness. Any path that you take that lays claim to wisdom must be a path that also is righteous. Wisdom and righteousness go hand in hand. An immoral path is not a path of wisdom. For example, 1 Thessalonians 4, Ephesians 5, 1 Corinthians 6 and many other passages warn against immorality, saying it will bring God's judgment. Therefore, any person who would lived an immoral lifestyle is not very wise. Those who would claim to be wise and mock those who are sexually moral show their own foolishness, not wisdom. How can you lay any claim to wisdom if at the same time you head down a road that leads to God's judgment?

The second characteristic is that of justice. Justice speaks of fairness. Fairness is based, not on riches, popularity or any other such thing, but on God's truth. Wisdom is influenced only by what God declares to be fair. Life may not be fair, but you must be, if you lay any claim to wisdom.

Therefore, a wise walk is one which is both righteous and just. Take note of your walk today. Will these two characteristics be true of you?

Take the wise path today, one which is both righteous and just.

October 9 - Read Proverbs 9

v. 18 But he does not know that the dead are there, that her guests are in the depths of Sheol.

Once again it is boldly stated. Once again we are told of the results of sexual immorality. The context in verses 13-18 is that of sexual immorality. Once I was told, "The Bible has much talk of sexual immorality, talk of things people do not talk about." Yet, you just need to go to Genesis 6 and you will see that it did not take long in human history for man to become very immoral.

The warning against immoral sexual behavior needs to be shouted from the roof tops because it is a warning that needs to be heard. Sadly, few are listening. Just look at the explosion of sexually immoral websites on the Internet. It did not take long for mankind to mess the internet up. That is what we humans do. We take the blessings of God and turn them into rebellion against God. The warning against sexual immorality in our verse and in this context is that it leads to death. See also 2:18-19; 7:27. People have taken something (sex) that God gave us for pleasure and turned it into death. We need to listen to the warning.

First Corinthians 6:13 tells us that, "...The body is not meant for sexual immorality...." We are constantly bombarded with invitations to this kind of immoral behavior, but as 1 Corinthians 6:18 says, we must flee. The invitation may seem inviting but you must understand that it leads to death.

Sexually immoral behavior leads to death, so flee from it.

October 10 - Read Proverbs 10

v. 20 The tongue of the righteous is choice silver; the heart of the wicked is of little worth.

The tongue and heart are linked throughout God's Word. You just need to go and look at what Jesus said in Matthew 15:16-20 where He said that the words found on the tongue come from the heart. Now the tongue can try to hide the heart, but sooner or later it gives the heart away. Here they are linked and parallel.

The thought is that there is value in listening to the righteous. Their words, like choice silver, are rare and valuable. The righteous are not perfect and neither are their words. Yet, their words, generally speaking, are well worth hearing. The righteous tend to speak words of wisdom (v. 21). The righteous speak with biblical thinking and speak of biblical truth.

Not so the wicked. The wicked, generally speaking, have nothing worth hearing. The wicked speak of things that are contrary to God's truth. Their philosophy of life, their wisdom, and their manner of life are all set against God's truth. Their words, listened to long enough, will draw you away from God's Wisdom.

In this world you will hear the wicked talk constantly. This being true, you need to counterbalance that by spending time with the righteous. The more you spend time with the righteous, the more you will hear things of value and the better off you will be for it. The more you spend time with the wicked, the more you will hear things that are of little worth.

Spend time with the righteous, for their words are valuable.

October 11 - Read Proverbs 11

v. 25 Whoever brings blessing will be enriched, and the one who waters will himself be watered.

The context of this verse is verses 23-26. It concerns sowing and reaping. Of course, the most recognizable verse on this subject is Galatians 6:7, "Do not be deceived: God is not mocked, for whatever one sows, that will he also reap."

This verse states the positive side of the story, as do the others in the context here. Verse 23 says, "The desire of the righteous ends only in good…." Verse 24 states, "One gives freely, yet grows richer…" Verse 26 continues, "…but a blessing is on the head of him who sells it (grain)." Verse 27 also says, "Whoever diligently seeks good seeks favor…"

There are many ways that this truth has been stated throughout history. For example, it has been said, "What goes around comes around." The basic idea is that doing good to others will come back on you. It simply states a general principle of life. When you do good to others, good will return to you.

This is not meant to be some sort of selfish motivation for doing good. In fact, when you do good for the sole purpose of getting good, it does not work. But, when you are good to others, or as stated in this verse, "brings blessing" or "waters," it will come back on you. As stated earlier, it is the principle of sowing and reaping. Though we live is a world so infected by sin, this principle is still valid.

Bless somebody today!

October 12 - Read Proverbs 12

v. 24 The hand of the diligent will rule, while the slothful will be put to forced labor.

This is another verse that speaks to the issue of hard work versus laziness. From Genesis to the book of Revelation, from creation on earth to eternity in Heaven, the Bible speaks and illustrates the reality of man working. Some seem to want to find a way around this truth.

Find yourself in a crowd of people working on a project. If you take the time to look around, you will find people who work hard at not working hard. Some people will find ways to get out of work. Some people are lazy right down to their very bones. There are all sorts of reasons for this, but whatever the reason, God makes clear that laziness is not good.

Even here we find great value in working diligently, "the diligent will rule." While we also see the ugly results of laziness, "the slothful will be put to forced labor." The picture given is that there is value in hard work and that those who don't want to work will eventually be forced to do that which they so badly wished to avoid.

So we learn that those who work diligently will find themselves on top while those who are slothful will find themselves on the bottom. As I said, this is the way it has always been and always will be. Those who are unwilling to work may at times get things for nothing, but they will find that slothfulness reaps unpleasant results.

Be diligent and avoid laziness for laziness brings no good thing.

October 13 - Read Proverbs 13

v. 8 The ransom of a man's life is his wealth, but a poor man hears no threat.

I have found in life that wealthy people are often unhappy and that those who are poor are often wishing for wealth so they can find happiness. They don't know that wealth does not give what so many think it offers.

Sure there are some advantages in having money, but there are disadvantages. The advantages don't necessarily outweigh the disadvantages, either. We find an advantage to having wealth in this verse. If you have a lot of money, and your life is ransomed, you may be able to pay the price. That certainly is an advantage to having great wealth. Yet, the unstated reality is that one's very wealth is the cause of the threat.

Notice that a poor man "hears no threat." No one seeks to ransom a poor man because they know he can't afford to pay the price. There would be no reward in taking a poor man for what would you gain? Of course, the argument made here is purely hypothetical for an action such as this is never rewarding. But, the argument being made is that there are advantages and disadvantages to being poor and wealthy. One is not better than the other. Seeking to be rich, thinking that it is the cure for all the ills of man, is pure nonsense. Don't get caught up in this kind of thinking.

Beware of the flawed beliefs concerning wealth.

October 14 – Read Proverbs 14

v. 34 Righteousness exalts a nation, but sin is a reproach to any people.

All men everywhere have their ideas of what is good for a country. In history, we have seen many forms of government, each group thinking that theirs was the best form. There are many ways we can approach this question of government, but there is one thing of which we can be sure: Right living matters!

There is something that will lift a country up, and that same thing absent will destroy a country. "Righteousness" is that thing. This is true because there is a God. God desires that men live righteously and when they do, He blesses them and their country. If there is one thing that people ought to think about looking for in their leaders, this is it. They should look for leaders who live this way and leaders who seek a society that is based on righteous living.

The opposite is also true. Any people who seek leaders who will live and do that which is contrary to God's Word are seeking leaders who will destroy their country. The Bible is full of countries, and so is history, whose people have sought to rebel against God and have in so doing destroyed their countries. One such example is Sodom and Gomorrah (Genesis 18-19). They rebelled against God's moral laws and the judgment of God fell on them.

Far more important then finances, health care, and all sort of other issues is what will a country do in relation to God's moral laws. Many issues are important, as those just mentioned, but God's moral issues top the list.

It is God who causes one country to rise and another to fall, so seek what is right in His eyes.

October 15 – Read Proverbs 15

v. 32 Whoever ignores instruction despises himself, but he who listens to reproof gains intelligence.

There are some choices in life that if made are made to one's own peril. These choices show that people despise or hate themselves. Some choices are obvious, but some not so much.

Here we have an example of the choices that once made, show people despise or hate themselves. The example we find here is that of not listening to instruction, which may come in the form of a reproof. There are some people who are unwilling to respond to a rebuke, even when done in complete love. We have seen elsewhere in Proverbs that some people may attack the person who rebukes them (9:7-9). We must get past these kinds of responses.

When a rebuke comes our way, we must be receptive to it up front. We should then take the rebuke and consider it. We must meditate on it and determine its value, considering who gave it, the intent with which it was given, and the content of it. Proverbs says a great deal of good about the person who listens to a rebuke and a great deal of bad about the person who does not. We see that very truth stated again here. Therefore, we must do all we can, with humility of heart, to consider a rebuke which comes our way.

Treat yourself properly by listening to a rebuke and gaining intelligence.

October 16 – Read Proverbs 16

v. 28 A dishonest man spreads strife, and a whisperer separates close friends.

Here we see two of the worst kinds of speech that can come from the mouth of any person: lying and gossip. In speaking of these two sins, and that is what they are, we are pointed to the results of these two actions of the mouth.

Speaking of the first, we see that "dishonesty spreads strife." Hatred, anger and greed do the very same thing, according to Proverbs. When people pervert truth, that is to turn it upside down, they spread strife. Strife refers to quarrels. So, one who lies or distorts the truth spreads quarrels. It is like scattering seed, this person scatters quarreling all over the land. People have found all kinds of ways to lie, and to cover it up in their own minds, so that to them it is not considered lying. If you intentionally say something or leave something out with the purpose of giving the wrong impression, it is a lie. The result is not good, for by your actions, you cause quarrels for people who react based on those lies.

The second one stated here is the act of whispering or gossip, which refers to speaking in low tones so that you do not get caught while back-biting or slandering others. Your purpose is to hurt others by what you say. This kind of speech can separate even close friends. This kind of speech is so ugly, yet so powerful, that it can rip apart best friends.

Lying and Gossip, let neither one ever be upon your lips.

October 17 – Read Proverbs 17

v. 23 The wicked accepts a bribe in secret to pervert the ways of justice.

The courts of any land are the place where men should seek justice. Yet, it is the place, at times, where injustice takes place. It is a well-known fact that bribes can pervert justice in any court, in any land.

The point of this proverb is that the person who accepts the bribe is wicked. It is not talking about the person who offers the bribe, but the one who accepts it. Most people would agree that offering a bribe is wicked. At the same time, we should also realize that the one who accepts the bribes is just as wicked. I would think that this is also a well-known fact, but my fear is that maybe people justify receiving a bribe.

The point, in fact, is that God's moral standard is being revealed here. As God views it, the person who accepts a part in an evil scheme is as wicked as the person who thought up the wicked act. It does not matter why the person accepts the bribe. Whatever the reason, accepting a bribe perverts justice. Yet, more than that, the person who accepts the bribe is wicked. It is a statement of his character and a statement of God's view of such a person.

It is wicked to pervert anything that happens to a person who comes before the court seeking justice. All such actions are pure selfishness at the expense of some person and his family. All too often the guilty get away with evil while the innocent get convicted of that which they did not do.

Don't ever be involved in accepting evil actions to the harm of others.

October 18 – Read Proverbs 18

v. 19 A brother offended is more unyielding than a strong city, and quarreling is like the bars of a castle.

There are some truths that are simple and a known reality. This is one of them. It is a truth that must be considered in our actions towards each other. It must not be overlooked.

This is a warning to us all that we should be careful not to cause an offense. Once a person is offended, it is as hard to get through to that person as it would be to get through a strongly defended city.

It seems that relatives are so easily offended and so difficult to mend fences with. This is even more so when the offended person is a close relative, such as a brother. Further still, usually the nearer the relative, the greater the divide. The chain, once broken, is not easily fixed. I'm sure this is a truth that needs no convincing as to its validity.

You should take care in dealing with people, especially family members. Knowing how hard it is to fix these grievances, we should not cause them. It seems so often that we treat family members worse than others.

Yet, while all of this is true it should not stop you from a monumental effort of love to fix every broken relationship. Romans 12:18 tells us that if there is a broken relationship, it should not be your fault. Let the fault rest with the other person. Do all in your power to follow Matthew 18:15-17 to try to fix the relationship if possible.

Beware of offending others, especially family members.

October 19 – Read Proverbs 19

v. 8 Whoever gets sense loves his own soul; he who keeps understanding will discover good.

There are often things that we can do that have great benefit to ourselves. For example, eating right has great benefit to you as it will make you healthy. The same goes for regular exercise. It is also true that attending church on a regular basis will have great benefit in your life. The same goes for regular time spent in God's Word and in prayer. Many more examples could be given of things done in life that benefit the doer.

Here is such an idea. If you seek after and get sense (wisdom) it will benefit you. Wisdom is one of those things that has great value and is worth chasing after. Once gained, it will benefit you greatly. It is the opposite of some things in life that people chase after, but do not have the value they might think, such as wealth. The wisdom spoken of here is not worldly wisdom, but the wisdom that comes from God. It is of great value and has great value for the person who attains it.

Some people spend their whole lives chasing after things that just do not benefit them for the long term. The thought of this verse is to keep you from doing that and to show you what is worth chasing after. Life is so short and we waste so much time on things that just do not matter. This verse can guide you towards what is useful and keep you from what is not.

Chase after the wisdom of God and you will do yourself well.

October 20 – Read Proverbs 20

v. 3 It is an honor for a man to keep aloof from strife, but every fool will be quarreling.

It is good to know what to chase after and also what to steer far from. It is good to know which path to avoid and which one to take. In most things in life there is a way to take and a way to avoid.

Here we see a way to be avoided. Strife here refers to quarreling or disputes. A person who avoids quarrelling finds honor. Now, it is not avoiding quarreling at all costs. It is not running from anything which may lead to a quarrel. Some people do this and so stand for nothing and are unwilling to take a stand for that which is right. I think of the age-old saying, "All that it takes for evil to flourish is for good men to remain silent." On the other hand, honor is found in wisely dealing with situations and so avoiding quarrels. There are times when one has to take a stand even if quarreling may result.

The thing is that the wise in heart have no desire to quarrel, but fools are often getting into quarrels. They do not have the sense to avoid them, and once in them, often make them worse. So in general, we find wise people avoiding quarrels and foolish people quarreling. The way we should live our lives is like the wise and when we do, we will find honor! Any fool can quarrel, but it takes wisdom to avoid it.

Find honor in wisely avoiding quarrels, and so avoid the path of fools.

October 21 – Read Proverbs 21

v. 1 The king's heart is a stream of water in the hand of the LORD*; he turns it wherever he will.*

When you think of a king, you think of the most powerful man in that form of government. The king has control of his nation like no other. Yet, God has control of the king like no other. He can use the king to either flood or fertilize his fields. God is the hand behind the hand that moves the world.

God has used powerful men to do His bidding. He had used kings in the Bible like Nebuchadnezzar, Cyrus, Artaxerxes and Belshazzar. He has also used kings in extra-biblical history to do the same. It reminds me of a game that I played a lot with my wife when we were first married called *Risk*. You would sit and try to take over the world and use your armies to do your bidding to control the world. Yet, the world has always been in God's control. He used good and bad kings to do his work. No person, and no king, is above His authority for He is sovereign and in total control.

We must understand this truth and see the world with this in mind. Having understood this, you will better be able to deal with all that happens in this world, and not worry about the actions happening around you. You will have more peace knowing that God is at work in the events of the world, working things according to His plan and timetable. Nothing, and no one, is beyond His control.

Knowing God is at work in the leaders of the world, trust this world to His control.

October 22 – Read Proverbs 22

v. 2 The rich and the poor meet together; the Lord is the maker of them all.

It is often thought that the rich and poor have very little in common. When you look at the rich and poor, you would think that they have nothing in common. But they have one very important thing in common, among others, and it is that the Lord is maker of both.

They share a common origin, God. God's hand is behind both of them. The rich at times think they can treat the poor with disdain, but they should remember that God is their maker (14:31). The poor also sometimes treat the rich in the same way, but they should not forget that God is also their maker. There is often animosity between these two groups of people and people often try to use that to their advantage. People will often try to make that gap even wider. This is done without considering who the maker of both is. This is done without God in mind.

If you are poor, before you attack those who are rich, consider this truth. If you are rich, before you seek to treat the poor with contempt, don't neglect this truth. If you seek to use one group against the other, keep this truth in mind. Any action which omits this truth is done to the peril of those are at work. Whether you are a king, or rich, or poor, God's hand in your life is a certainty.

Be careful in your treatment of others, for God is the maker of all.

October 23 – Read Proverbs 23

v. 17 Let not your heart envy sinners, but continue in the fear of the LORD all the day.
v. 18 Surely there is a future, and your hope will not be cut off.

This world has been infected by sin. It permeates every part of it. It can be seen by looking at who gets ahead and who does not. Understanding this makes it easy to recognize that those who do not follow God often get ahead in life, and those who do, don't. It is a natural thing for a world so affected by sin.

This being true, one might tend to envy the wrong people. If you do not look at life with eternity in mind, you might look at those who do wrong, and envy them, but this would be a very dangerous mistake. Success in this world should not be the motivating factor in your life for doing right or wrong, or for following God or not. These two verses are a commentary on Psalm 73. Asaph did this very thing. He let his heart envy the arrogant, and it almost messed up his life. The only thing that saved him was entering the sanctuary of God and looking at life from an eternal perspective. He realized that the wicked, no matter how successful in this world, only had this world to live for. He made the right choice and turned to God, realizing that there was nothing on earth he desired besides God. To be near God was good enough for him. Having gained the whole world would be worthless without God.

Chose God over this world every single day!

October 24 – Read Proverbs 24

v.30 I passed by the field of a sluggard, by the vineyard of a man lacking sense,
v. 31 and behold, it was all overgrown with thorns; the ground was covered with nettles, and its stone wall was broken down.
v. 32 Then I saw and considered it; I looked and received instruction.
v. 33 A little sleep, a little slumber, a little folding of the hands to rest,
v. 34 and poverty will come upon you like a robber, and want like an armed man.

Passing by a field and seeing what had happened taught a lesson. The field was owned by a sluggard (a lazy person). It was owned by a man who lacked sense. He was a man who did not work the way he should have. Laziness will do the same as a robber who breaks into your house and steals all that you have. Either way, you end up with nothing, and it does not take much laziness. Note verse three and the repeating of the word "little."

This truth goes for one man, or many men, or even a whole nation. If a man or a nation loses its work ethic, it will begin a backward fall that is no different than if a robber breaks in and steals all that you have. Once you start giving things away for no work or little work so that people get something for nothing, the danger is there. People who lose the incentive to work will become their own destruction. They will lose what they have.

Do not let laziness steal away all that you have.

October 25 – Read Proverbs 25

v. 4 Take away the dross from the silver, and the smith has material for a vessel;
v. 5 take away the wicked from the presence of the king, and his throne will be established in righteousness.

What is the most important thing in a country? It is healthcare? Is it social security? Is it the economy? Or, is it some other issue that is often talked about during every election?

Going to the Word of God, the answer to this question is easy, very easy. The answer is that the single most important issue to any country is the issue of morality. The story of Sodom and Gomorrah tells us this. The story of Israel in the Old Testament tells us this. We know this from every country mentioned in the Bible and what happened to them. We know that from these verses right here. Proverbs 14:34 makes this truth clear.

When, as a country, we look to a new leader and walk into the voting booth, there is no issue more important than this one. When you are all alone and God's eyes are watching you, there is no more important matter than this one. This is the issue that will keep America moving forward, or will cause it to cease to exist. The leaders who began this country understood this, but many of the leaders today have lost sight of this, and so have many of the people who vote for a new leader. The truth of the verse five cannot be stated too strongly. The president and those who advise him must be concerned with honor and morality, or our country is in trouble. A wicked society can last only so long before the judgment of God comes.

Know that wickedness ensures God's coming judgment.

October 26 – Read Proverbs 26

v. 21 As charcoal to hot embers and wood to fire, so is a quarrelsome man for kindling strife.

A fire needs the right stuff to make it burn. By using charcoal or the right kind of wood you could have a blaze going. I have always loved building fires, from when I was a Boy Scout to the fireplace my in-laws had. The smell of wood burning in the summer at night is one thing I sure love. I can picture it in my mind, people sitting around a campfire at the edge of a lake, singing songs and cooking marshmallows.

On the other hand, the fire of a quarrel is not something that is good. Quarreling can be very ugly, especially in a church or a family. It can separate people and cause harm that endures for generations. A quarrelsome person is perfect for getting that kind of fire going. The quarreler feeds the fire and keeps it going. His temper makes the quarrel even worse (15:18). This kind of person needs to be kept away from quarrels. This kind of person needs to be kept in check during quarrels. This kind of person needs to look in the mirror and consider his actions when found in the midst of a situation which is headed in the wrong direction. Honestly looking at yourself and others when situations are turning troublesome can help in dealing with difficult issues. Using wisdom, when handing people, can keep life from turning ugly.

Be wise, and keep the quarrelsome person far from quarrels, if possible.

October 27 – Read Proverbs 27

v. 13 Take a man's garment when he has put up security for a stranger, and hold it in pledge when he puts up security for an adulteress.

Have you ever loaned money to someone to try to help him and never been paid back? This mistake happens to a lot of people, far too many people. The issue one must consider in loaning money is the person who is asking for the money and whether he is a worthy risk.

This proverb is almost a carbon copy of 20:16. The idea is that you must consider the character of the one who is receiving the money if you plan on getting your money back. There are certain people that a loan should not be given to without getting some kind of security to ensure you will be paid back. Here the security is the man's clothes or something that would guarantee you get paid back. If you are unwilling to do this, you run the risk of not getting your money back. I am of the opinion that we should not lend money unless we are willing to just give it to the person in question. In this case, it would not matter if you get paid back. Yet, if you want the money in question back and the person is a risk, get some kind of security for the loan. Banks do this all of the time. It puts more in your favor of getting your money back.

Security for loans makes sense, so get some if you loan money.

October 28 – Read Proverbs 28

Do morals matter when electing leaders? When going to the voting booth should we consider the moral values of those we elect? A careful reading of Proverbs 28 gives us the answer. Read Proverbs 28 looking for what is says about the morals of those for whom we vote and you will find the following:

v. 2 When a land transgresses, it has many rulers, but with a man of understanding and knowledge, its stability will long continue.

v. 4 Those who forsake the law praise the wicked, but those who keep the law strive against them.

v. 5 Evil men do not understand justice, but those who seek the LORD understand it completely.

v. 8 Whoever multiplies his wealth by interest and profit gathers it for him who is generous to the poor.

v. 12 When the righteous triumph, there is great glory, but when the wicked rise, people hide themselves.

v. 16 A ruler who lacks understanding is a cruel oppressor, but he who hates unjust gain will prolong his days.

v. 18 Whoever walks in integrity will be delivered, but he who is crooked in his ways will suddenly fall.

v. 28 When the wicked rise, people hide themselves, but when they perish, the righteous increase.

Morals matter, whether in private life, in public life or in government. We must consider a person's morals when it comes time to vote. Those who lead must be moral and must stand on proper morals or those who follow will reap the result.

Vote with morals/values in mind! Vote based on the principles of God's Word.

October 29 – Read Proverbs 29

v. 27 An unjust man is an abomination to the righteous, but one whose way is straight is an abomination to the wicked.

The righteous and the wicked can be contrasted in so many ways. One of these ways is the way they view each other. They see one another as an abomination. The word abomination here means someone or something that one detests, abhors, or loathes.

The thing that creates this separation between the two is that their paths are opposites. The wicked person's way is unjust, which means deviating from a right standard. The righteous person's way is straight, that is, it is one that follows the right standard. The standard is God's way or truth. So they each look at each other's lifestyle and it is repulsive.

The righteous and the wicked cannot see eye to eye on life because they are headed in opposite directions. Now for the righteous, the situation is different, for he used to be on the path of the wicked (Ephesians 2:1-10). So he knows all about this path and this path continually calls out to him to come back, and if he is not careful, he may heed the call.

The thing that has made the path of the wicked to be so repulsive to him is that he has come to understand the righteousness of God (Philippians 2). Having understood it, his old path had become an abomination. He must continue to keep his eyes on Christ so that his eyes do not become clouded.

Keep your eyes on Christ and the way of the wicked will be seen for what it is.

October 30 – Read Proverbs 30

v. 10 Do not slander a servant to his master, lest he curse you, and you be held guilty.

Slander is not good. It is something we should cleanse our mouths of. Our verse speaks of a slander of a specific kind, that of slandering a servant to his master. This kind of slander might be thought, by some, to be acceptable, but it is not.

In modern terms, we are talking about slandering a worker to his boss. The idea is that we should respect their relationship and not interfere. People need to learn what involves them and what is out of bounds for them. This is an example of what is out of bounds for one to get involved in. Here the concern is to protect the worker of unjust attacks from someone outside of the relationship. You are not involved and so you should not involve yourself. If you do, you will be accountable for the false charges. In this case, the curse is deserved, for your actions are wrong and uncalled for. People tend to meddle in things that do not involve them. The warning here is to stop.

There may be a variety of reasons why someone might take this kind of action. Maybe she is trying to get his job. Maybe, she does not like him and so is just trying to cause him trouble. And maybe, just maybe, she is evil. Whatever the reason, we are reminded here to mind our own business.

Don't meddle in things that do not involve you.

October 31 – Read Proverbs 31

v. 11 The heart of her husband trusts in her, and he will have no lack of gain.

A woman of value, a woman that a mother would choose for her son, is a woman who can be completely trusted. Trust is one of the characteristics that a relationship, a strong relationship, is built upon. Without it, there can be no intimacy in a marriage. This amazing chapter of an excellent wife begins its description with one of the most important attributes – trust.

If I were going to hire someone for a job, it is the first attribute I would seek. If I were going to go into battle with an enemy, it is the characteristic I would look for in those who stand at my side. So, certainly if I were looking for someone to spend the rest of my life facing the good times and bad, the sicknesses and health, the riches and poverty, trust would be high on the list. This is extremely important concerning the person to whom I would say, "I do."

Trust is needed for intimacy. Trust is essential to a great marriage. So, I think it is no accident that it is listed first in regard to the excellent wife. The term "trust" means to rely on, believe in, to have confidence in. When a young man finds this kind of woman, he is a long way toward finding a woman worthy of marrying. This is also true for a woman looking for a man. Being able to trust your wife in every area of life is an awesome thing. I know for I have found such a woman.

Young men, in considering whom you will marry, keep "trust" high on your list.

November 1 - Read Proverbs 1

v. 31 therefore they shall eat the fruit of their way, and have their fill of their own devices.

There is value is being wise. Wisdom benefits those who seek it and get it. Good things happen when a person gains wisdom and knowledge and also chooses to fear God. Fearing God is the place where wisdom and knowledge begin (1:7).

While this is so true, many reject it. Jesus said that those who are on the wise road are few (Matthew 7:13-14). Proverbs teaches that anyone can gain wisdom, but many reject it. The book of Proverbs is full of the benefits of gaining wisdom. Having read these devotions and the book of Proverbs for ten months, you have been able to learn these benefits. Yet, what happens to those who reject God's wisdom? This you have also read about. Even here in the first chapter of the book of Proverbs, we see the result of rejecting wisdom.

Those who reject wisdom, "... shall eat the fruit of their way and have their fill of their own devices." Stated simply, they will reap what they have sown. Every action has a reaction, even every lack of action. By neglecting to choose to be wise, one will walk in foolishness and reap the consequences. Verse 32 tells us that the person who rejects wisdom and so turns away from God will be destroyed. There are only two roads, one leads to life and the other leads to destruction.

Choose a relationship with God and gain wisdom and life.

November 2 - Read Proverbs 2

v. 20 So you will walk in the way of the good and keep to the paths of the righteous.

Is this what you want for your life? Do you want to do "good" and keep to a path that is "righteous?" Is this what you are after in life?

If you look at the context of this verse, you will notice that this is a result of getting wisdom (2:1-4). In fact, it is the 5th of five benefits of becoming wise that are mentioned in chapter two of Proverbs. Those who love God and desire to live for Christ want this to be true of their lives. It means more to them than success, riches, power or popularity. Living a life that walks in the way of good and keeps to the path of the righteous is so very important.

Yet, you must have known by this time that this is a promise of wisdom. And, wisdom is attained by those who are rightly related to God, seek it in prayer and spend much time in the Word of God. Why is it then that the thing believers want so desperately (wisdom) which is found by spending much time in the Word of God, finds believers spending so little time in the Word of God?

There may be several answers to this question. But here, it may be simply stated that if we want these things to be true of our walk, it takes daily time in the Word of God, receptive and prayerful digging.

If you desire a righteous walk, spend time in God's Word.

November 3 - Read Proverbs 3

v. 29 Do not plan evil against your neighbor, who dwells trustingly beside you.
v. 30 Do not contend with a man for no reason, when he has done you no harm.

How a person treats his neighbors is a sign of whether a person knows God. Take a seat on a street corner anywhere in the world and watch how a person deals with his neighbors, and you will learn who knows God and who does not. Watch a traffic jam and see who sits on their car horn or who is yelling at the street workers, and you will learn a lot about their relationship with God.

What does your dealings with your neighbors say about you? If your first reaction to the question is to berate your neighbors while defending your own actions, you are already revealing your heart. God tells us what he expects of us concerning how we treat our neighbors. Here we are told how to treat someone who has trusted us and done us no harm. Alford Plummer once said, "To return evil for good is devilish; to return good for good is human and to return good for evil is divine." The statements we find in these two verses are statements of the obvious, but nonetheless need to be stated. God wants us to know that we should never do harm to people who trust us and have not harmed us. Our neighbors should be able to trust that the one who follows Christ would never do them wrong.

Live in such a way that your neighbors may never be sorry for having trusted you.

November 4 - Read Proverbs 4

v. 2 for I give you good precepts; do not forsake my teaching.

The vast majority of the proverbs found in Proverbs are teachings of a father to his son. Look at the first verse of chapter two through verse seven and you will see this. You will also notice this in many other places in Proverbs. Here we see a father, Solomon, talking to his son and encouraging him to listen to him and to not reject what he tells him.

Solomon was the wisest man who ever lived except for Jesus. The wealth of sitting and listening to him would be tremendous. He talked to his son about everything from morality to money. It would have been an awesome thing to sit and listen to a father with such wisdom. It would be great to be able to sit with our children and be just that wise and be able to teach them proverbs that were just as full of wisdom as his.

Wait one minute! You can! God made sure that the proverbs Solomon taught his children were written down and preserved for every dad and mom living today. You have a wealth of information before you, overflowing with wisdom, just waiting for parents to saturate the minds and hearts of children today. Parents are filling the minds of their children with all sorts of things today, from books to the TV. Some of it has value and some of it is pure junk. But Dads and Moms, why miss out on the chance to fill your child's mind and heart with the wisest sayings of all?

In this book sits the proverbs of the wisest of the wise, teach them to your children.

November 5 - Read Proverbs 5

v. 16 Should your springs be scattered abroad, streams of water in the streets?
v. 17 Let them be for yourself alone, and not for strangers with you.

We are living in a society where many children have never seen their fathers and many children do not know who their fathers are. How sad! Why is this happening? It is happening because of the rampant sexual immorality that is taking place in our society.

Proverbs 5 may be one of the most important chapters in the Bible for men on how to avoid sexual immorality. It is a warning to men about the consequences of committing adultery. The principles can also be applied to women, but this is a chapter where a father is speaking to his son about being a moral man. We need more of this happening today in our country.

The part of this warning we find in these verses pertains to children. The warning to men is that they make sure that their children are not shared with others as a result of committing adultery. "Springs" is a reference to children. It may refer to children men have with the adulteress or children they have with their wives, or both, who are then shared with others because of divorce. Either way this happening is never a good thing. It leaves destroyed lives all over the place.

The temptations to sexual sin comes in many different forms, but whatever form they take, the Bible makes clear that you should run from them (1 Corinthians 6:18). The temptation may look good at first, but as these verses tell us, the end result of sexual sin is very ugly.

Flee sexual immorality. Why destroy children?

November 6 - Read Proverbs 6

v. 29 So is he who goes in to his neighbor's wife; none who touches her will go unpunished.

No, it can't be. No one would believe it, at least, not those who live according to the life-style of Hollywood. TV shows and movies all seem to indicate that free morality with no moral standard is the way to go. Many within this way of thinking would say that to think any other way is stupid.

Here is what God says, "none who touches her will go unpunished." Now there are many in our world who would say that this statement is simply not true. But here is what God says in Ephesians 5:6, "Let no one deceive you with empty words, for because of these things the wrath of God comes upon the sons of disobedience." Additionally, here is what God says in 1 Thessalonians 4:8, "Therefore whoever disregards this, disregards not man but God..." So what we learn is that God will deal with sexual immorality and those who practice such a life-style will be punished. No one will escape!

The only hope a person who has been involved in sexual immorality has is to repent of his or her sin and turn to God for forgiveness. Anything short of this will result in God's punishment - period. God has set a moral standard and there is no such thing as grayness when it comes to sex. This is one of the reasons America is in such danger.

Know this: Those who are sexually immoral will be punished.

November 7 - Read Proverbs 7

v. 26 for many a victim has she laid low, and all her slain are a mighty throng.

We look back to the days of Noah and see what God did to a world that turned its back on Him. We see what happened to Sodom whose morals were missing. We remember King David who at one point was a man after God's heart. We are even reminded of Solomon who God used to write the book of Proverbs. We even can look to Samson for an example.

As we look at all of these examples, and many more, we see this verse proven true. It is not just weak men who fall. Strong moral men have fallen to such sin. It has been men who have been in the wrong place at the wrong time. It has been men who have taken their eyes off of the goal. It is men who have, even but for a moment, lost sight of righteousness. And, it has not just been men.

Temptation is common to us all. We need to take steps to make sure that we do not give in to its lure. We must never lose sight of the fact that sin, sexual sin, is never right. This is yet another warning to avoid sexual sin –"her slain are a mighty throng." How many warnings do we need?

Jesus said that we need to "watch and pray" so that we do not give in to temptation. Daily, stay in His Word, and come before the throne of grace.

Heed the warning and don't be numbered among those who have been slain.

November 8 - Read Proverbs 8

v. 5 O simple ones, learn prudence; O fools learn sense.

Do we always have to remain where we are at? Or, do we have to wait until we are white-haired before we move forward? What I mean is this: Do we have to wait until we are old before we become wise? Do we have to go through the entire "school of hard knocks" before we learn sense?

The truth is that we do not have to and that we can become wise long before then. Wisdom calls out to everyone and invites us to become wise. We do not have to remain in a state of foolishness only to pass it once we are old and gray. In fact, even then, some don't get there.

As we have seen, there are a number of ways we can gain wisdom. For example, learning from God's Word (Psalm 119:97-104), gaining from life's trials and asking God (James 1). In Psalm 119, the writer tells us that he was wiser than his enemies, teachers and even the aged because of the Word of God. Wisdom, true wisdom, comes from God.

The so-called wisdom of the world does not stand up to the wisdom of God. Wisdom is not found in some secret place where only a few can find it. Therefore, we all can get it if we really want it and are willing to put in the effort to get it. Ask God for it, go to His Word and learn from the trials He brings you through.

Seek wisdom in the right places, and you will gain it.

November 9 - Read Proverbs 9

v. 17 "Stolen water is sweet, and bread eaten in secret is pleasant."

In chapter nine we find a contrasting offer between Wisdom and Folly. They both speak as a woman and each offer what they have to give. The first is wisdom and the offer is found in v. 1-12. The second is folly and the offer is found in v. 13-18.

What we read in this verse is folly speaking of the value of what she has to offer. The major offer of folly and why you should choose it is found here. People fall for the lie over, and over, and over. It is sad, but people buy into this line of reasoning. In fact, you may have at some point bought into it too. You may have bought into it many times, most have.

What folly is saying is that her offering is exciting and satisfying. And, to a point, this is true of sin, if it were not, people would not be so quick to rush into it. There is a certain sense in which doing things with the possibility of being caught lends an excitement to the activity, in this case, to sinful activity. Here stolen water and bread may be a reference to sinful sexual activity. This sometimes happens with couples when they get involved in sexual immorality and then get married. They sometimes find that the passion is gone once married and wonder why. It is just one more way in which sexual immorality destroys those who choose it.

Don't let the excitement of sin lure you into rebelling against God.

November 10 - Read Proverbs 10

v. 24 What the wicked dreads will come upon him, but the desire of the righteous will be granted.

Ever see things going in the opposite directions? I have. I saw the football team I did not especially like winning and the one I loved losing. I have seen some succeed while others have failed. Here we see people going in opposite directions

Notice, "What the wicked dreads will come upon him" but "the desire of the righteous will be granted." We are not told what the wicked dread. But, we are told in 11:23 that their expectations will end in wrath (God's judgment). Hebrews 10:26-29 tells us that the wicked will face judgment at the end of their lives. It may be that the thing the wicked dread is God's judgment. Either way, what he fears, God will bring upon him (Isaiah 66:4). In the end, the wicked will be punished.

Yet, in the opposite direction, the righteous will get what they desire. Though it sometimes does not seem that way, God will give the righteous what they desire. If I may speak without pride, I know what the righteous desire. They desire to be with God. They desire to be in Heaven worshipping God. They desire to be removed from the curse of sin. They desire to see their Savior and praise Him for all eternity. In the end the righteous will be rewarded.

Don't be fooled, in the end the righteous, not the wicked, will get the desires of their hearts.

November 11 - Read Proverbs 11

v. 26 The people curse him who holds back grain, but a blessing is on the head of him who sells it.

There are two ways to live life. One way is the way of selfishness and the other is the way of selflessness. Sadly, I would say, most choose the first. I would also say that most don't see themselves as having chosen the first.

I see selfishness all of the time in my pastoral duties. I certainly see it outside of the church, but even inside of the church. Selfishness comes in many degrees, from those who are sometimes selfish, to those who are totally selfish. It can be seen in those who only want to talk about themselves and their issues and don't hear a word others say. It can be seen in those who only want to do what makes them happy and don't have time for others unless it makes them happy. It can be seen in those who are loners (18:1). And, as we see here, it can be seen in those who "hold back grain" meaning they think of themselves first.

What should be noticed in this verse is the reaction to these two ways of life. People "curse" those who are selfish. It may not always be verbally stated but people do not like selfish people. Selfish people often have no friends for the very fact that they are selfish. These kinds of people wonder why they don't have friends and usually blame others for the lack of friendship.

Reject selfishness! Choose to be selfless for the selfless are the ones who are blessed.

November 12 - Read Proverbs 12

v. 25 Anxiety in a man's heart weighs him down, but a good word makes him glad.

No one needs to be convinced of the truth in the first half of this verse. We all know what anxiety does to us. "Anxiety" means worry, or today we might use the term stress. Anxiety makes us discouraged and disheartened. It makes us feel like we have a 100 pound weight on our shoulders.

There is much in God's Word about how to deal with worry. Passages like 1 Peter 5:7 and Philippians 4:4-13 come to mind to help us with the problem of anxiety. Here in Proverbs we are given a very practical weapon to help fight the battle of anxiety. The help here is not for the person who is worried but for those who would help such a person. Their help may even include using the verses stated above.

The help here is that of a "good word." The right word at the right time can help a person who is burdened down with worry. The right word can make the anxious person "glad." This is what we all need to know. We can help people who are hurting from anxiety and stress. Yet to do this, we must look beyond our own hurts and see the needs of others. We need to spend our day looking to comfort rather than to be comforted (2 Corinthians 1). This is the very thing that God has called us to do and what we are told here will work.

Look for an opportunity to give a good word to a heart that is weighed down with anxiety.

November 13 - Read Proverbs 13

v. 5 The righteous hates falsehood, but the wicked brings shame and disgrace.

Does truth matter? This is a question that certainly needs to be asked. We are living in a day when it seems that most people just don't care about truth. In fact, many people do not believe there is such a thing as absolute truth. People believe that truth is just different shades of gray and that truth is dependant on how you look at issues. People believe that you can totally disagree on a given issue and both still have truth on your side.

Why have we come to this place in history? Might it be that we are here because people have also lost a desire for righteousness? Righteousness and truth go hand in hand, and you can't have one without the other. So, if we lose righteousness then we lose truth. The righteous hate falsehood (a false word or action) and love truth, but this is not true of the wicked. One contrast between the righteous and the wicked is seen in their concern for truth. The wicked have no problem with falsehood and so bring shame (shame - cause to stink) and disgrace on themselves and others.

The righteous hate falsehood because God hates falsehood (12:22). The wicked have no relationship with God so to them the issue is mute. See how a person deals with falsehood and truth and you have a window into their soul. What does your view of truth and falsehood say about your soul? Do you loosely play with the two, or like God, do you hate falsehood and love the truth.

Don't be put to shame by falsehood – hate it!

November 14 – Read Proverbs 14

v. 29 Whoever is slow to anger has great understanding, but he who has a hasty temper exalts folly.

We all get angry at one time or another. Sometimes that anger is sinful and sometimes it is not. Anger is an emotion given to us by God to help create energy so that we may find solutions and solve issues. One must use it with great care and wisdom.

Here we have a contrast between two ways of using anger. One way is to be slow in getting angry and the other is to be quick in getting angry. If you have read God's Word, even in little bits, especially Proverbs, you know that the first is the right use of anger. God's tells us to be slow in getting angry. It is the fool who gets angry in haste. This verse tells us "slow anger" shows understanding or wisdom.

"Hasty anger" displays folly or foolishness. If you fly off the handle, as some people call it, you are acting like a fool. If every little thing sets you off, as others call it, you are acting like a fool. If you get angry fast, it shows that you have no or little self-control. If you get angry in this way, you have sinned and played the fool and most likely you have done or said some things which you wish you had not.

You must learn to control yourself. You must learn the truth about yourself and what God says concerning your anger. The Bible says, "Be angry and sin not."

Slow down, that is, slow down your anger.

November 15 - Read Proverbs 15

V22 Without counsel plans fail, but with many advisers they succeed.

Everyone wants to succeed, yet some do and some don't. There are reasons for that. One of the reasons is that the ones who succeed seek and listen to advice. Usually those who don't succeed are those who think they know it all and are above the help of others. They believe they can do everything without anyone.

Not seeking and taking advice is the way of those who do not succeed. Proverbs 12:15 says, "The way of a fool is right in his own eyes, but a wise man listens to advice." And, Proverbs 26:12 says, "Do you see a man who is wise in his own eyes? There is more hope for a fool than for him." It is wise to seek counsel knowing that two or more heads put together tend to be better than one all by itself. For example Proverbs 20:18 says, "Plans are established by counsel; by wise guidance wage war." And also Proverbs 11:14 states, "Where there is no guidance, a people falls, but in an abundance of counselors there is safety."

There are so many variables in life. There are so many possibilities to deal with. Life is so uncertain. We need to help each other. God has created us for community but pride or selfishness often keeps us from it. People try to go through life on their own and miss the value of what God is doing in all of us. Counsel from advisors has great value.

Seek and be receptive to advice, it will help you on the road to success.

November 16 – Read Proverbs 16

v. 26 A worker's appetite works for him; his mouth urges him on.

Find someone who is hungry and you will often find a person who is more ready to work than someone who is full of food. A person who is hungry, and who knows the only way to eat is to work, is driven by his hunger.

There is nothing wrong with people sometimes being hungry and out of food. That hunger will work for that person. Some people think that hunger is the worst thing that could ever happen to anyone. The truth is that hunger can work in a very positive way by driving the hungry person to working for his food. This is why the vast majority of people in the world go to work each day. So, even an empty stomach can be useful in people's lives.

Having said that, I also know some people are so lazy that they would rather starve than work. In fact, I have seen people wanting food work harder to get it by begging than if they went out and got a real job. But, even though they may not work a real job, they are doing something because they are driven by an empty stomach.

I think sometimes we are too quick to jump in and help and so we cause people to learn wrong actions such as begging for food. They learn wrong ways of getting their needs met. Being needy, being hungry, is the very thing that God has put within us to cause us to do the right thing.

Know that hunger can have a positive influence in a person's life.

November 17 – Read Proverbs 17

v. 5 Whoever mocks the poor insults their maker; he who is glad at calamity will not go unpunished.

There are many reasons why a person may be poor. Laziness is a very bad reason, but there are a number of reasons that may not be in a person's control. One such reason may be a poor economy.

Sadly, there are some among us who would look down on and even ridicule the poor. There are some who want nothing to do with the poor and try to keep a path far from them. Those who would be part of this group must understand that doing these kinds of things and more, insults not just the poor but their Maker. Insulting their Maker is a very grave action indeed, for their Maker is none other than God (22:2). It is not that God makes them poor, but that God is the Maker or Creator of all men, including the poor and the rich. So when you insult any person whom God created, you are insulting God himself (Matthew 25:40, 45).

The poor seem to be insulted more than the rich since people think they can get away with it. When one laughs or is glad that a person has ended up poor or needy, it is no light thing. Those who would do the above must understand that their actions deserve to be punished and they will be. If not by man, they will be punished by God. It is sometimes calamity that leads a person to poverty, and no one should laugh when others fall, even if it is your enemy who falls.

Be careful of how you treat others, for in doing so you also treat God the same.

November 18 – Read Proverbs 18

v. 13 If one gives an answer before he hears, it is his folly and shame.

Numerous times over the last few weeks it has hit me that people just don't listen. There are many reasons why people don't listen. But, the truth is that people have very poor listening skills.

I don't want to spend time writing about the reason why this happens. I would rather talk about the truth of it happening. I don't think I have to convince anyone that people are very poor at listening and at times it includes all of us. Yet, it includes some far more than others. In either case, it is not good to speak before listening.

Here we are told that this action of answering before listening is "folly and shame." "Folly" means foolishness. You are being foolish when you speak to someone without first listening to what he has to say. The wise person knows it is much wiser to use more of what God gave us two of, than using what God gave us one of. Having two ears and one mouth may be the way God created us for a reason. All too often it is sin that makes us use our mouth more than our ears. It is sin, from anger to pride, that causes such actions. We also know from this verse that it is a lack of wisdom that would make people act this way.

"Shame" means dishonor or disgrace. People who have a low regard for what others have to say, or who are so self-absorbed that they need to talk without listening, act shamefully or disgracefully, and so dishonor all involved.

Be quick to use your ears and slow to use your mouth!

November 19 – Read Proverbs 19

v. 23 The fear of the LORD leads to life, and whoever has it rests satisfied; he will not be visited by harm.

The Bible says much about the fear of the Lord. Here we are told of some of the benefits of fearing God.

The first is that it leads to life. When one is in a proper relationship with God, the result is life. Jesus touches on this life in John 10 where he says that the purpose for his coming was to give us life and life abundantly. This life is not just existence, but *abundant* life. When one trusts in Jesus as his personal Savior, He takes sin and death from him and gives him life.

Added to this is a life that finds satisfaction in God and in life. In Psalm 73, the Psalmist said that he had almost messed up his life for he had envied and desired what the wicked had. But, he came to his senses and said, "Whom have I in heaven but you? And there is nothing on earth that I desire besides you." David said in Psalm 1," "The Lord is my shepherd; I shall not be in want."

Added to this is that one will not be "visited by harm." It's not that we will always escape bad events, for we surely won't. But, it's that nothing harmful or evil will happen that should cause your total ruin. God watches over those who are rightly related to Him so that all things work together for their good (Psalm 121; Romans 8; 2 Corinthians 12).

Trust God, today, with your life.

November 20 – Read Proverbs 20

v. 24 A man's steps are from the Lord; how then can man understand his way?

Sometimes life can be very confusing. We sometimes wonder why we are where we are. It most definitely is hard to figure out what God is doing in our lives. We often ask the age-old question, "Why?" when things don't go as we had hoped.

God is sovereign which means that He is in control of all things. While He does give us some freedom of choice, it is His plans that will be carried out. His plans are so detailed that He will release demons during the tribulation at the very year, month, day and hour that He foreplanned (Revelation 9:15). We have choices and those choices have responsibilities and impact on our lives. Yet, it is the will of God that determines what happens.

So, we plan but God does the directing (16:1, 9). It is His purpose that wins out (19:21). This does not make us robots, but our free will can never trump God's Sovereignty. We must plan and prepare (4:25-27; 14:8; 19:2; 21:5, etc.) for God will hold us responsible for the things we do. But, in the end His will prevails.

Since God is directing our steps it means we will never fully understand our path in life. This might be hard to comprehend but that is the way it is. Knowing this should keep us from continually spending so much time trying to figure it out. This truth should actually give us more peace about what is happening in our lives for it shows that Romans 8:28-30 is true.

God is moving in your life, trust Him and don't waste time trying to understand.

November 21 – Read Proverbs 21

v. 25 The desire of the sluggard kills him, for his hands refuse to labor.
v. 26 All day long he craves and craves, but the righteous gives and does not hold back.

In the Bible, we often see a contrast between the righteous and the wicked. We expect this comparison. But, here we see a contrast between the righteous and the sluggard (lazy). This may not have been expected by most but it is seen here. Why?

A student of God's Word knows that this contrast is seen in several parts of the Bible. Certainly here in Proverbs we see it. We are often encouraged to not be lazy in Proverbs. There is the example of the ant found in Proverbs 6 that does this very thing. In 2 Thessalonians 3:6-13 we are told to 'keep away from" and take "note" of any person who is lazy. What we learn is that being lazy and being righteous do not equate. We often equate righteousness with "spiritual" things but here we see righteousness equated with a very down-to-earth practical thing – hard work.

Another contrast is pointed out here. The sluggard's cravings will destroy him because he is unwilling to work in order to fulfill them. On the other hand, the righteous not only see their needs met but also give to help others. So the righteous are workers and givers, in contrast with the lazy who are neither.

Let your righteousness be seen today through working and giving to help others.

November 22 – Read Proverbs 22

v. 9 Whoever has a bountiful eye will be blessed, for he shares his bread with the poor.

Whenever I come across a verse that speaks about those who will be blessed, it peaks my interest. I want to know how that happens and to whom it happens. Here we are told who will be blessed and why they will be blessed.

The one who will be blessed is the person with the "bountiful eye." "Bountiful" means "good." It is the opposite of an evil eye. It speaks of a person who looks at others wanting to help them instead of seeking to use them for his own benefit. A person who has a good eye is generous and a person who has an evil eye is stingy (23:6). People who are stingy with what they have do not have a good eye, for they put themselves first. But, a good-eyed person puts others first and seeks to help them.

Now, notice what the good-eyed person does. "He shares his bread with the poor." This is the reason that he will be blessed. His heart is seen in his actions and his actions are seen in helping others. His desire and his actions help the poor. Through his eyes the poor are people in need and people whom he seeks to help. It is in helping the poor that you are truly blessed. Whatever you think about the poor is seen through your eyes.

People often find many reasons to be stingy with what they have, but a good-eyed person will use none of them. They will always do what they can with what they have to help those in need.

If you want to be blessed, help the poor.

November 23 – Read Proverbs 23

v. 22 Listen to your father who gave you life, and do not despise your mother when she is old.

v. 23 Buy truth, and do not sell it; buy wisdom, instruction, and understanding.

v. 24 The father of the righteous will greatly rejoice; he who fathers a wise son will be glad in him.

v. 25Let your father and mother be glad; let her who bore you rejoice.

You will never know what is in the heart of a parent until you become one. I only know that because I am now a parent. Growing up I did not always understand why my parents did and said what they did and said to me. But, now as a parent, I understand better. And, the one thing I understand now better than ever is what the actions of a child do to the heart of a parent.

If a child does what is wise, his parents' hearts will be filled with joy. If a child does what is foolish, his parents' hearts will be filled with pain. It is only a parent who can know how sweet the joy is and how bitter the pain is. The challenge of this passage is a call to live your life in such a way as to give your parents joy, not pain.

It is the child who is characterized by obedience, wisdom and righteousness that will make his parents joy-filled. The opposite of these things will grieve his parent. As your parents look at your life, which fills them: Joy? Or, pain?

Live your life so that your parents will be filled with joy.

November 24 – Read Proverbs 24

v. 3 By wisdom a house is built, and by understanding it is established;
v. 4 by knowledge the rooms are filled with all precious and pleasant riches.

I am surprised but I guess I should not be. I'm surprised by all of the people who believe a good home is easy to come by. Two people coming together cannot make a great home without wisdom, understanding and knowledge.

It takes these three things to make a good marriage. Not every couple who says "I do" will have a good marriage. They may all hope they will, but we know that half will not. It is very sad that so many end up that way, but God's Word in verses like these warns us all of this truth. It is those who reject wisdom, understanding and knowledge and neglect them that fail.

It takes these three things to raise and discipline children. Good children do not happen by accident. Young people and adults may be able to have children, but that does not mean they can raise them right. These three things are essential to raising healthy, well-established children. The problem with children is bad parents, parents who try to do the job without these three things.

I have been a pastor for over thirty years and have seen this truth played out many times. It can relate to a family or any endeavor people attempt. From my perspective, the best place to find all three is in the Word of God. God's Word will equip us for every good work.

Gain these three and apply them to your family, and everything you attempt in life.

November 25 – Read Proverbs 25

v. 11 A word fitly spoken is like apples of gold in a setting of silver.

I have been places where the wrong thing was said at the wrong time and the atmosphere could not be any worse. I have also seen the right thing said at the right time and it could not get any better for all involved.

The word "fitly" means at the right or proper time. It is saying the right thing at the right time. Oh, how I wish this would always be true of the things I say! This is what we should all seek for the words that flow from our mouths. Yet, having lived over fifty years in this world, I know it is not always true of me or others. To say the right thing at the right time is as beautiful as the most beautiful of jewelry.

Fit words may include anything from an encouragement, to a challenge, to a word of counsel or even a rebuke. These words properly timed are very good indeed and bring joy (15:23). Even something as simple as an honest answer can be put into this category (24:26). To speak fitly, consistently and with proper timing, one must be careful in speech and full of wisdom. You cannot honor God if you neither care what you say to people nor care what people think of your words.

Well-chosen words, spoken at the proper time, come from a heart filled with love and a mind swelled with wisdom. Some may get there by accident occasionally but to consistently get there does not happen accidently.

Seek God's help so that your speech may be as beautiful as the finest jewelry.

November 26 – Read Proverbs 26

v. 22 The words of a whisperer are like delicious morsels; they go down into the inner parts of the body.

This is one of those truths that is repeated twice in Proverbs. It is here and also in 18:8. In fact, it is repeated word for word and so we should take notice.

A "whisperer" is a "gossip." A gossip is a talebearer who spreads slander. A gossip is a peddler who picks up slander in one place and then utters it in another. According to Romans 1:28-32, gossip comes from a depraved mind. Now that is a pretty strong statement, but that is what is stated about a gossiper and her gossip. In the context here, v. 20-22, we can see that nothing good comes from gossip and it only makes matters worse.

In the verse for today we see two truths about gossip. First, it is attractive to our sinful hearts for "delicious morsels" means "things greedily devoured." Sadly, people love to hear gossip. We can also see this from all of the gossip magazines that are sold in stores. It is also seen in the TV shows that are gossip-based.

Secondly, gossip wounds deeply. Notice that it goes "down into the inner parts of the body." The words of gossip hurt a lot more than we were ever told they would in the ancient nursery rhyme "Stick and stones may break my bones but words will never harm me."

Gossip separates close friends (16:28). It makes quarrels worse (26:20-21). It hurts people (18:8). It is condemned (Leviticus 19:16).

Refuse to listen to gossip and avoid the gossiper.

November 27 – Read Proverbs 27

v. 23 Know well the condition of your flocks, and give attention to your herds,
v. 24 for riches do not last forever; and does a crown endure to all generations?

Money, money, money… Nearly everyone wants more of it and nearly everyone thinks they have too little of it. Often people think that more of it will make them happier. Most think if they have enough of it, they will be able to sit back and take life easy for all of their needs will be met and they will be good for life. But, it is just not true!

The Bible contains many warnings about money and what we think of it. For example, there is the warning in Luke 12:13-21 of the farmer who did really well for himself but he did not realize he would not live long enough to enjoy it. Then, there is the warning of Jesus found in Matthew 6:19-24 that you can't serve God and money. There is also the story of the rich man and Lazarus in Luke 16:19-31 which shows that money in this world does nothing for you in the next. Even in Proverbs 23:4-5 we are warned of the foolishness of chasing after money. Also in Proverbs 3:10, we are commanded to honor God with our wealth and to give Him the firstfruits of all we have.

Here we are warned that "riches do not last forever." Our trust must always be in God and not the size of our bank accounts. The other day I saw a list of famous athletes who had become rich but afterwards had declared bankruptcy. Never trust the amount of money you have, for it can be gone in an instant. Always put your trust in God.

Put your trust in God not riches.

November 28 – Read Proverbs 28

v. 12 When the righteous triumph, there is great glory, but when the wicked rise, people hide themselves.

History confirms this to be true in nation after nation. Life confirms this to be true. The Bible is full of examples of this truth in country after country. It is always better when the righteous triumph. When the wicked do, bad things always happen especially to the righteous.

"Hide" here refers to the righteous going into hiding from their wicked rulers. The truth is that the wicked do not like the righteous and when they are in power they do not sit passively by and leave the righteous alone. No, they seek them out and seek to do them harm. This is why during the tribulation there will be many martyrs. This is why we have seen this very thing throughout history.

The wicked do not lead the way the righteous do. When the wicked rule they seek to do away with those who do not agree with them. This is why when the righteous rule there is far more freedom than when the wicked rule. The wicked claim the opposite, but it is not true. The world, or a particular country, is always better off when the righteous rule. Sadly, even the righteous are sometimes fooled into thinking that morals do not matter and so it may not be bad if the wicked are in authority. Even in America we often see the righteous voting for the wicked to rule, wicked meaning those who do not share the same moral values as the righteous. The righteous who fall into this trap often don't understand this truth until it is too late.

Do all you can to help the righteous triumph.

November 29 – Read Proverbs 29

v. 23 One's pride will bring him low, but he who is lowly in spirit will obtain honor.

When the issue of pride is discussed, people usually think that they are not among those who are proud. The reality is that we all battle with the sin of pride. Some would even fit into the category of being very proud but often don't see themselves in this light.

How do you know if you are proud? If you feel like you are better than others or too good to hang around some people, you are proud. If you make fun of or are constantly criticizing others, pride may be found in your heart. Pride may be welling up within you if you have problems with authority. Pride may have walked into your life if you have a hard time accepting correction. These are a few of the signs that pride is a sin that has come home to roost in your life.

The issue of this verse is not figuring out if you are proud. This verse deals with the consequences of pride. Like other verses in Proverbs, and the rest of the Bible for that matter, pride is condemned and warned against. One such example is Proverbs 16:18 which says, "Pride goes before destruction and a haughty spirit before a fall." Pride will bring a person low as we see here. Pride which lifts a person up in his heart will result in bringing a person low. This is why you should evaluate whether your heart is full of pride.

Beware of pride! It will bring you only bad results.

November 30 – Read Proverbs 30

v. 29 Three things are stately in their tread; four are stately in their stride:
v. 30 the lion, which is mightiest among beasts and does not turn back before any;
v. 31 the strutting rooster, the he-goat, and a king whose army is with him.

There is an old saying, "Stop and smell the roses." This phrase may go back as far as 100 years. It originated in the United States. I think it is known by most people. It means to slow down and take time to notice what is going on around you. It is often said to people who are moving too fast and not noticing their surroundings.

The wise person takes time to learn from God's creation. Some things he learns are major and some are minor, but he learns none the less. I remember once while bow hunting spending over an hour watching an inch worm crawl up and down a tree. I was fascinated by that little worm. We can learn a great deal by exploring God's creation.

Here Agur compared a king to the lion, the rooster and the he-goat. He stopped and took the time to see how each of these was so similar.

Wisdom tells us that rushing here and there in life is not good. Life is busy, but the wise know when to slow down. The wise know the value of sitting and watching, of sitting and evaluating, of sitting and meditating. In this chapter, Agur gives us several things he learned about life by comparing animals and man. I can picture him in my mind, sitting and watching and learning.

Learn the value of slowing down at times and learning from your surroundings.

December 1 – Read Proverbs 1

v. 8 Hear, my son, your father's instruction, and forsake not your mother's teaching,
v. 9 for they are a graceful garland for your head and pendants for your neck.

Sadly, we are living in a time when the family is falling apart. Many, too many, children are growing up in homes where their mother and/or father are not living with them. As many homes look forward to the Christmas holiday, far too many homes care more about what presents will be given to the children in those homes than the teaching that is happening between parents and children.

These verses are telling children to make sure they listen to their parents' instruction. Yet, in many homes very little instruction is happening. Parents, spend time teaching your children. "About what?" you may ask. Anything and everything should be the topic of parental instruction. Parents, teach your children about God first and foremost (Deuteronomy 6). Afterwards teach your children about all of the other issues of life, from character to morality, to life in general.

Now, in other homes parents are spending time with their children "bringing them up in the discipline and instruction of the Lord" (Ephesians 6:4). Children who live in these kinds of homes ought to be grateful for the actions of their parents. These kinds of parents understand their God-given responsibilities and take actions to fulfill them. Children in these homes should value and listen to their parents' wisdom.

Value and obey your parents' teaching and do not turn from it.

December 2 - Read Proverbs 2

v. 1 My son, if you receive my words and treasure up my commandments with you,

So much is missing today in so many families. This is especially true when it comes to fathers. Many children growing up in America do not even know who their father is. I hate the term "biological father." This term is used because of the mess we have in families today and dads often not being known.

For awhile, many in America have been insinuating that fathers are not needed. They are! Fathers need to be a part of every family. Unfortunately, rampant immorality and divorce have caused problems with this. In the case of moms with no husbands, they need to work within the church and or their family to involve men in the lives of their children. But, the best way is for fathers to be involved. Sadly, even within families with fathers, dads are often "no-shows". Men also must wake up to their God-given role in the family.

Here in this verse, we find a father talking to his son about the words of instruction and commands he passed on to him. Being a man in today's world is very stress-filled, with little down time. But fathers must spend time with their children teaching them about God and life from God's Word. Yet, sadly, many men are seldom in God's Word themselves.

If you don't know what to teach your children, just use this devotional as a starting place. And, on a regular basis teach them and the value of living according to God's Word.

Fathers, be found faithful in teaching your children Biblical truth.

December 3 - Read Proverbs 3

v. 19 The LORD by wisdom founded the earth; by understanding he established the heavens;
v. 20 by his knowledge the deeps broke open, and the clouds drop down the dew.

I am utterly amazed every time I look into my reef tank in my house. What is a reef tank? It is an aquarium with live rock, salt water fish and corals. The beauty of the fish and corals is astounding. One would think that someone sat down and painted the fish with the lines and varying colors. Someone did – God!

I have finally been able to get all of the tests of the water parameters close to where they are in the ocean. How did that happen? It was done by figuring out how God does it and trying to replicate that process in the tank. Everything in the tank works to help everything else out in the tank. While I cannot perfectly match what God has done in creation, I can do things to replicate the process and it works. When you understand the process, you understand the wisdom that went behind it. You also understand that it could not happen by chance. The great wisdom and understanding behind creation argues for a wise and understanding creator. Once you understand this, you begin to understand creation's relationship to the Creator.

Creation is not an accident and neither are you. Both have purpose. Both fit together with perfect wisdom from an all-wise Creator. Generally speaking, man has rejected this Creator (Romans 1). Don't you! Keep in mind that He has a plan for your life and for creation (Romans 8).

Look at creation and marvel at the wisdom it took to bring it, and you, into being.

December 4 - Read Proverbs 4

v. 14 Do not enter the path of the wicked, and do not walk in the way of the evil.
v. 15 Avoid it; do not go on it; turn away from it and pass on.

There are two paths: the path of the wicked and the path of the righteous (v. 10-19). People think that there is somehow a middle road. There is not. There are only two, which is what Jesus also said in Matthew 7:13-14. We all face a choice as to which path we will take.

Here wisdom tells us to avoid the wicked path. To choose the path of the wicked is not wise. The path of the wicked is one of wickedness and violence that must be participated in even before sleep (v. 17). It is full of deep darkness and causes people to stumble (v. 17). Six times in these two verses (v. 14-15) we are warned to reject the path of the wicked.

Why such strong warning? Remember this is a father speaking to his son about life. He is talking to him before he has made the choice as to which path he will choose. His warning comes with the hope of stopping him from choosing the wrong path.

The path of the wicked is one in which people invite us to join (Proverbs 1:10). It is one which we may be tempted to choose (Psalm 73). It is one which the majority of people have chosen (Romans 1). So this warning serves value not only for the young son but also for every person who may be tempted to join the wicked.

Reject the path of the wicked knowing there is nothing of eternal good there.

December 5 - Read Proverbs 5

v. 8 Keep your way far from her, and do not go near the door of her house.

What great advice! This chapter may be the best chapter in the Bible about how to avoid sexual immorality. It consists of practical instruction concerning morality that a father gave to his son. Oh how it is so needed today!

America needs men who will be men of morality. America needs men who will be faithful to their wives. Men need to hear that being moral is the only path to take in life. But, they also need to hear practical instruction on how to be and stay moral. That is what you will find here in Proverbs 5. As part of that, this father told his son – Stay away from immoral women. That instruction is so simple but often so neglected.

Men, you are not strong enough to play with sexual temptation. The best way and the only way to deal with sexual temptation is to run from it. This is the example of Joseph (Genesis 39). Men must avoid places and people who may tempt them. Men must be wise about where they go and who they are with. Men must be wise about spending time with the opposite sex. The advice found in this verse is so simple yet very wise. Men who neglect this advice are in great danger and are so foolish.

When Proverbs 7:26 says, "for many a victim has she laid low, and all her slain are a mighty throng," it is a warning to men to be very careful. He who disregards this advice is foolish and on a dangerous path.

Be wise and careful about who you spend time with and where you go.

December 6 - Read Proverbs 6

v. 19b ...one who sows discord among brothers.

What might be the worst sin in a church? That question might raise a lot of answers. A look at the New Testament should give us a clue. At least, in my opinion, I think it would be false teaching. Second Peter 2:17 tells us that utter darkness is reserved for them. Revelation 2 and 3 is speaking to seven churches concerning the issue that was condemned more than any other, false teaching. Well I could go on, but I really want to get to the second, which I believe, is that of sowing discord among brothers.

This is a sin that God speaks of as being really, really bad. In fact, here in Proverbs it says that He hates it (v. 16-19). In Titus 3:11 it says that a person who does this even after having been warned is warped, sinful and self-condemned. In Romans 16:17 we are told that "such persons do not serve our Lord Christ, but their own appetites."

What are we to do with such a person? First, make sure you are not that person. Make sure that if there are divisions, you did not start them nor are you making them worse. Second, warn such people not do to such sinful things. Third, warn others concerning them as we see happen in Titus and Romans. Fourth, if they do not listen, have nothing to do with them with the hope that this action will help them to get right with God. For further study see Romans 16:17-19; Titus 3:9-11; 1 Corinthians 5:11-13; Matthew 18:15-17 and 2 John 10.

Do not cause divisions knowing that God hates such practices.

December 7 - Read Proverbs 7

v. 7 and I have seen among the simple, I have perceived among the youths, a young man lacking sense,

Oh, how often this statement has proved itself true! Young men or women are lacking in wisdom. There is no doubting this. Parents, life, and especially God's Word, amongst other things, help young people to learn to be wise as they grow older. It is truly awesome when you see a young person with the wisdom of an older person.

In the context of this verse and chapter, this particular young man shows his lack of wisdom by going to the wrong place at the wrong time. Here he is heading near the immoral woman as darkness is falling. As I said, it is the wrong place at the wrong time.

This is where parent's teaching can step in and help a young person, who does not have the sense enough on his own, to avoid this kind of error. This is where God's Word can make a young person wiser than his years. As the moral climate drops, people with morals must step in and help young people by being a moral compass for them. This world is so accepting of immoral behavior or behavior that is so close to the edge that young people and even older people fall off into immorality.

When I spend time with young people, one of my hopes is that I may help them to avoid the mistakes of someone lacking sense. I would like to see children grow up without having a bunch of stories of how they did things they wish they had not.

Become wise beyond your years and help others along the way to do the same. (Psalm 119:97-104)

December 8 - Read Proverbs 8

v. 6 Hear, for I will speak noble things, and from my lips will come what is right,

In Proverbs 8 wisdom speaks! Wisdom is given a mouth and it calls out to all who will listen. Those who lack sense have the opportunity to gain it. Even fools, if they will listen, can learn sense.

That is the key! We find ourselves so willing to talk and so unwilling to listen. Listen more often than you talk. Yet, we use our mouth far more than our ears. May we all learn to use ours ears, and not our mouth, especially when wisdom speaks.

Real wisdom, godly wisdom, is noble and right. It is worth every moment we give to it. Wisdom must move through our ears into our brain and down to our hearts. We have spent just about a year on a daily basis listening to wisdom speak. Proverbs is the Book of Wisdom in the Word of God. It teaches us practical things that must go from eyes to ears to brain to heart and then to our feet. As we continually read this great Book of Proverbs and let our ears hear it, we must allow our mind to meditate on its truth. It must then settle in our heart. Finally, it must become part of our character and our walk.

There is so much value in the Bible for everyday living that to turn away from it shows one is lacking in any sense whatsoever. When wisdom speaks, we must listen. To do anything else is sheer lunacy.

When wisdom speaks – LISTEN!!!

December 9 - Read Proverbs 9

v. 7 Whoever corrects a scoffer get himself abuse, and he who reproves a wicked man incurs injury.

v. 8 Do not reprove a scoffer, or he will hate you; reprove a wise man, and he will love you.

v. 9 Give instruction to a wise man, and he will be still wiser; teach a righteous man, and he will increase in learning.

I have referred to these verses in counseling and life as much as any. This is one of those truths that you learn from years of experience or by reading Proverbs.

Whenever you seek to correct someone, you must ask the question, "To whom am I talking?" Jesus said this very thing in Matthew 7:6. You must determine, the best you can, the heart of the one you seek to correct. Is his heart open or hard? Sometimes you only learn this by correcting him. Other times, you know this through interaction with the person in question.

Know this: if you seek to correct a scoffer, you will be abused and injured in one way or another. The scoffer will hate you for seeking to correct him. He will throw all kinds of accusations your way. The accusations may look like these, "Who do you think you are?" or "The Bible says don't judge," or other accusations similar to these. He may even try to harm your reputation with others for having the audacity of trying to correct him. In having these responses to correction, he reveals his heart.

Now, the wise person reacts totally different to correction. He will love you for having cared about him and will be even wiser.

Know that people can have two opposite responses to correction based on their hearts.

December 10 - Read Proverbs 10

v. 26 Like vinegar to the teeth and smoke to the eyes, so is the sluggard to those who send him.

Go to your cupboard right now and grab some vinegar and take a drink. No? Well go sit in an enclosed room and light a fire and then put it out and sit for a while in the smoke. No? You say that neither one sounds good? Keep that in mind the next time you think about hiring a sluggard. Or, keep in mind what it does to your boss if you are considering being a sluggard at work.

A sluggard is a lazy person who determines to put little or no effort into what he is doing. It is a person who would rather sleep or lie on the couch all day than work. It is a person who is always counting the days to his next day off or the days until he can retire. It is a person who is wasting his life and the abilities that God has given him. It is a person who could do so much more but chooses to do so much less. It is a person for whom God has strong words (2 Thessalonians 3:6-15).

Vinegar is sour tasting and smoke is irritating to the eyes. Neither one sounds like a good proposition to choose. So the sluggard is an irritant to those who would hire him. He does not do what he should, and even if he attempts to do something it is done so slow that he drives his employer crazy. Yet some people, instead of working at work, seek to do as little as possible and try to get away with as much as possible.

Be careful in choosing workers. If you choose a sluggard to work for you, he will irritate you until the day you fire him.

Don't choose a sluggard to work for you and don't be a sluggard because sluggards tend to irritate people.

December 11 - Read Proverbs 11

v. 28 Whoever trusts in his riches will fall, but the righteous will flourish like a green leaf.

There are many things you could put your trust in: health, friends, parents, government, strength, armies, God, or as stated here, riches. We are warned here that the person who puts his trust in riches will fall. The indication also is that the righteous do not put their trust in riches.

Our complete and total trust must be in God alone. He alone will never disappoint us. The Psalmist said in Psalm 28:7, "The LORD is my strength and my shield; in him my heart trusts, and I am helped; my heart exults, and with my song I give thanks to him." Just think what would have happened to godly Job if he had put his trust in his riches and then lost them as he did. He would have betrayed God (Job 31:24-28). To have money is not wrong, but no one should ever put his trust in it. It is not worthy of our trust. Only God is worthy of complete trust and total trust.

Very few people would ever admit to trusting in money. Yet, many do so. When you are struggling financially, in spite of doing all that you can, in spite of putting God first and seeking His righteousness first, what happens in your heart? Is it full of joy and trust or is it full of worry and fear? Do you have the same joy when your bank account is empty as when it is full? What do you really trust?

Trust God, not riches, and flourish like the righteous.

December 12 - Read Proverbs 12

v. 19 Truthful lips endure forever, but a lying tongue is but for a moment.

The comparison here is between that which lasts and that which is but a moment. This is the comparison we should think about in all things. Usually the sinful thing is the thing that is but a moment. The right things are the things that last. People often forget about eternity and choose the temporary. The eternal is the thing that shows the value of something. Jesus endured the cross for the joy set before Him – our eternal salvation (Hebrews 12:2). Paul said he overcame trouble by looking at the eternal (2 Corinthians 4).

Lying is often done for quick fixes. Truth is chosen because of the eternal weight of doing what is right (v. 22). Truth endures but lies do not last. Not only do lies not last, but neither do liars. In this verse the tongue is put for the person. "But for a moment" is literally "blinking of the eyes," referring to any movement of the eye which lasts only for a moment. What is said should always be considered in light of eternity.

Much is said about lying and truthfulness in Proverbs. Lying is always rejected and truthfulness is always embraced. It does not matter if it is a big lie or a little "white" lie. It is always rejected. Here this is done by comparing truth and lying to that which is lasting. Choosing that which lasts is the better choice. Don't be tempted to lie for the sake of the moment.

Truth lasts. Always choose it.

December 13 - Read Proverbs 13

v. 11 Wealth gained hastily will dwindle, but whoever gathers little by little will increase it.

Certainly around Christmas time people think about money. They think about their ability to buy presents for the ones they love. They think about whether they should buy what they can't afford with a credit card only to spend next year paying for it. They think about how they wish they had saved throughout the year so they would have money now to spend.

There it is: "whoever gathers little by little will increase it." People often think in January that saving $5 - $10 per week or per month is just not worth it. They think it will not add up. People think that saving $25 per month when they are 25 will not add up, so they wait until retirement is upon them and they have not saved anything.

Most people do not save little by little or seek to make money little by little. They often think that they have to win the lottery or get into some get rich quick scheme to get anywhere in life. The reality is that those who don't know how to handle money when they have little might gain much in a hurry but lose it very quickly. This is especially true of anyone who would gain it quickly by wrong means. At times, this can be seen in those who inherit large sums of money. Because they never learned how to handle it, they lose it as quickly as they gained it. Think about it in terms of eating. Eat little by little and you will do well, but it you shove food into your mouth as quick as you can, you will be one sick puppy, losing what you have eaten.

Most things done in haste don't end well; grow what you have in a disciplined way.

December 14 - Read Proverbs 14

v. 30 A tranquil heart gives life to the flesh, but envy makes the bones rot.

People are taking all kinds of pills to do what this verse could fix in a moment. Pills that people take often don't work and come with many side effects. Friends, there is a better way.

We are told here that a person being right emotionally and spiritually benefits his physical body. But, when you are not right spiritually and emotionally it can have a detrimental affect on your physical body. This can be seen in King David. In Psalm 32 and 51, King David speaks of the physical effect his sin had on him until it was confessed. Envy, which is sin, can rot away the bones. I have heard from various sources that as much as ninety percent of people who see doctors for physical illnesses have not physical, but stress-caused, illnesses.

A healthy heart can go a long way in keeping the body healthy. Fill your heart with trouble, and the impact on your body can be tremendous (bones rot). Keep your heart where it ought to be and it will go a long way in keeping your body healthy. You can exercise all you want, but if your heart is not kept healthy, your body becomes unhealthy.

A tranquil heart is a heart at peace. It comes from being rightly related to God (Romans 5:1). A tranquil heart is assured as one makes sure that his thinking is biblical in every aspect. As God's wisdom fills your mind and heart, you see life from His perspective and it gives peace beyond understanding.

Become spiritually and emotionally healthy and your body will thank you.

December 15 – Read Proverbs 15

v. 6 In the house of the righteous there is much treasure, but trouble befalls the income of the wicked.

Wow! Walk into some houses today and you will find all sorts of goodies, while in others you will find emptiness. The cry of the righteous is that the wicked get ahead in this world and the righteous fall behind. But, not according to this verse, it is the righteous that have a house full of treasure.

Let me take the last first. The wicked do often appear to have all sorts of treasure. In looking around you may see wicked people who have no love for God swimming in the toys of this world. This verse does not say the wicked have no income but that their income comes with trouble. For example, in Proverbs 1, we are told not to join with the wicked that are "greedy for unjust gain." They are only setting an "ambush for their own lives." Their income takes away their very lives. The story of Achan (Joshua 7) is a prime example of this and what it does to one's family.

A house where there is the fear of the Lord and even a small meal has far more value than a house full of feasting gotten wickedly (v16-17). A house full of the God's wisdom is full of treasure worth far more than any amount of money (16:16). Though one may not have the riches of this world, he may still be rich (2 Corinthians 6:10). The righteous know, but sometimes need to be reminded, that a home where God is foremost is a home where there is much treasure. No amount of Christmas gifts could ever replace such treasure. And, the righteous must teach their children this important truth.

Choose righteousness over wickedness and you will always be on the winning side.

December 16 – Read Proverbs 16

v. 25 There is a way that seems right to a man, but in the end it leads to death.

This verse is a repeat of 14:12. God said it twice so we would not miss it.

It is sad, but it is true. We have a hard time seeing our own errors and mistakes. We tend to think that every course we take is right. We tend to want to prove to others that we are right and they are wrong.

For example, there are the paths that lead to Heaven or Hell (Matthew 7:13-14). Most people take the path that leads to Hell (destruction). Most people think they are right even though they are wrong. Even at the point of standing before God, those headed to Hell still think they are on their way to Heaven (Matthew 7:21-23).

These verses are warnings to us that we need to go past what seems right to us. You or I cannot be the basis for choosing our path. The path that leads to death seems right to the one on that path. We tend to be poor judges of the right path. So, there must be something other than ourselves that we use to determine if a path is right or wrong. Just think of what the world uses to choose their path – "If it feels good" or "I did it my way." These cannot and must not be the basis for choosing right and wrong paths to take. I would submit to you that the best place to go to determine right and wrong is the Word of God.

Look beyond yourself for determining what path is right, look to the Word of God!

December 17 – Read Proverbs 17

v. 10 A rebuke goes deeper into a man of understanding than a hundred blows into a fool.

Are you teachable? This issue is gigantic in Proverbs and in rest of the Bible. One thing that made the apostles so useable for Jesus was that they were teachable. Find a person who is not and you have found a problem person. Proverbs 26:12 says, "Do you see a man who is wise in his own eyes? There is more hope for a fool than for him."

A "man of understanding" is not bothered by being rebuked. Why? The reason is that such a person is teachable. He wants to learn. He wants to grow wise. He is open to rebuke because he has a deep desire to grow. When he is rebuked, he takes it seriously and considers what has been said. He takes time to investigate the validity of the rebuke and tries to determine where he may have failed and how he may learn from the rebuke. This is what the wise do and that is one of the reasons he has grown wise.

On the other hand, a fool is not teachable. A fool hates being rebuked and is offended when he has been rebuked. He does not desire to be corrected when wrong. He would rather correct than be corrected. The comparison here says that a fool can be beaten and still not learn as much as a man of understanding who has simply been verbally corrected. Watch how a person reacts to a rebuke and it will tell you which camp they fit into, the understanding camp or the foolish camp. Are you teachable?

Keep a teachable spirit and wisdom will never leave you.

December 18 – Read Proverbs 18

v. 10 The name of the LORD is a strong tower; the righteous man runs into it and is safe.

When in trouble, where do you run? When you are in need, to whom does your mind go first? The great men and women of the Bible did what this verse states. They ran to God!

"The name of the Lord" stands for God Himself (Exodus 34:4-7). In fact, if you just look at the names of God in the Bible, you can learn a great deal about who God is. When in trouble the righteous run to Him because they know where to find security. Even the wicked, at times, run to God when in trouble. The righteous know that He is a strong tower who will keep them safe (safe means safely above the danger). Towers were often built for battle to keep armies above the trouble. In battle, it was a safer place to be than down on the ground.

My favorite Psalm puts it this way, "I lift up my eyes to the hills. From where does my help come? My help comes from the LORD, who made heaven and earth" (Psalm 121:1-2). Great peace comes into one's heart when you know that in times of trouble you can run to the Creator of the universe. The righteous know that they can run to Him. They know that He will never turn them away. They know that He is always there for them. They know that His help is the best help anyone can have. Check out the cry of the Psalmist in Psalm 61:1-3.

Need a safe place? Run to the strong tower! Run to God!

December 19 – Read Proverbs 19

v. 27 Cease to hear instruction, my son, and you will stray from the words of knowledge.

Do you know when you are in trouble? Do you know when you are heading for a cliff? Do you know when trouble is just outside the door? It is when you stop listening.

This verse tells us that the person who stops listening (hearing and obeying) to God's Word is going to go astray. People go to church, but are they listening to what is being preached? Have they closed their ears to the truth being proclaimed? Sometimes it seems that way. Others have stopped going to church altogether and so closed their ears to God. Truth must be heard and applied or it does a person no good. This is exactly what Jesus said in Matthew 7:24-27 as He concluded the Sermon on the Mount. Jesus' half brother, James, also said the same thing in James 1:22-25.

Sadly, people often go through life going to church, just going through the motions week after week, and year after year, but there is no change in their lives. Yet, people look at their lives and think that they are fine and right before God. God's Word must be acted upon. You must not turn a deaf ear to God's truth. The moment you close your ears and stop listening and responding, you begin to stray from knowledge.

You must continually have your ears open (v. 20). Wisdom is not a place that you attain and stop. Wisdom is a matter of continually growing and learning. Wisdom is seen in those who seek more wisdom and not in those who say, "I have arrived and now I'm finished."

Keep listening and you will keep learning and growing; stop and you will stray.

December 20 – Read Proverbs 20

v. 7 The righteous who walks in his integrity— blessed are his children after him!

We are coming to the end of the year, and you may be thinking about what you will leave behind this year.

Parents, what will you leave your children at the end of your life? What will their inheritance look like? Will it be worth very much? Will it be something of value?

When we think of an inheritance, we often think of money or goods. If we are rich, our children will get a good inheritance, and if we are poor our children will not get much of value, we think. But this is not the whole story. There is something much more valuable we can leave our children than money or goods. It is a walk of integrity.

A walk of integrity is a walk of moral goodness. It is a life that is pleasing to God. It is a walk that is absent of hypocrisy. This kind of life leaves children in a place of blessing with God (Exodus 20:4-6). It is the kind of life that causes your children not to have to hide who they are because of something that you have done. It is the kind of life that causes them to be grateful that they had you as a parent. It is important to know that leaving your children this kind of life has far more value than any monetary amount you could ever leave them. So what kind of life are you leaving your children? Wherever you are at, make sure from this day forward you leave your children an inheritance worth leaving.

Make sure you walk with integrity!

December 21 – Read Proverbs 21

v. 11 When a scoffer is punished, the simple becomes wise; when a wise man is instructed, he gains knowledge.

People who are seeking wisdom gain wisdom even from something as negative as a scoffer being punished. The punishment of those whose lives are not right teaches the simple that his path is a wrong path. The simple realize that a scoffer is headed in the wrong direction and so he must not follow the lead of the scoffer.

This verse is similar to Proverbs 19:25 which says, 'Strike a scoffer, and the simple will learn prudence, reprove a man of understanding, and he will gain knowledge." Those who are willing to learn can learn even from those who are not willing to learn, such as the scoffer. In this case, it is learning from the punishment of the scoffer. We live in a world where those who do wrong sometimes get away with it, at least temporarily. But, there is enough evidence that doing the wrong thing gets punished. The simple learn this truth by seeing them get punished.

In so doing, the simple make the decision to follow a different path. Only a fool would see this evidence and continue in the same direction as those who are being punished. Sadly, many do that very thing. And so, here we see three different mindsets: The scoffer, who is closed-minded, only learns when he is punished, and often not even than. The simple, who may need vivid pictures to startle him into truth. And, the wise man, who learns by simple instruction without the need of either. What does it take for you to learn?

Be open and ready to learn, continually seeking truth and wisdom.

December 22 – Read Proverbs 22

v. 2 The rich and the poor meet together; the LORD is the maker of them all.

It is interesting to see how much polar opposites have in common. Sometimes people look and act as if they had nothing in common. Here, we find the case of the rich and poor. Though they are on the opposite end of the spectrum when it comes to riches, they have something in common. The Lord is the maker of both.

God created mankind, all men both rich and poor. In fact, not only is God the creator of both, but He is the sustainer of both (29:13). The fact that man is created by God and that his life is sustained by God is a truth that must not be missed. This truth is saturated with wisdom and is so sadly missed when people believe in evolution. Throw out Genesis 1 and you miss the foundation for life. It is no wonder that people often have no idea how to treat one another.

Since God is the maker of both, the rich and poor have a common origin and responsibility towards God. The rich often feel like they can treat the poor badly, while the poor often feel they can do the same, just in different ways. The relationship between these two groups is often strained. Maybe, if they would just grasp their common origin and what it means, this could be fixed. And, it is being fixed in churches across the world.

The rich must understand that when they oppress the poor they insult their Maker (14:31). The poor do no better when they do not treat the rich in a loving way. An understanding of where we all come from can fix so many of the evils in our world.

Rich and Poor, be careful how you treat each other for we all have a common origin.

December 23 – Read Proverbs 23

v. 5 When your eyes light on it, it is gone, for suddenly it sprouts wings, flying like an eagle toward heaven.

The "it" here is riches or wealth. This verse gives the reason why we should not wear ourselves out to get rich. What is the truth concerning riches?

Riches are fleeting. It is as if they sprouted wings like an eagle and flew away. Banks have always built buildings with brick and stone trying to give the idea that the money that they hold for people will always be there. They want people to think it is safe with them. But there are all sorts of ways to lose money or the toys that you have. Riches are fleeting!

Just read about all of the sports people who have made it big. They have made millions doing their thing. Then they retire. The money stops coming in, and they lose what they have made. They are often found penniless and broke. It is so hard to make money and so easy to lose it. Riches are not secure!

People who are poor seek to become rich thinking that once they are, life will be secure. But, it is so untrue. Riches are not secure! Just look at those who seek to be rich by winning a lottery. Many who have won are often later found with nothing. Only a fool would seek to be secure by having something that is so unsecure. It is sad that most people only learn that lesson when it is too late.

Have a proper view of riches and don't buy into the thinking of most concerning it.

December 24 – Read Proverbs 24

v. 23 These also are sayings of the wise. Partiality in judging is not good.

Partiality in anything is not good. So, it is certainly not good when it comes to judging. No one would say they judge others, but the reality is people do it all of the time.

For example, we judge our kids differently than other kids. What do we say? "If my child hadn't hung around those kids he would be OK." The truth may be that it was my child who messed up the other parent's child. But most parents would not entertain such an idea. Why does this happen? It is because we often show "partiality in judging." To do so is not good at any time.

This is also true when it comes to the courts. We see someone do something bad and we want him to be thrown in jail and the key placed where it could never be found. But, our attitude changes when it is our own child. When it is our own child or someone we know, we plead mercy or say he was judged too harshly or that it is not fair.

It is also seen when we get a ticket for speeding. I was once told that a person saw the State Police while speeding and slowed down. By the time she was caught, I was told, she could not have been speeding. She said she should not have gotten a ticket because she had slowed down, and besides, other speeders go much faster then her. She wanted to be treated differently than others.

To show partiality in judging is not good, so don't do it.

December 25 – Read Proverbs 25

v. 21 If your enemy is hungry, give him bread to eat, and if he is thirsty, give him water to drink,

v. 22 for you will heap burning coals on his head, and the Lord *will reward you.*

The way to change the heart of an enemy is by doing "good" to her. In so doing, you will cause her to be ashamed of her actions.

There is an ancient Egyptian custom where a guilty person would carry a pan of burning coal on his head to indicate repentance. The coals represented the pain of his guilt. The goal was that the heart of the enemy would soften and you would no longer be enemies.

God rewards this kind of behavior because it is behavior that represents the character of God (Matthew 5:43-48). God rewards us for acting the way He does and for doing what He would want us to do. His desire is that we act like He would towards others. As Christians who represent God, we should be consumed with acting like He would. It reminds me of the bracelet that people often wear that asks, "WWJD" or "What would Jesus do?" It reminds us that we should only do those things that Jesus would do.

It should not be that we would act like our enemies. We should confront our enemies with good. When they do us evil, we ought to return their evil with good. This is the Biblical way to respond to those who would hurt us (Romans 12:12-21). This is the way that Christians ought to act and the way that we so often fall short.

Be careful how you treat your enemies, God is watching.

December 26 - Read Proverbs 26

v. 6 Whoever sends a message by the hand of a fool cuts off his own feet and drinks violence.

In life, we often have to depend on other people. Sometimes it is a planned thing and at other times it is a quick decision that must be made in a hurry. It is here where we can get ourselves into trouble.

We think that sometimes we have to make a decision that we don't want to make. So, we may think that we must sometimes depend on someone we would rather not depend on. But, buyer beware! Anyone who would depend on a fool is in great danger. Sending a message by the hand of a fool will create a mess. This may be contrasted with Proverbs 25:13 which states the opposite.

Fools are not qualified for anything. They are not even qualified to carry a message to another person for in some way they will mess it up, that is just what fools do. The warning here is not to entrust anything to a fool, not even the sending or carrying of a message. If you must depend on someone, consider his character even for something as small as carrying a message. A fool is a danger to everyone around them. A fool is a moral degenerate who messes up anything and everything, and so why put your trust in such a person?

If you must rely on someone, make sure it is not a fool.

December 27 – Read Proverbs 27

v. 12 The prudent sees danger and hides himself, but the simple go on and suffer for it.

A wise person knows when to stop. A wise person knows when enough is enough. A wise person knows when the danger of going forward is not worth the risk and as a result makes the decision to stop and hide from the danger. This verse is a repeat of Proverbs 22:13.

The simple have no such wisdom. The simple are bullheaded and will move forward and stop at nothing. The simple do not know when it is time to stop, so they move forward and reap the results of their actions. The simple have not learned that there are times when stopping is better than continuing to move forward.

Successful people often move forward in the face of danger. Successful people are people who have often faced danger and won. The wisdom comes in knowing when the danger is so great that one must stop and hide. Wisdom knows when the risk is not worth the reward and finds reward in stopping. Stopping and hiding from danger may cause all sorts of ridicule from others. Stopping and hiding may not be an easy thing to do. Society does not look well on those who do such things. Yet, the wise know when it is the right time. They have learned this through time spent in God's Word, time spent listening to the wise, and time spent dealing with life.

Learn this lesson before you suffer for moving when you should have stopped and hid.

December 28 – Read Proverbs 28

v. 14 Blessed is the one who fears the Lord *always, but whoever hardens his heart will fall into calamity.*

Here "fearing God" and having a "hard heart" are set in contrast. The first is seen as something worth having, while the second is something one should run from. Having the first results in blessing. Having the second results in calamity.

Fearing the Lord is talked about often in God's Word. It describes one who has a healthy awe of God and so loves and obeys Him. The key word that I see here is the word "always." Satan told God that Job would stop fearing him if God removed his blessing from Job's life (Job 1-2). Yet Job was blessed because he feared God in the first place. Satan was wrong about Job. Sadly, he is not wrong about so many who claim to fear God. It does not take much these days for those who claim to fear God to turn away from Him. So the one who is blessed is the one who fears God "always" like Job and many others in the Bible.

On the other hand, I often find people who do not fear God have hard hearts. It is the very fear of God that keeps one's heart from becoming hard. The person who chooses not to love and obey God often becomes hard towards the things of God. I have found myself saying, to people who have admitted their sin, that there was no value in talking to them about their sin, if they are set on disobeying God. To which they have agreed. How sad! (Hebrews 3:7-19)

Fear God and do not let your heart become hard.

December 29 – Read Proverbs 29

v. 3 He who loves wisdom makes his father glad, but a companion of prostitutes squanders his wealth.

The actions of a child will either bring his parents joy or sadness; either honor them or bring them shame. Children should consider how their actions will affect their parents. This often is not a consideration of young people in this generation. It used to be that young people sought to be careful what they did with their family name.

Only a parent knows how much joy or sadness a child can bring. Thankfully, my children have brought joy to my life. When a child is doing what is right and seeking a path that honors God, the joy to his parent is great. The decisions of a child who is wise make the heart of his father glad beyond any words that could be said. I think every parent desires that his children will be wise and when they are, he is filled with joy.

Yet, the opposite is also true. When a child becomes the companion of prostitutes or any other people who live foolishly, he drains all that a father has. Here it is said in terms of his wealth, but that is only part of the picture. The foolish choices and actions of a child drain a father. I have watched many fathers and mothers over the years drained by the actions and choices of their children.

Consider how your actions today will either bring your parents joy or sadness.

December 30 – Read Proverbs 30

v. 20 This is the way of an adulteress: she eats and wipes her mouth and says, "I have done no wrong."

The adulteress sees her actions as no big deal, kind of like eating a meal. To her adultery is OK. To her adultery is not wrong.

The adulteress has deceived herself into thinking that adultery is not wrong. She may say things like: "My marriage is not good."," My marriage never was good." or "His marriage is not good.", "His marriage never was good." or "We get along so well! How can it be wrong?" or "God wants me to be happy." Or, many other such things even to the degree that one person said, "This relationship must be God's will."

What we see happening here is that the adulteress has set aside the Word of God for her own selfish heart. This woman has created her own standard of right and wrong. This woman has set herself up as God. But, this woman is not alone. She is the picture of any person who would set aside God's moral standard for her own. She is the picture of any person who has convinced herself that wrong is now right. She has, and all who follow her have, turned God's standard upside down and sought to fulfill her own selfish heart.

But, there is a price to be paid. When you contradict God, at that moment you will have to answer to God for making that choice and offering it to others. Doing such things have consequences and they are clearly spelled out in Romans 1:18-32. As we near the end of the year, this is a perfect verse to consider in seeking to be wise.

A wise person agrees with God, so the more you agree with Him, the wiser you will be.

December 31 – Read Proverbs 31

v. 12 She does him good, and not harm, all the days of her life.

This mother has listed for her son the characteristics of an excellent wife. Every unmarried man should look for these characteristics in his potential wife, and every unmarried woman should seek to have these characteristics in her life. The list covers many different areas of life and gives us the reason why her husband trusts her. Take a look at what makes a woman an excellent wife:

- She does her husband good, not harm. – v. 12
- She is not lazy. = v. 13-15, 27
- She is wise in dealing with family finances. – v. 16-19
- She cares for the needy. – v. 20
- She does not worry, but makes her family ready for life – v. 21-22
- She is clothed with strength and dignity – v. 24-25
- She is wise and kind. v. 26
- She is rightly related to God. – v. 30
- She is not proud. – v. 31

Young unmarried women, unmarried women, and even married women should compare their lives with what they see here. They should strive to be this kind of a woman. They should also look at Ephesians 5, 1 Peter 3 and Titus 2 for other characteristics of an excellent wife.

This kind of woman should be praised by both her children and husband. This kind of woman would make a man proud to marry her. This kind of woman would make a man's life far more than what it could be had he not met her. I know, for I married this kind of woman.

Find a woman like this and you have found an excellent wife. Become a wife like this and you become something very precious indeed (v. 10).

Endnotes

1 *The Holy Bible: English Standard Version*. 2001. Wheaton: Standard Bible Society.

2 Henry, Matthew: *Matthew Henry's Commentary on the Whole Bible: Complete and Unabridged in One Volume*. Peabody: Hendrickson, 1996, c1991, S. Pr 27:2

3 Buzzell, S. S. (1985). Proverbs. In J. F. Walvoord & R. B. Zuck (Eds.), *The Bible Knowledge Commentary: An Exposition of the Scriptures* (J. F. Walvoord & R. B. Zuck, Ed.) (Pr 13:24). Wheaton, IL: Victor Books.

4 Swanson, J. (1997). *Dictionary of Biblical Languages with Semantic Domains: Hebrew (Old Testament)* (electronic ed.). Oak Harbor: Logos Research Systems, Inc.

5 Swanson, J. (1997). *Dictionary of Biblical Languages with Semantic Domains: Hebrew (Old Testament)* (electronic ed.). Oak Harbor: Logos Research Systems, Inc.

6 Swanson, J. (1997). *Dictionary of Biblical Languages with Semantic Domains: Hebrew (Old Testament)* (electronic ed.). Oak Harbor: Logos Research Systems, Inc.

About the Author

Thomas J. Sica became a Christian as a teenager, in the 1970's. In 1982, Tom graduated from Liberty University, was ordained, and started a church, which he still pastors more than thirty years later. He has been married for thirty-two years, and has two children and two grandchildren.